William
Faulkner

TWO DECADES of CRITICISM

———

Edited by

FREDERICK J. HOFFMAN

& OLGA W. VICKERY

———

Michigan State College Press

1954

———

William Faulkner:

TWO DECADES OF CRITICISM

Preface

THE EDITORS of this book have arranged and selected these studies of William Faulkner with the aim of providing a collection of maximum usefulness. The arrangement of the essays has been made with the object of helping the reader to see Faulkner from four points of view: first, with respect to his regional "place"; second, in terms of his work as a whole; third, in the matter of his methods and especially of his style; and, finally, in terms of individual works. Except for the first essay, all of the contributions date from 1939. While there were many interesting notes and reviews of Faulkner before that date, it marks the beginning of serious critical examination of his work.

The introduction is designed primarily as a means of indicating both the *scope* of Faulkner's critical reception and the *kinds* of criticism. The bibliography, while necessarily selective, is the result of careful research and contains as full an accounting of the subject as space will permit. Since there have been hundreds of reviews, and these have often echoed and borrowed from each other, only a small number are listed; they were chosen when either the suggestions made in them or the importance of the reviewer seemed to warrant inclusion. Two reviews are reprinted[1]—Elizabeth Hardwick's and Andrew Lytle's on *Intruder in the Dust*; and these principally because they represent two opposing views of that novel, which has not yet received a full-length study.

The editors have collaborated closely in the selection of the contents. The introduction was written by Mr. Hoffman, the bibliography compiled by Mrs. Vickery. Miss Martine Darmon contributed the translations of the essays of Jean-Paul Sartre and "Rabi."

William Faulkner: Two Decades of Criticism is neither a

1. While Robert Penn Warren's essay is a review (of Malcolm Cowley's *Portable*), it is so extensive and goes so far and so competently beyond its subject that it can scarcely be classified as a contemporary notice.

tract nor a symposium. The essays reprinted were written at various times and under the influence of several kinds of critical persuasion. They possess the great merit of their occasions; they are more than "appreciations" or notes taken down hastily on a trip to Jefferson. They should, therefore, be read as a group of intelligent studies that settle some issues and raise others, and in any case should contribute significantly to the reader's understanding of an important and sometimes difficult artist.

April, 1951

F.J.H.
O.W.V.

Contents

William Faulkner:

An Introduction

i

IN AN ESSAY published in *Commentary* (October, 1950), Leslie
Fiedler expressed an understandable exasperation over the mis-
conceptions with which critics have obscured the "actual"
Faulkner.

It has taken me ten years of wary reading to distinguish the actual
writer of *The Sound and the Fury* from a synthetic Faulkner, compounded of sub-Marxian stereotypes...;and I am aware that there
is yet another pseudo-Faulkner, derived mostly from the potboiling
Sanctuary, a more elaborate and chaotic Erskine Caldwell, revealing
a world of barnyard sex and violence through a fog of highbrow
rhetoric. The grain of regrettable truth in both these views is lost in
their misleading emphases; and equally confusing are the less hysterical academic partial glimpses which make Faulkner primarily a historian of Southern culture, or a canny technician whose evocations of
terror are secondary to Jamesian experiments with "point of view."[1]

Criticism has certainly been busy offering us many versions of
"that writin' man of Oxford." From the start, however, much
of it has been largely blocked by certain concerns with "society,"
"naturalism," and "the human condition." The strange genius
from Mississippi seemed often to violate preconceived standards
of taste, or capriciously to disregard sober warnings from his
critics. That he should deliberately have announced (in the
Preface to the Modern Library edition of *Sanctuary*, 1932) his
intention of exploiting the horrible and the obscene confirmed

1. See "R.W." (Reed Whittemore), "Notes on Mr. Faulkner," *Furioso*,
Summer, 1947, for a parody of Faulkner criticism.

1

these critics in their worst fears. Faulkner's announcement there that he had written his novel as "a cheap idea, . . . deliberately conceived to make money" was the beginning of the most persistent of all types of Faulkner criticism.

It is necessary to see this point of view in terms of its setting. The critics who first attended to Faulkner's work were largely of two persuasions: they were either in the "humanist" or in the "leftist" tradition. In either case, they sought a virtue of statement in literature and were much distressed when they failed to see it. It was not possible to ignore the call to responsibility, as Faulkner seemed to be doing, and remain unpunished. From the beginning of the 1930's, therefore, he was classified as a writer who had ignored the largest demands upon social taste and moral discretion. His work did not have "spiritual resonance"; it exploited obscenity and horror for their own sake or as a "cheap idea"; he did not wish for a "better world" but hated the present and brooded over the collapse of the past; he was abnormally fond of morons, idiots, perverts, and nymphomaniacs. He was, in short, the leading member of a "cult of cruelty" school of modern writing.

The leading spokesman in this attack upon Faulkner's work was Alan Reynolds Thompson, whose essay, "The Cult of Cruelty" (*The Bookman*, January–February, 1932) provided a statement of its terms. Faulkner and Robinson Jeffers, said Thompson, have established a new "school" of writing, a "tendency which we may call the cult of cruelty." Cruelty is, of course, "inherent in human nature," but there is a genuine difference between early American and modern exploitations of horror. The modern "cult" is motivated by "a pessimistic skepticism, to which morals and aspirations are merely customs and dreams, and the world is an inhuman mechanism." The work of these writers, it develops, is a consequence of blind and purposeless naturalism, a "dead end" to which the errors of the American naturalists have been leading us. Thompson agreed that the horrible is a legitimate means of achieving a great aesthetic effect, and he pointed to Oedipus and Lear as examples. But this is not the effect achieved by Faulkner; he failed "to transmute the raw material in such a way as to give [his readers] a purely aesthetic effect." His appeal is not to the mind, but to the viscera. "The response to beauty involves the higher powers of the mind. These cannot endure when the gross animal instincts are aroused."

This is the kind of criticism which, with many variations of tone and motive, pursued Faulkner through the 1930's and continues to be heard. It was frequently combined with an expression of irritation over his perversities of style and method. The two most obvious qualities of Faulkner's writing, said Granville Hicks (*The Bookman*, September, 1931), are "his preoccupation with unpleasant subjects and his experimental approach to the novel as form." As for the first of these, "The world of William Faulkner echoes with the hideous trampling march of lust and disease, brutality and death." Hicks was not without admiration for the achievement: *The Sound and the Fury* and *As I Lay Dying* seemed to him remarkable experiments in form. But he was obliged to ask a question which has since been echoed many times in Faulkner criticism: "Have we here some new, some sharply individual view of life creating for itself new forms, or a keen but mechanical intelligence posing for itself problems that it loves to solve?" His answer to that question met exactly the terms of many of his contemporaries. Faulkner was, he said, playing a game with his readers, "a game in which he displays tremendous ingenuity and gives pleasure to the reader by stimulating a like ingenuity on his part." It is even possible, said Hicks, that the order of some of Faulkner's novels was decided upon perversely, that he had been fond of "inventing his stories in the regular form and then recasting them in some distorted form." It is to Conrad Aiken's great credit that this notion, while not entirely refuted, was at least largely ridiculed in Aiken's *Atlantic Monthly* essay on Faulkner's style and method (November, 1939). Hicks's discussion of Faulkner's whimsical "game" continued, however, to afford reviewers an opportunity to complain about and to mock the style, as well as to excuse their own bewilderment. Reviews of the fiction throughout the decade emphasized the "unusual" complication of plot and the needless involution and redundancy of style. This form of objection was not unrelated to the major accusation contained in Thompson's essay: the style and the method were linked at best with moral uncertainty (see F. R. Leavis's review of *Light in August* in *Scrutiny*, June, 1933), at worst with a wicked preoccupation with irrational and subnormal forms of behavior.

Perhaps the most extreme example of the latter critical approach is the work of Camille J. McCole, first published in the *Catholic World* in 1936, then enlarged as a chapter of his *Lucifer at Large* (1937). McCole found nothing virtuous or honest either in Faulkner's intentions or in his work. Faulkner was a salesman of vice, the leader of those writers who "set themselves up in a rather profitable literary business with unmitigated cruelties and abnormalities as their regular stock-in-trade." McCole was merciless, uncompromising, and inaccurate[2] in his cataloguing of the "gruesome gallery" of "idiots, perverts, degenerates, and introverts." The plot sequences are largely and hopelessly confused; the style is intolerably dense and absurd; the horrors are compounded by Faulkner's insufferable interest in idiots and morons. Only *Sartoris* escaped the slaughter; it was Faulkner's "best book." But, said McCole, Faulkner had shrewdly discovered that such a book did not sell, and it was then that he "turned so deliberately to the exploitation of cruelty."

Such shouting was after all an extreme form of protest; the critics who followed the leads of Thompson and Hicks, or who in their own way came to similar conclusions, were usually neither so strident nor so careless. Their objections to Faulkner possessed a common air of regret that a great talent had not as yet found its direction or purpose, was too self-indulgent, lacked self-

2. Typical inaccuracies: the setting of *Sartoris* is Jefferson, Missouri; Whitfield (*As I Lay Dying*) is the father of three of Addie Bundren's children; Snopes (any Snopes?) is a "pervert, reminiscent of one of Anderson's Winesburg degenerates...."

discipline, and seemed determined to stay in the blind alley of naturalism. Harlan Hatcher (*Creating the Modern American Novel*, 1935), commenting upon the "monstrous beings" who inhabited the novels, had regretfully to admit that Faulkner "defines the farthest limits to which the innovations and revolts that were at one time necessary to the continued well-being of our literature can be carried without final self-defeat." Philip Henderson (*The Novel Today*, 1936), after providing the usual catalogue of Faulkner's subjects, offered a not-unexpected comparison with Erskine Caldwell. The latter's *Tobacco Road*, said Henderson, is greatly superior to any of Faulkner's novels because Caldwell "shows us why his agricultural morons are as they are and indicates how their individual helplessness can be remedied by large-scale collective farming on the part of both whites and blacks." A social conscience made Caldwell genuine; lack of it made Faulkner cheap and aimlessly melodramatic.

Concessions were usually made; there were "hopeful signs," or in one or another novel Faulkner seemed free of his otherwise damaging preoccupations. Halford E. Luccock (*American Mirror*, 1940) saw in the horror, especially of *Soldiers' Pay*, "real data for a spiritual and moral estimate of war, and its effects, and for the spiritual history of a decade." Percy Boynton (*America in Contemporary Fiction*, 1940) saw a close parallel between abnormality of vision and aberration of judgment: ". . . it is not without significance that the technique is simpler and the content more lucid in the tales which have the greater normality, or that they become more intricate and elusive in the tales of abnormality; that, in short, technique becomes a compensation for content as content sinks in the scale of accepted values." Oscar Cargill (*Intellectual America*, 1941), while he thought that the Compsons of *The Sound and the Fury* "are so lacking in intrinsic worth that we do not really care what happens to them," and was satisfied to call *Absalom, Absalom!* "a dull book, dull, dull, dull," did hopefully point to the future as it was suggested by the publication of *The Hamlet*; a sequel, he hoped, might show Faulkner at his determined best to "come to grips with his protagonist. Then we shall know the wherefore of the Bilbos and the Huey Longs." Herbert Muller (*Modern Fiction: A Study of Values,* 1937) provided an intelligent statement of Faulkner's "technical mastery of his materials, . . . a remarkable ability to project highly original characters," but suggested that his promise of closer attention to "the main march of human affections" had as yet not been realized, was in fact dissipated in *Absalom, Absalom!* Muller concluded that the fiction was of a kind that "powerfully stimulates the imagination without greatly refining or enriching it, making it a more efficient instrument in controlling human experience." George Snell (*The Shapers of American Fiction: 1798-1947,* 1947) admired, among other things, the "affirmative attitude" he saw in "The Bear" of *Go Down, Moses;* perhaps, he said, "for once, we have seen an American writer emerge from the wild miasmal depths where Brown and Poe and Melville were at home, into freer attitudes where a view of humanity in its workaday aspects is possible." Snell did not deny, however, that the "demonic tragedy" of Faulkner's South was after all "the fundamental fructifying principle of his art."

Leftist criticism, when it did not ignore Faulkner, severely chastised him for writing in ignorance or defiance of the brave new world in the making. For all that, they sought in the fiction for hopeful signs of social consciousness. V. F. Calverton (*Modern Monthly*, March, 1938) defended Faulkner from his leftist critics who had accused him of lacking an interest in important modern issues, by saying that the South was "semi-feudal," "bankrupt and degenerate, living upon forgotten frontiers of experience...." To speak of "the class struggle," therefore, would have been to point up something that scarcely existed. Edwin Berry Burgum (*The Novel and the World's Dilemma*, 1947) suggested that Faulkner's studies of the South are portraits of American decadence in general. Burgum even tried to invest Jason Compson of *The Sound and the Fury* with a kind of desperate tragic dignity: "Caught in the vicious circle of the family pattern, he only hastens their decline into a commonplace vulgarity. But he is struggling to maintain some command over his destiny and theirs." Burgum saw a social significance in *Sanctuary*, "a Southern variant of a social interpretation of American life long since established in our fiction." It lay, briefly, in Faulkner's remarking in that novel "not only that decadence is characteristic of the region as a whole, but that even more of it is to be found in the more respectable classes." Barbara Giles (*Masses and Mainstream*, February, 1950) was less charitable. Acknowledging Faulkner's new "concern" with the South's "burden" (seen in "The Bear"), she nevertheless showed profound irritation over the attitude of Gavin Stevens in *Intruder in the Dust*; what right had he to ignore "all genuine movements rooted in history (both North and South) for the true liberation of the Negro." And she concluded by classifying Faulkner as a member of a "dying class" who "cling to their self-loving myths of the past, glorifying themselves with the gaudy legends of their ancestors until the sound of their own names becomes to them like 'silver pennons downrushing at sunset.' "

These judgments, however varied and original they may individually have been, demonstrate a common preconception with respect to what Faulkner's work should have been, a standard, or a variety of standards, to which it largely did not succeed in conforming. In the course of these deliberations, some attention was necessarily paid to Faulkner as a Southerner and to his region, either by way of extenuation or of an additionally severe stricture. In large part, the faults lay with the author, and these faults were partly a consequence of the literary "creed" he had been trapped into accepting, partly of his own overbearing hatred of "modernism" which had blinded him to the virtues of progress. Two essays (chapters of books) demonstrate these two forms of explanation especially well. The first, by Harry Hartwick (*The Foreground of American Fiction*, 1934), accused Faulkner of having followed the wrong "naturalism," or rather, of having wandered into "a kind of blind alley" from which there is no escape.

The vital tradition of naturalism, which is at heart broad in its sympathies and warm in its "passionate recognition" of life, cannot rest upon such a specialized, reptilian art as that of Faulkner's; it requires thought to justify its style and meaning to adorn its emotion. It should be a "mansion of philosophy," invigorating as well as vigorous, and a source of inspiration for all those who draw their values from Nature rather than Man, not a haunted house, dark and cold, inhabited only by spiders and morons.

In this extreme view, Faulkner is discovered exploiting atrocities for his morbid pleasure in them, and without any "moral concern," which is the only excuse for an attention to the ugly and the cruel: "his books lack what might be termed 'spiritual resonance.' "

The second essay, by Maxwell Geismar (*Writers in Crisis,* 1942), at least possessed the virtue of a sincere and often intelligent effort to understand the work. Geismar's major contention did not fully appear until near the end of his long chapter, during which he had diligently attended to what he thought were Faulkner's thematic concerns. His hatred of "modern woman" and of the Negro, the "twin furies" of the novels, was, in Geismar's estimation, a form of scapegoat device, "a dangerous quirk of the psyche,...a trick which may end by deceiving the trickster."

For it is in the larger tradition of reversionary, neo-pagan, and neurotic discontent (from which Fascism stems) that much of Faulkner's writing must be placed—the anti-civilizational revolt rising out of modern social evils, nourished by ignorance of their true nature, and which succumbs to malice as their solution.

Geismar discovered the evidence for this rejection of "a developing American maturity" in Faulkner's obvious dislike for the Female and his hatred of the Negro. Joanna Burden is the primary scapegoat victim, as Joe Christmas becomes the malicious and corrupt instrument of destruction. The murder and the lynching are, said Geismar, the crucial expression of "his contempt for modern maturity which displays itself so eloquently in the variety of perversions which the writer contrives for his characters." This is a part of a thesis-ridden interpretation of Faulkner which at best might claim the merits of originality and a strenuous effort to provide proof. It did, however, lose sight of many facts in the fiction, ignored the all-too-obvious exceptions to it, and led to misinterpretations of various and interesting kinds. The conclusions are not unlike Hartwick's, but the procedures followed in the course of arriving at them are quite different; Geismar attempted to answer the question *why* with something more than a cliché of literary history or a prevailing expression of discontent with horrors. He was also alive to the problem of literary merit, though his occasionally shrewd observations concerning style and method were soon enough overwhelmed by the insistent plodding of a search for evidence.

This, then, was the first (as it continues to be the predominating) critical view of Faulkner's work. Many others took up the refrain and echoed the objections. The reviews were quite often duplications of the points raised in the longer studies. Critics like Pelham Edgar, H. S. Canby, and Bernard Fäy rang few changes upon the general indictment (*The Art of the Novel from 1700 to the Present Time*, 1933; *Seven Years' Harvest*, 1936; "L'École de l'infortune," in *Revue de Paris*, August 1, 1937). Only occasionally was there recognition either of the sources of Faulkner's preoccupation or of his genuine talent as an artist, his genius for formal and rhetorical expression. Faulkner could himself have learned nothing from these warnings and expressions of distress; they could only fortify him in his determination to write as he needed, and to remain aloof from all criticism but his own.

ii

Favorable criticism of Faulkner, said Robert Daniel (*Perspective*, Autumn, 1950), began in 1939. Except for isolated observations (such as Robert Penn Warren's, in an essay otherwise devoted to T. S. Stribling), studies of his work were largely devoted to expressions of disgust, horror, and distress over what

Faulkner was doing or failing to do. An important element of criticism was lacking—a sympathetic effort to understand Faulkner on his own terms, a willing suspension of distress. Certain matters had scarcely been touched. One of these was the region to which Faulkner had early decided to devote himself. Another was his fictional strategy—the reasons, if any were to be found, for the strangely original methods he was using with almost every publication. In 1939, Conrad Aiken published his essay on Faulkner's style in the *Atlantic Monthly*. It was followed in the spring of 1941 by a longer and more perceptive study by Warren Beck (*American Prefaces*).[3] Since then, few serious considerations of Faulkner's work have neglected the place in his fiction of the specially functional language and syntax, or have failed to acknowledge the way in which, as Aiken put it, the sentences "parallel in a curious and perhaps inevitable way, and not without justification, the whole elaborate method of *deliberately withheld* meaning, of progressive and partial and delayed disclosure, which so often gives the characteristic shape to the novels themselves."

The year 1939 was the date of another important essay, George Marion O'Donnell's "Faulkner's Mythology" (*Kenyon Review*, Summer, 1939),[3] an essay which established the pattern of a very distinguished form of interpretation. Its main lines of consideration were taken up subsequently by several other critics, and it has in general been acknowledged as one serious way of seeing Faulkner's work as a whole. An important contribution of O'Donnell's essay was its insistence that Faulkner "is really a traditional moralist, in the best sense." This, in the face of what had been the majority conviction concerning Faulkner's "immorality" and "nihilism," was a most necessary assertion.

O'Donnell based his interpretation upon the belief that Faulkner was "a traditional man in a modern world." The fiction had therefore followed the line of such a man, who observed, in his region of the South, "the conflict between traditionalism and

3. These essays are included in this collection.

the anti-traditional modern world in which it is immersed." The points of view are represented by the Sartorises and the Snopeses. These two groups become in O'Donnell's interpretation not so much persons as polar antitheses in a conflict of moral codes. The Sartorises (not only as a family, but as a type of person) act "traditionally"; that is, they act always with an "ethically responsible will." The Snopeses "acknowledge no ethical duty." In such terms ("a struggle between humanism and naturalism") the works are examined. In each case the Sartorises and the Snopeses figure, but not always in simple conflict. Often the opposition leads to important insights: Quentin Compson, for example, is the sole representative (in *The Sound and the Fury*) of the Sartoris tradition. The rest of the Compsons have either gone over to the Snopes world or have found one or another means of withdrawing from it. The two poles of act and view are sometimes uncomfortably narrowing, and O'Donnell's essay must take the consequences of a too inflexible ordering of the fiction. Quentin's view of the tradition, for example, has become "formalized"; that is, he has lost an accurate sense of the tradition and substitutes a romantic version of it. The crucial issue is, of course, Candace's act, which O'Donnell calls her "yielding to the amorality of the Snopes world." Quentin's tragic effort, futile as it proves to be, is to "transform meaningless degeneracy into significant doom." The two classes of society are not economic but moral divisions; the Bundrens belong to the Sartoris tradition, and the progress described in *As I Lay Dying* is "not unlike that of the medieval soul toward redemption." The Bundrens are therefore able to "carry a genuine act of traditional morality through to its end." This is to push the novel to an extreme—the opposite of that view which called it a grim farce. As other critics have pointed out, it is scarcely either an ignoble comedy or a formal morality. O'Donnell's considerations of the other novels reveal the stresses and strains of his view: *Sanctuary* is a failure because in it Faulkner suffers the defects of Quentin Compson; he has become a formal rather than a vital traditionalist. *Light in August* presents to O'Donnell an "allegory," in which Gail Hightower stands for the "Formalized Tradition," impotent before the "Snopes," Joe Christmas. Faulkner has here given in to the fascination of the "antagonist"; the "Snopes" character dominates the reader's attention and enlists his sympathy. Such a view, carried with a grim and inflexible persistence through all of the work, can lead occasionally to strange commentaries: as in the case of O'Donnell's description of *Mosquitoes* as a "Snopes-world Bohemia." But the essay proved to be of considerable service to Faulkner criticism: first, in suggesting a means of viewing the work as a continuous whole; second, in insisting on Faulkner as a serious, a "moral" writer in the face of scores of assertions to the contrary; third, in raising Faulkner's characters from the level to which other critics had consigned them; and, finally, in providing illumination for the problem of his use of history. It was natural enough that, when *The Hamlet* appeared, two years after O'Donnell's essay, it should be claimed not only as a part of the canon but also as an additional proof of O'Donnell's judgment. Robert Penn Warren, reviewing that novel (*Kenyon Review*, Spring, 1941), fitted it into the pattern: the contrast in this case was "between the non-aristocratic Frenchman's Bend world, unconscious of its past, and the Snopes world, which Ratliff, the characteristic Faulknerian commentator, recognizes as the enemy."

The fullest and in many respects the most ingenious adaptation of O'Donnell's construction of Faulkner came in 1946, when Malcolm Cowley published the Viking *Portable Faulkner*. Except for short stories and such longer works as "The Bear" and "Old Man" ("half" of *The Wild Palms*), the necessities of Cowley's form of order did not permit publication of Faulkner's works as a whole. The work of editing the *Portable* was undertaken at a time when Faulkner's books were almost entirely out of print; since then, they have returned, been reissued, and their author has once more become a familiar and much-discussed figure. In his introduction, Cowley attended with devotion and care to the geographical and historical revival of Yoknapatawpha County. The selections themselves recall that history, from 1820 to 1940;

Faulkner's additional remarks on the Compsons push the dates back as far as 1745 and forward to 1945, a full two centuries accounted for. The "legend" which dominates Cowley's selection is explained in some detail in his introduction:

The Deep South was settled partly by aristocrats like the Sartoris clan and partly by new men like Colonel Sutpen. Both types of planters were determined to establish a lasting social order on the land they had seized from the Indians (that is, to leave sons behind them). They had the virtue of living single-mindedly by a fixed code; but there was also an inherent guilt in their "design," their way of life; it was slavery that put a curse on the land and brought about the Civil War. After the War was lost, partly as a result of their own mad heroism (for who else but men as brave as Jackson and Stuart could have frightened the Yankees into standing together and fighting back?) they tried to restore "the design" by other methods. But they no longer had the strength to achieve more than a partial success, even after they had freed their land from the carpetbaggers who followed the Northern armies. As time passed, moreover, the men of the old order found that they had Southern enemies too: they had to fight against a new exploiting class descended from the landless whites of slavery days. In this struggle between the clan of Sartoris and the unscrupulous tribe of Snopes, the Sartorises were defeated in advance by a traditional code that kept them from using the weapons of the enemy. As a price of victory, however, the Snopeses had to serve the mechanized civilization of the North, which was morally impotent in itself, but which, with the aid of its Southern retainers, ended by corrupting the Southern nation.

Included in this variant of O'Donnell's interpretation is the crucial struggle between Sartorises and Snopeses; but the "burden" of conscience which Cowley gave the former is an additional insight into the history of Faulkner's people. The editing in this case was necessarily that of paraphrase and crucial quotation. As in the selections made, so in the introduction, too little attention was paid the separate "integrities" and unities of the works themselves. This is not to say that Cowley did not possess most excellent insights into Faulkner's art; his discussion of that art as well as of its weaknesses was one of the most perceptive and

acute so far published. Cowley, however, had little respect for
Faulkner as a novelist; he was considered best as a writer of
novelle, such as "The Bear." It seemed unnecessary, therefore
(as well as impossible, given the strategy of the *Portable*'s organization), to consider Faulkner a novelist. The novels are thus
shabbily treated, and none of them comes through with even an
adequate sense of their original structure and method. What *is*
accomplished in the *Portable* is a vivid evocation of imaginative
reality; it is both fuller in its documentation than is O'Donnell's
essay and less handicapped by the limited perspective which a too
narrowly conceived thesis caused in O'Donnell's case. In consequence of Cowley's work, the influence of Thompson, Canby, and
Hicks had considerably subsided; and Cowley, with O'Donnell
and others, encouraged and insisted upon a serious attention to
what Faulkner was saying. A major weakness in both O'Donnell
and Cowley was that they did not sufficiently emphasize the importance of Faulkner's *way* of saying it.

Warren's long review of the *Portable Faulkner* (*The New
Republic*, August 12 and 26, 1946) marked a further step in
the consideration of Faulkner's subject as it offered valuable suggestions for another kind of critical study. Warren gratefully
acknowledged Cowley's introduction as "one of the few things
ever written on Faulkner which is not hagridden by prejudice or
preconception and which really sheds some light on the subject."[4]
He then proceeded, after reviewing Cowley's statement of "the
legend," to examine crucial matters related to Faulkner's treatment of the legend and its region. Warren's discussion of nature
as a means of formulating judgments of Faulkner's people was an
admirable extension and correction of O'Donnell's rather more
abstract view of "tradition." Two important issues concerning
Faulkner's people gave Warren an opportunity to correct certain
misconceptions: those pertinent to the "poor white" and the
Negro. In each case the thesis contained in Geismar's *Writers in*

4. See also Caroline Gordon's review, in the *New York Times*, April 5,
1946, in which she thoroughly approved of O'Donnell and Cowley as
having seen Faulkner correctly and "as he wants to be seen."

Crisis was taken to task, as was his inaccurate view of the role of humor in Faulkner's work. The review concluded with a number of acute observations on technique, the principal value of which was that they were suggestive beginnings for a further range of Faulkner studies—studies that Cowley had scarcely indicated in either his introduction or his selection. "To what extent," Warren asked, "does Faulkner work in terms of polarities, oppositions, paradoxes, inversions of roles? How much does he employ a line of concealed (or open) dialectic progression as a principle for his fiction?" These questions, together with his query concerning Faulkner's development of "symbolic motifs," were perhaps the most fruitful brief challenges thus far offered in the history of Faulkner criticism. They also pointed up a division in that criticism which still exists. O'Donnell had, after all, suggested what Warren called "the main symbolic outline of Faulkner's fiction," but he had only incidental attention for technique, symbol, and form, and then only by way of implementing a thesis or explaining it. The major question was unanswered: had Faulkner written novels, short stories, and *novelle* which independently stood, or had he written a "history" or made a "moral" examination of the South's past tradition and present "burden"?

Delmore Schwartz's "The Fiction of William Faulkner" (*The Southern Review*, Summer, 1941) did not answer that question, but raised many others. It belonged to the beginnings of the newer Faulkner criticism, but was made less useful than contemporary pieces because of its failure to achieve sharp definition and classification. Schwartz found a total of nine "themes," and these proved, on closer examination, to be only subdivisions of major concerns. They were, furthermore, not always rewarding or acute statements (the poor white and the peasant; the primitive, the abnormal, and the virtually insane; the city slicker and the village slicker; etc.). Some suggestion of what were Faulkner's larger concerns did, however, come through: "The conflict between the idea of the Old South and the progressive actuality of the New South has brought Faulkner to the extreme where he can only seize his values, which are those of the idea of the Old South, by imagining them being violated by the most hideous crimes."

Other important insights into Faulkner's work and worth, some of them found in brief reviews, marked the growing maturity of Faulkner's critical reception. Kay Boyle (*The New Republic*, March 9, 1938) had early recognized Faulkner's genius and had insisted that it be seen in terms of the entire work; it "resides in that entire determined collection of volumes which reveal him to be the most absorbing writer of our time." Three of Warren Beck's essays demonstrated his sharp intelligence with respect both to Faulkner's views and his technique. The first ("Faulkner and the South," *Antioch Review*, Spring, 1941) showed Beck's recognition of Faulkner as a "Mississippian who has transcended provincialism without losing artistic devotion to a locale." The essay put much emphasis on what Beck called a needed expiation for the "sin of human slavery" and stressed Faulkner's "moral sense," his "humane point of view" as a necessary critical means of acquiring perspective upon Faulkner's concern with violence. The most important question Beck asked here (important by way of challenging contemporary protests against the violence) was this: "Is he really riding on a momentum of a waning, vitiated romance that lends his narratives a scandalous interest, or do the evils pictured conform fundamentally to observable and characteristic acts of men, and do these evils pictured stand proportionately silhouetted against an implied background of enduring ideals?" The second of the essays (*College English*, May, 1941) posed the question of Faulkner's point of view, as this is seen modifying and "tightening" the sensibilities of his characters. The simplicity of some of his persons is in the direct line of an honest recognition of the tensions existing in his world. That world is not merely governed by "nihilism," though Faulkner's protagonists are frequently (usually) defeated. That they are defeated is not a proof of " a denial of values" but an acknowledgment of the very real presence of evil and of "the precariousness and difficulty of rationality."

The thematic interpretation of Faulkner, proceeding largely

from O'Donnell, was once more taken up by Russell Roth ("William Faulkner: The Pattern of Pilgrimage") in the best of a series of essays published in *Perspective*, Summer, 1949. The prevailing order that Roth saw in Faulkner's work is discovered largely in his point-of-view characters: beginning with the "young aesthete" of the novels of the 1920's, and moving from there to what Roth calls the "middle-aged ethicist," Horace Benbow, whose task is "to make the humanistic Sartoris values prevail in a particular case in the naturalistic Snopes world." In *Light in August,* Roth noted "a major shift." Faulkner, no longer satisfied with the "Sartoris ethic" (rendered almost wholly ineffectual in the figure of Hightower), seeks a new "vantage point." The redeeming figure Faulkner has finally discovered is Isaac McCaslin of *Go Down, Moses,* whose character "would appear as an attempt to work back to this fountainhead of intuitive strength and humility from the ruin of the Old Southern aristocracy." McCaslin is Sartoris revived and strengthened, and in him are both "the humanistic motivation and, most important, the ability to act. . . ."

The service performed by these essays, from O'Donnell to Roth, was largely the necessary one of redressing the balance of view, of forcing the reader away from incrimination and empty protest to a serious and sympathetic reading of Faulkner's larger intention.[5] The criticism had its own risks. A great improvement

5. Other sympathetic studies, not considered here, include Dayton Kohler's "William Faulkner and the Social Conscience" (*College English,* December, 1949), which relies largely upon Cowley's definition of "the legend" and continues it in the light of Faulkner publications that had appeared since the *Portable* (1946). Of especial interest is Vincent F. Hopper's "Faulkner's Paradise Lost" (*Virginia Quarterly Review,* 1947), which remarks, of Faulkner's world, that it is "indisputably infernal" and deliberately so; that there is and can be no compensating "Paradise Regained"; and, finally, that Faulkner has remained "pure romanticist, with most of the romanticist's traditional reactions. He wallows in gloom and despair." A strange variant upon the thematic study is James T. Jackson's "Delta Cycle: A Study of William Faulkner" (*Chimera,* Autumn, 1946), which considers Faulkner's work in terms of seasonal analogies, with much stress upon an historical reading of the actual South as it bears upon Yoknapatawpha County. Thematic readings of Faulkner's work began also to be seen in the reviews of the 1940's,

over the captious and impatient dismissal of Faulkner by the "cult of cruelty" reviewers and critics, it did nevertheless involve a need to force novels and stories into a pattern, or to slight them when they did not quite yield to thematic pressure. Certain errors of interpretation, largely the result of a narrowness of view, persisted through most of the criticism. *As I Lay Dying* continued to be a novel of heroic denial and obligation; the character of Vardaman continued to puzzle the critics; and novels of great subtlety of form (such as *Absalom, Absalom!*) were too often merely summarized, a procedure that almost invariably distorted them.

iii

For many years after the publication of an author's first book, his reputation must rely upon the reviews and notices his work receives. In many respects, Faulkner's career has depended more than most upon such treatment. Hundreds of reviews have been published, ranging from brief notes to longer "studies."[6] As in any other case, the history of these reviews provides a footnote to the career of popular and semipopular taste. That history has its definable stages: in the 1920's, Faulkner was scarcely known and indifferently reviewed; in the period from 1929 to 1932, when a large share of his best novels appeared, he was given much attention, but it was hesitant and puzzled when not downright indignant; after 1946, the date of the *Portable*, each new Faulkner publication was recognized widely and some effort made to consider it in the light of past achievement; finally, since

---

the O'Donnell and, especially, the Cowley interpretations having eventually reached the reviewers. A marked increase of this type of criticism is noticeable, beginning with the appearance of the *Portable*, which demanded a full view of the work.

6. I am indebted to Mrs. Vickery for many of the references used in part three of the introduction. This survey of reviews has, of course, had to be reduced in length, and reactions to certain of the works have been ignored. The most regrettable omission is the reviewing of *Pylon*, interesting because English and French attention to it greatly exceeded the American. (F.J.H.)

1948 and the controversial *Intruder in the Dust*, reviews have been disturbed over the "polemical Faulkner," the "preacher," and the garrulous Gavin Stevens.

In the case of *Soldiers' Pay*, Faulkner's first novel, the reviews were concerned chiefly to "place" it in the tradition of post-war fiction, to which it, to all appearances, belonged. As such, the novel seemed to promise nothing more than an addition to that literature. Even here, however, lines were drawn. Thomas Boyd called the novel "Honest but Slap-dash" (*Saturday Review of Literature*, April 24, 1926), and described its characters as "vague, abnormally behaving characters who waver uncertainly and fantastically. . . ." The English reviews were largely patronizing: Mr. Faulkner has talent, is fortunately young and may outgrow the faults so obvious in this tale. One English reviewer went to the opposite extreme (*The New Statesman*, June 28, 1930) and considered Faulkner superior to both Lawrence and Hemingway: "I can remember no first novel of such magnificent achievement in the last thirty years." In the reviews both of this and of the next novel (*Mosquitoes*) there are several discerning references to Faulkner's imitativeness of style, to the "echoes" from late-nineteenth-century poetry. *Mosquitoes* deservedly received severe criticism and short shrift. A *New Republic* review (July 20, 1927) pointed out its second-rate satiric "cleverness" and its "labored sophistication."

The reviews of the second "period" are both more numerous and more varied. In *Sartoris* the reviewers sensed the beginning of a larger and perhaps more enduring preoccupation than those found in the first two novels. "In *Sartoris*," said an unsigned review in the *New Statesman and Nation* (April 2, 1932), "we are given a picture of the South, of four generations and two wars, tossed at us apparently haphazard, yet more complete, because more stimulating to our imaginations, than in many volumes of detailed family chronicles." The sense of family tradition, new to his fiction, was recognized elsewhere as well, though reviewers were for the most part unfavorably disposed. Willard Thorp, writ-

ing in *Scrutiny* (September, 1932), called the novel a product
of the influence of *Beau Geste* and *Death of a Hero*, complained
of its repetitions and bad literary "echoes," and went on to say:
"Faulkner, if he goes on at this rate, can easily lead the pack that
helps the *Saturday Evening Post* sell mouthwash to 50 million
Americans." L. A. G. Strong, however, spoke in the *Spectator*
(February 27, 1932) of Faulkner's genius, in fact, suggested that
he was one of a very few to whom the term *genius* could be applied. In general, the English reviews, which adopted a "watch-
and-wait" attitude, were kinder than the American. The most
penetrating review of *Sartoris* was written, some eight years or so
after its publication, by Jean-Paul Sartre (*Nouvelle Revue française*, 1938) and was, of course, aided by Sartre's knowledge of
the fiction published by Faulkner since 1929.[7]

    The Sound and the Fury challenged critical skill as no other
modern American novel had thus far done. Reviewers were quick
to see the exceptional uses to which Faulkner had put the stream-
of-consciousness technique, and not unwilling to suspect that the
novel was a work of extraordinary talent. L. A. G. Strong, from
the beginning an ardent Faulkner supporter, said of this novel
(*The Spectator*, April 25, 1931) that its difficulty is worth mas-
tering, since the method is indispensable to the effect needed.
Henry Smith (*Southwest Review*, Autumn, 1929) agreed, and
added that Faulkner had been able to combine a study of provincial life with certain important universal overtones. The refrain
of reviewers seemed generally to applaud the method both in spite

7. The French have, of all Europeans, been the most enthusiastic and
the most critical. For information about French reactions, see the interesting (though sketchy) essay, "What French Readers Find in William
Faulkner's Fiction," *New York Times,* December 17, 1950, and also
Sartre's "American Novelists in French Eyes," *Atlantic Monthly*, August,
1946. The most diligent of French sponsors of Faulkner have been Maurice E. Coindreau, Maurice le Breton, and Sartre. In *L'Age du roman
americain* (Paris, 1948), Claude-Edmonde Magny has provided (pp. 196–
243) the best study of Faulkner's work as a whole available in French
criticism. See also "Faulkner, et la génération de l'exil," by "Rabi"
(*Esprit,* January, 1951), reprinted in this collection.

of and because of its difficulty.[8] But there were several exceptions:
Francis L. Robbins, for example (*Outlook and Independent*,
October 16, 1929), who complained that the novel betrayed a
regrettable distrust of "familiar values" and that the "subjective
analysis" weakened a potentially great theme. The London *Times
Literary Supplement* (May 14, 1931) saw little but "skill" overcome by a concern with "pathological delinquency." *The Sound
and the Fury* can be credited with beginning the serious general
concern over Faulkner as an artist. Even those reviewers, like
Thompson and Hicks, who had scarcely been willing to grant him
distinction, admitted to admiration for the formal experiment.
Evelyn Scott's pamphlet study of the novel, published in the same
year as the novel (1929), was the first extended analysis of the
form and point of view of a Faulkner work and was in that
sense a landmark in Faulkner criticism.

Annoyance over *As I Lay Dying* seems to have been motivated in two ways—the obscurity of the method and the un-
pleasantness of the content. A grudging admission of Faulkner's
"talent" usually acompanied these complaints, but the remark in
the *New York Times* (October 19, 1930) was characteristic of
the general reaction: "Content compels us to put this book in a
high place in an inferior category." In short, the novel was called
an "uncommonly forceful book, though not a pleasant one" (*The
New Republic*, November 19, 1930). Admiration of Faulkner's
talent was combined with horror over his "pageant of degeneracy." Clifton Fadiman (beginning a series of "clever" dis-
paragements) found it difficult to acknowledge Faulkner as an
important writer. He is clever, said Fadiman, but tedious and
morbid; he does have an interesting mind, "untouched by the
major intellectual platitudes of our day." Only Maurice le Breton
found the novel "relatively simple" (*Revue Anglo-Americaine*,
June, 1936), the writing "precise and vivid."

8. The strongest of American endorsements appeared in the *Sewanee
Review* of January, 1930, written by Abbott Martin, who claimed for
Faulkner a greater artistry than Joyce's.

The objections to Faulkner had to this time been fairly confined to qualifications of earnest or puzzled admiration. With the
publication of *Sanctuary*, they became more overt and bold. Each
page of the book "is a calculated assault on one's sense of the
normal," said Fadiman; and, though he considered it an improvement over *As I Lay Dying*, he thought it overcharged with the
faults of "excessive eagerness." Faulkner evokes only fear, said
John Chamberlain (*New York Times*, February 15, 1931),
"whereas Dostoyefsky evokes both fear and exaltation." The great
share of the novel's reviews complained of that lack of "exaltation," of the grimness of the horror, the "sadistic cruelty," and the
lack of "warmth." Literary talent is wasted on a "morbid theme";
the characters are of no interest save to the neurologist or crim-
inologist.[9] When the novel was praised, it was often because the
reviewer (like Herschel Brickell, *North American Review*, April,
1932) thought Faulkner courageous in telling "the truth" about
the South, and in refusing to "kneel in the romantic temple." In
the *Saturday Review of Literature* for October 20, 1934, Lawrence S. Kubie subjected the novel and its author to psychoanal-
ysis. This view and the letters written in answer to it provide an
interesting commentary on Faulkner's fate among the reviewers.
Sanctuary, said Doctor Kubie, was that type of literature which
"represents the working out in phantasy of the problems of
impotence in men, meaning by impotence a frailty in all spheres
of instinctual striving." Horace Benbow's struggle in Lee Goodwin's behalf is actually a struggle against his own "impotence and
powerlessness [*sic*]." The only persons of the novel "who take
life in the body with simple, earthy realism" are Lee and Ruby
Goodwin. At least one of the correspondents thought Kubie had
not gone far enough; J. R. Oliver felt that "Along these lines of

9. Henry Seidel Canby (*Saturday Review of Literature*, March 21,
1931) added his voice to those who accused the novel of indulging in a
depraved and morbid subject; he added that such an indulgence distorted
the American scene, which is infinitely varied and many-shaded; the novel
therefore "exaggerates a potentiality of human nature at the expense of
human truth."

overcompensation lie all the attempted rapes, all the cruelty and bullying that are so vividly described in Mr. Faulkner's book."[10]

Faulkner's first collection of short stories, *These Thirteen*, provoked a number of interesting reviews, perhaps really a tribute to the succession of important novels produced in the years 1929–1932. The book proved an occasion for several "total" estimates. Grenville Vernon (*The Commonweal*, January 20, 1932) rather definitively underscored the "regret" so often seen in the reviews: that a man of so much talent should be so entirely concerned with "the malevolent and disgusting." A perverse genius, a Baudelairian romanticist, his appearance in literature is a sad indication of what is possible in an age deprived of faith. Lionel Trilling (*Nation*, November 4, 1931) objected to Faulkner's lack of "largeness of reference." "A Rose for Emily," for example, is "pure event without implication." "Dry September" and "Victory" escape the impeachment "because they are aerated by the writer's acceptance of the common, an acceptance which by no means limits the originality, even idiosyncrasy of their vision and style. Beside them the rest of the stories, for all their success in their own terms, have a subtle kind of stuffiness, shut off as they are in their interesting but hermetically sealed universe." Robert Penn Warren, however, in one of his first statements (*Virginia Quarterly Review*, January, 1932) found the opposite values in Faulkner's work. The narrow identification of theme and locale gives the stories their strength; the "feeling for place" strengthens the sense of reality which is always profound in Faulkner's characters. Far from being "trivial" or isolated and strange, "A Rose for Emily" is his best achievement. The publication of *These Thirteen* served, in these and other reviews, to mark off clearly as at no

10. In *Saturday Review of Literature*, November 10, 1934. One of the most discerning reviews of *Sanctuary* appeared in the *Nouvelle Revue française* (1933): André Malraux's "Préface a 'Sanctuaire' de W. Faulkner." Its approval of the novel was explained in this way: Certain great novels derive their strength from the fact that their authors are capable and are able to "submerge" them in a single dominating preoccupation: as D. H. Lawrence "s'enveloppe dans la sexualité," Faulkner buries himself "dans l'irrémédiable."

time hitherto the lines of critical reaction. The wide disparity between Trilling's and Warren's views was indicative of the sharpness of division: Trilling temperately stating a need for "social reference," Warren recognizing the strength that is given by a preoccupation with place and limitation.

Light in August caused a sharper division of opinion than had previously been seen. The period of puzzled admiration was over. Faulkner had now produced a number of books; and the novel itself was not "experimental" in any obvious sense. The expression of outrage was vehement and outspoken. Faulkner provides intense depictions of horror together with vague hints of meaning, said Geoffrey Stone (*The Bookman*, November, 1932); in his preoccupation with horrors he flees reality. Other objections were to Faulkner's refusal directly to give information, his "roundaboutness" in developing his narrative; this often as a result of bad planning, a needless and reckless luxuriance of style.[11] Such reviewers as J. Donald Adams saw in *Light in August* a "turn toward the better" (*New York Times,* October 9, 1932): the work of a man who has been "desperately hurt, a man whom life had at some point badly cheated," but who gives signs of recovering his balance. Sponsors of Faulkner found the novel equally stimulating as proof of a maturing genius: the preoccupation with evil seemed to them more clearly justified and more exactly defined, the intricacy of form as significant as that of *The Sound and the Fury* and more profoundly relevant.

A similar division of views was seen in the reactions to *Absalom, Absalom!* The parade of objections was of course led by Clifton Fadiman's *New Yorker* review (October 31, 1936): "every person in *Absalom, Absalom!* comes to no good end, and they all take a hell of a time coming even that far." Fadiman discoursed on what he called the "Non-Stop or Life Sentence" of the novel, citing statistics, and discussed the method of "Anti-Narrative, a set of complex devices used to keep the story from being

11. Strangely, Maurice Coindreau (*Nouvelle Revue française,* 1933) hailed *Light in August*'s clarity, comparable, he said, with that of a novel by Willa Cather.

told . . . as if a child were to go to work on it with a pair of shears. . . ." Perhaps significant of the reviewer's tastes, Fadiman concluded with a qualified approval of James T. Farrell's *A World I Never Made*: at least "what [Farrell] knows is important, what he says is clear. . . ." There was widespread agreement with Fadiman concerning the "Anti-Narrative" of *Absalom, Absalom!*, and not a little exasperation over what seemed a perversity of method carried too far. Such figures as these were employed to describe the obscurity: a man dealing cards and secretly hiding the joker; reading the novel at times little easier than trying to knit with barbed wire; an extravagant puzzle; a mixture of fog and dreams. Bernard De Voto complained (*Saturday Review of Literature*, October 31, 1936) that "When a narrative sentence has to have as many as three parentheses identifying the reference of pronouns, it signifies mere bad writing and can be justified by no psychological or esthetic principle whatever." Life is short and *Absalom, Absalom!* is very long! Faulkner's friends among the critics acknowledged the "density" of style and the complication of method, but while admitting the former explained and sometimes defended the latter with suggestions of Conrad and James. The method of "multiple narrators" provoked references not only to these but also to Ford Madox Ford.[12] William Troy suffered from the same need to defend what he was not certain of understanding (*Nation*, October 31, 1936): Faulkner is best understood as a lyric poet, said Troy; and his fiction provides no "norm" to which the reader can have access. "His imagination posits isolated people, actions, gestures, even speeches, broods upon them until they take the full shape of his vision, and then attempts to relate them in some sort of pattern." In short, *Absalom, Absalom!* proved a crucial test for Faulkner's admirers as it seemed definitive proof of the long-standing objections of his detractors. Not even Troy (who disapproved of the scheme of "multiple narration") saw clearly the relevance to Quentin Compson of the Sutpen story or came clearly to recognize its

12. See Graham Greene, "The Furies in Mississippi," *The London Mercury*, March, 1937.

speculative nature. The complexities of style were almost universally called an extreme case of Faulkner's suffering from a lack of the advantage, as Mary Colum put it, "of threshing out his technical ideas around a café table."[13]

Except for Malcolm Cowley and Stephen Vincent Benét, *The Hamlet* was received with disfavor, on the usual counts of its unintelligibility, obscenity, and lack of purposeful direction. The Snopeses are all bad; there is an unnecessarily long documentation of this fact. "It's a nice bucolic idyl of insanity, avarice, cruelty, rape and murder, centering around the meanest passel of white folks this side of a nineteenth-century novel."[14] The principal objection was to the "spectacular" accumulation of evil, large and small, with no relieving contrast. Ratliff seemed to most reviewers scarcely to have existed. Benét, however, saw his importance as a specially designated Faulkner personality (*Saturday Review of Literature*, April 6, 1940): "He doesn't, it is true, get anywhere in particular, but his disillusioned comment represents the defeated virtues of civilization—at least by comparison with the Snopeses."

The abundance of reviews of *Intruder in the Dust* testified both to the "arrival" of its author as a literary celebrity and to the controversial nature of the work itself. The long direct statements made by Ike McCaslin in *Go Down, Moses* had prepared the discerning reviewer somewhat for the "shock" of Gavin Stevens in this novel. As a consequence of its directness, the novel became the subject of sharply drawn lines of interpretation. Everyone admitted the greater "explicitness" of Faulkner's text, most reviewers with regret. Edmund Wilson's *New Yorker* review (October 23, 1948) stated most sharply the two objections to the book: those to its too false directness of polemical statement and to its defeating and finally needless involutions of style. Of the

13. "Faulkner's Struggle with Technique," *Forum and Century*, January, 1937.
14. *Newsweek*, April 1, 1940. *Time*, on the same day, was as extravagant in its praise as *Newsweek* was generous with its abuse. A reviewer for the *Spectator* (September 27, 1940) was apparently so bored by the book that she misplaced its events in a "Kentucky village."

latter Wilson said that they are too often "the casualties of an indolent taste and a negligent workmanship" not seen so abundantly in his earlier prose. As for the "tract," the novel contains "a kind of counterblast to the anti-lynching bill and to the civil-rights plank in the Democratic platform." One inference drawn from this novel by Faulkner's apologists was stated by Malcolm Cowley (*The New Republic*, October 18, 1948): "Now one can clearly see what so many readers formerly overlooked: that these are Faulkner's people and that he loves them in a fashion fierce and proprietary." But the major question (except for critics like Barbara Giles of *Masses and Mainstream*) was not so much Faulkner's right to "love" these people, but rather the propriety of Gavin Stevens' "lectures": had not the "point" of them been most brilliantly and dramatically made in the first seven chapters, and especially in the very fine narrative of the Lucas-Chick Mallison tensions? Some reviewers (like Harvey Breit, *New York Times*, September 26, 1948) were willing to maintain that Stevens' arguments had been more than satisfactorily "particularized." Irving Howe (*American Mercury*, October, 1948) spoke of Faulkner's extreme use of the "official" Southern rhetoric, but found that use "significant" and exciting. On aesthetic grounds it may have to be rejected, but the sincerity of its anger is profound and meaningful. Dan S. Norton (*Virginia Quarterly Review*, Winter, 1949) thought otherwise: Gavin's role is to intervene, to violate the experiential pattern from which Chick Mallison should come to his special realizations. This was the primary objection— to a "special pleading" which, whatever its independent virtues, violated the context and caused an imbalance of narrative and recourse to blunt persuasion. In the end, the reviews of *Intruder in the Dust* provided a remarkable cross section of a considerable body of criticism, of an artist firmly established and widely read. The bulk of the reviewing was now addressed to the question which Faulkner answered (or, at least, to which he gave his own answer) in the long speeches and not to the particular experience dramatized on the courthouse square and in the graveyard. The extremes of rejection and acceptance of the novel were seen in

the condescending and somewhat wrongheaded review of Elizabeth Hardwick (*Partisan Review*, October, 1948) and the sober
and total endorsement of Andrew Lytle (*Sewanee Review*,
Winter, 1949).[15]

Perhaps no novelist of our century has suffered so persistent
an attack in his lifetime of writing, as no author has been more
valiantly defended. The reviews demonstrate a progress from
obscurity to a falsely motivated popularity (in connection with
the notoriety of *Sanctuary*) to what was almost a unanimous bewilderment (over the complexities of *Absalom, Absalom!*), and
finally to his present *succès d'estime*. Faulkner was subjected to
the abuse now conventionally expected in the case of most
modern writers; but he suffered additional abuse, on the grounds
of his own "regional" peculiarities and his apparent "lack of interest" in the "larger implications and responsibilities" of his
work. The reviews provided abundant repetition of the "cult of
cruelty" thesis first set down at the beginning of the 1930's; they
revealed critics trying to define and describe Faulkner's "South"
and to see a thematic discipline governing the work; they also
demonstrated a concern over form, diction, language, and artistry,
by way of meeting the successive challenges offered by the novels.
In many of them were to be found germinal suggestions for the
longer and more careful studies of Faulkner's novels which have
appeared in the last few years. These are, after all, the beginnings
of a substantial criticism, to which reviewing is always and properly subordinate.

iv

Almost every critic and reviewer who has had anything to
say about Faulkner has made some comment on his style. One of
the principal complaints registered against him from the beginning had to do with his "perverse" maneuvering of syntax, his
reckless disregard of grammatical "decency," and the exorbitant
demands he has made upon the reader's attention. Joseph Warren

15. These are reprinted in this collection.

Beach (*American Fiction: 1920–1940*, 1941) stated well the reader's genuine distress:

Half the time we are swimming under water, holding our breath and straining our eyes to read off the meaning of submarine phenomena, unable to tell fact from figure, to fix the reference of pronouns, or distinguish between guess and certainty. From time to time we come to the surface, gasping, to breathe the air of concrete fact and recorded truth, only to go floundering again the next moment through crashing waves of doubt and speculation.

Not only the reader, but every character is "lost in the spool of his rhetoric," said Alfred Kazin (*On Native Grounds,* 1942), a rhetoric that is "perhaps the most elaborate, intermittently incoherent and ungrammatical, thunderous, polyphonic rhetoric in all American writing...." Faulkner's love of this rhetoric was explained at times on the grounds of his "Southern romantic" inheritance, at other times as a consequence of his constant "uncertainty" and attempts to evade discipline. Wyndham Lewis, writing in 1934 (*Men Without Art*), thought it merely "second-rate," cheap poetry masquerading as prose, and proceeded to document, by reference to three of Faulkner's novels, the working of his "slipshod and redundant artistic machine."

It was largely through the effort of Conrad Aiken, an American critic whose importance for modern literature has been underrated, that the "style" was seen as something more than the product of mere undisciplined whimsy. Admitting, perhaps too eagerly, that the style was "all too frequently downright bad," Aiken went on to point out what he thought was the reason (even the *necessity*) for it. The manner is an effort on Faulkner's part to make the reader "go to work," his reward being "that there *is* a situation to be given shape, a meaning to be extracted." Especially in the case of *Absalom, Absalom!*, Aiken demonstrated the advantages gained: there is no "*logical* point of entrance" in that novel; "we must first submit, and follow the circling of the author's interest, which turns a light inward toward the centre, but every moment from a new angle, a new point of view." There was no denying Faulkner's "exuberance," and especially in the earlier novels (through *Sartoris*) the rhetoric was rightly seen as scarcely identified with the needs of its subject. But critics had been so fond of pointing out the obvious excesses that they often substituted a listing of them for honest criticism. In the last ten years, the emphasis has been less on these "infelicities," more frequently on the close and significant relationship of language with structure—more than that, on the advantage gained from a richness of language. Warren Beck pointed out convincingly the effectiveness of Faulkner's "intervention" in his narrative; and in comparing two passages (from the early and the late version of "Spotted Horses") he showed how much the stylistic "voice" of the author added to the narration.

If technique and structure were interdependent in Faulkner's work, then it might be proved that the style had a significant purpose; but this conclusion awaited serious and careful examinations of text. The next step in criticism involved the reading of separate novels or short stories, with the aim of attending to technique in the spirit of Mark Schorer's "Technique as Discovery":

Technique is the means by which the writer's experience, which is his subject matter, compels him to attend to it; technique is the only means he has of discovering, exploring, developing his subject, of conveying its meaning and finally of evaluating it.

The problem of defining the narratives in terms of what the text reveals has scarcely yet been solved in Faulkner's case. Unlike Hemingway's (which has perhaps been too exhaustively and too tediously examined), Faulkner's work has just begun to yield its technical evidence. In the last decade, however, important beginnings have been made. The two Faulkner issues of *Perspective* (Summer, 1949, and Autumn, 1950), and the Autumn, 1948, issue of the *Kenyon Review* have been largely responsible for these beginnings. Much of this work is still speculative and therefore scarcely definitive. But such essays as the following are a fine earnest: Sumner Powell's on *The Sound and the Fury*, Phyllis Hirshleifer's on *Light in August*, Ray West's on "A Rose for Emily" (*Perspective*, Summer, 1949); Olga Vickery's on *As I Lay Dying* (*Perspective*, Autumn, 1950); Richard Chase's on *Light in August*, Lawrence Bowling's on *The Sound and the Fury* (*Kenyon Review*, Autumn, 1948); and William Poirier's on *Absalom, Absalom!* Irving Howe's re-examination of *The Wild Palms* (*Tomorrow*, December, 1949) is the only serious attempt to examine that work, which has for the most part been dismissed as two novels only indifferently related. Other investigations are under way, in the universities and elsewhere. They are long overdue, delayed by two decades of easy dismissal or cautious reserve, and perhaps also by Faulkner's own attitude toward the criticism of his work.

That attitude has been notoriously indifferent—perhaps rightly so, for Faulkner found little to learn from his early critics and does not seem to have suffered (at least not disastrously) from his isolation. Cowley, Mrs. Colum, and others have regretted his failure to seek out advice, to join some group of fellow writers around a café table for frequent discussion and exchanges of criticism. He has occasionally announced his indifference to criticism, has spoken of the speed with which he finished manuscripts; but there is evidence that these public expressions of scorn do not accurately describe his own concerns over his writing.[16] It is absurd to suggest that that writing is a "public concern," that Faulkner needs to submit to formal training. The isolation from schools and cafés has carried its own risks of absurdity (there are many suggestions, ideas, and images in his work which seem to have been lost or discarded before their full use has been developed); but one may hazard the suggestion that it was indispensable to Faulkner's way of writing and that the "treatment" (whatever it might have been) might well have caused more damage than good. Faulkner has achieved distinction, if not in spite of, then independently of, his critics. The criticism is itself useful for the most part to his readers; and it is with that conviction that the selections from it contained in this book are offered.

16. See Russell Roth, "The Brennan Papers: Faulkner in Manuscript," *Perspective*, Summer, 1949.

I. The Region

WILLIAM FAULKNER AT HOME

A. WIGFALL GREEN

"Faulkner," said the Muse, "look in thy heart and write," and Faulkner wrote of the pseudopolis Jefferson, in Yoknapatawpha County, in the heart of the red-hill section of northern Mississippi. Jefferson, probably named for the President of the Confederacy, is Oxford, in Lafayette County, the seat of the state university; Yoknapatawpha was probably suggested by Yocona (locally pronounced Yŏk'-ny), the name of a bordering county and river.

Repudiating the custom of the New Englander of placing a green in the center of the town, the Southerner placed the courthouse, the civic nucleus, within a square, about which commerce is usually concentrated. The Circuit Court of Yoknapatawpha, or Lafayette County, which has jurisdiction in the sensational trial in *Sanctuary,* affords, together with opossum hunting, the principal entertainment for the native. At the sessions of this court, the audience eats peanuts as though it would never consume the local produce; in the moving picture house, however, popcorn is devoured, frequently after a preliminary toss into the air, and unshelled peanuts are chucked at other members of the audience. Within the courtyard, pigeons which have attained the required state of burliness, and village idlers whose beards have become tobacco tinctured to the required saffron, vie in garrulity. In *Sanctuary,* Faulkner tells of "the young men pitching dollars in the courthouse yard." Gambling is a Mississippi diver-

Reprinted with permission from *The Sewanee Review,* Summer, 1932, pp. 294–306.

sion inherited from the river folk—wealthy Southern planters who
had much to lose and flotsam who had much to gain. Had Faulkner said "pennies," however, he would have been nearer the
truth for seldom is more than a nickel pitched at the line. Inside
this yard and on the pavement outside the fence is the town
curb market, where home-slaughtered, unrefrigerated meats,
exposed to the sun, are sold, and where, at harvest, scores of
negroes voraciously eat watermelons which they have broken
open against the curb; the rind, the seeds and the overripe centers
they discard on the pavement, forming a treacle so viscid and
so slippery that one's feet alternately stick and slide. The main
entrance to the tetragonal courthouse is distinguished by a granite
shaft upon which stands at attention a soldier of the War between
the States, one of a multitude manufactured in equivocal Ohio
and supplied to North and South alike.

Between the courthouse and the shops which surround it is
a street, in which until three years ago, swine wallowed. To the
east are a red post office of the Polk period and a one-story
department store which has grown little since the War. To the
west are a hamburger restaurant, a jewelry store which sells
victrola records, and a hardware store, the one which figures in
The Sound and the Fury. To the south are several drugstores
and the workshop of a cerement costumer, the hand on the shop
sign pointing, however, into the street rather than to the stairway
which leads to the second floor. To the north are a bank which
has remained open in spite of flood and drought, a beauty shop
which has withstood the sentiment against bobbed hair, the
establishment of an undertaker, at which, quite appropriately,
picture frames are made, and a grocery store bearing the cordial
sign, "Don't go elsewhere to get skinned; come in here." The
four-faced clock of the courthouse looks, respectively, at a
rutted, red-clay road leading to barren fields; at Washington
Street (a new-fangled name for Depot Street) leading to the railroad station; at South Lamar Street (named for Lucius Cincin-
natus Lamar II, onetime Secretary of the Interior under President
Cleveland), leading through a pleasant residential section to

Jackson, the capital; and at North Lamar Street, leading to merry Memphis past Holly Springs, the twin sister of Oxford, and past a huge oak under which Grant wiped the perspiration from his brow on his way to Vicksburg, an expedition mentioned in *Sanctuary*.

That Jefferson and Oxford are the same place is established by the statement in *Sartoris* that Jefferson is seventy-five miles from Memphis on a clay road, and on the Illinois Central Railroad between Chicago and the Gulf of Mexico, every detail of which applies to Oxford. The trip by train from Oxford to Memphis, which affords an outlet for money and inhibition, requires five hours: one hour to Holly Springs, a stopover of three hours, and another hour to Memphis, where the Mississippi plantation owner has been so prodigal of money as to establish the adage, "He squanders money like a Delta planter in Memphis after harvest." The trip "through the country" requires more than two hours of hard driving over treacherous gravel, dust, and sand, making one long for the return of the days of the linen duster. Heavy fogs and stray cattle increase the perils of the trip, not to mention looping the loop over bridges of rough-hewn timber which cover dry creeks and sluggish streams filled with pale green algae, through which lazy turtles snap at insects, and into which negroes place many lines attached to cane poles in the hope of enticing a sunfish for dinner. The road leads also past gum trees and undergrowth of brier and past sorghum mills which, in the autumn, emit the sweet savor of the new-crushed stalk; in winter, the withered sedge and overcast skies collude to depress. The Tennessee line is always greeted with a great yell, for ahead lies a concrete road leading to the comparative simplicity of the city, and freedom from the complexities of the small town. Yet, after a week end in the most sophisticated city of the South, one is willing and eager to return to one's servitude and to the reality which Faulkner has so well depicted in his novels, for Mississippi is ever a challenge, an inescapable portent.

Northern Mississippi, blighted but not benighted like several adjoining states, is yet the home of true chivalry, commingled,

of course, with the materialistic spirit of the Midwest, but yet
cultured and serene. The artificiality of the Southwest is replaced
by a bland ease which flouts worry and work. In *The Sound and
the Fury,* Faulkner says, "It's a good thing the Lord did something for this country; the folks that live on it never have. Friday
afternoon, and from right here I could see three miles of land
that hadn't even been broken," and it would have been the same
had the day been Tuesday!

One wonders, however, what the Lord did for this part of
the country except to fructify the cotton plant and its eternal
enemy, the boll-weevil. One of the characters in *The Sound and
the Fury* says truly, "Ain't nobody works much in dis country cep
de boll-weevil, noways." Yet despite the low price of picking,
fifteen cents a hundred pounds, the cotton seems to be picked and
ginned, although the ginner receives but three dollars—and only
a dollar and a half in some places in Alabama—for the ginning,
the hemp sack in which the cotton is bound costing sixty-seven
cents. Every shack on every plantation has cotton, the staple of
the South, piled on the tiny front porch as high as the eaves, and
every farm is sown with cotton to the very farmhouse door, no
room being left for truck gardening, with the result that, when the
harvest is bad or the price low, the poor whites have to beg for
food. Nearly every crossroad has a gin operating at capacity, although the roof admits rain and the floor groans with the weight
of the heavy machinery. Part of the cottonseed, which is sold at
ten dollars a ton, is often given in exchange for the ginning. The
earth about the railroad station in Oxford is wadded several
inches deep with cotton waste and cottonseed. Negroes may be
seen on any dusty or muddy road about Oxford driving oblong
wagons, made of unfinished timber, containing cotton, the product which has brought comparative wealth and extreme poverty
to this part of the country.

All Faulkner's novels show his familiarity with the Mississippi negro, who differs considerably from the negro of the South-
east. One of his best descriptions is that contained in *The Sound
and the Fury,* where he depicts a crazy, weathered negro church,

supporting with difficulty a box steeple, on the outskirts of Oxford. Faulkner tells of the barbaric decorations of multicolored crepe paper and folding Christmas bells, but he leaves unnoticed an immense sign bearing the pathetic inscription, HE. IS. RIS. In Oxford, the negro Second Baptist Church, so called because it is built on the site of the First Baptist Church, which was burned, affords good material for one interested in the Christian contortions of the negro.

The Oxford cemetery, with the negro plot beyond the white, where the distinguished are buried simply and the simple ornately, has given good material to Faulkner, who, in *The Sound and the Fury* and *As I Lay Dying*, describes the pompous graves in the burying ground of his own family.

All northern Mississippi is, to some extent, a cemetery, for decayed and decaying towns encompass Oxford, one of the most interesting of these being Old Wyatt, now comprising a single farmhouse, but a city more populous than Oxford or Holly Springs when the Tallahatchie River formed the chief means of conveyance between this section and the lower Mississippi. Among the ruins of Old Wyatt, which emits the vapors of a tomb, an occasional coin of the eighteenth century or a fragment of English blue porcelain is found; in the midst of this rank swamp country, a sense of forlornness and evanescence arises within one like that felt after reading *The Ruined City* in Anglo-Saxon literature.

The country about Oxford is a series of gulches, called humorously the Grand Canyons of Mississippi, perversely produced by Nature to supply the Delta with its silt in which cotton luxuriates. Often this erosion, for which there seems to be no preventive, destroys whole plantations, rendering the land uncultivatable and providing natural graves for cattle. Within some of the gulches, the stratification of the surrounding embankments, rising often more than fifty feet, is quite beautiful: twilight suffuses the dull gold walls with a rugged and ancient charm comparable to that of the cathedral at Exeter. Freshets have left, in many places, tiny, imperfectly rounded masses of sandstone which offered resistance when water was sucked spirally toward the center and found outlet by overflowing. These remains, most resembling the woody cup of the acorn, make grotesque ash receivers. Throughout the countryside, also, large mounds have survived, having been reared by Indians probably as a means of escape from flooded surrounding territory, and probably not for burial; about these mounds, arrowheads and other instruments of warfare are frequently found.

The two common types of Mississippi architecture appear in Faulkner's novels: the paintless, one-story cottage of the farmer, with porch, called locally a "hall," extending from front to back, and with rooms on each side; a high-vaulted roof protects the occupants from the sun. Most of Faulkner's characters live in this kind of house, but he lives in the other kind, the more ornate, two-story mansion of the wealthy planter, with columns extending from the lower porch to the roof, and a balcony inside the pillars.

In this country, says Faulkner, "I was born in 1826 of a negro slave and an alligator." How the mother alligator must have shed tears over her offspring! In reality, Faulkner was born in 1897 at New Albany, Mississippi, where his father, Murry T. Faulkner, who, until last year, was business manager of the University of Mississippi, was connected with the family railroad which his father, John W. T. Falkner—the "u" is a recent restoration—an Assistant United States District Attorney from 1886 to 1888, and his grandfather, Colonel William C. Falkner, had built. Colonel Falkner, William's great-grandfather, was a first lieutenant during the Mexican War, and, during the Civil War, as a colonel, he saw service at Harpers Ferry. On November 5, 1889, he was elected to the legislature of Mississippi, on which day he was assassinated in Ripley, Mississippi, by R. J. Thurmond, who was acquitted. There is no doubt that the lovable Colonel Bayard Sartoris, who, in Faulkner's *Sartoris*, served as aide-de-camp to Jeb Stuart in Virginia, is Colonel William C. Falkner, and that John Sartoris is a combination of John W. T. Falkner and Colonel Falkner. Faulkner says in this novel:

It showed on John Sartoris' brow, the dark shadow of fatality and doom, that night when he sat beneath the candles in the dining-room and turned a wineglass in his fingers while he talked to his son. The railroad was finished, and that day he had been elected to the state legislature after a hard and bitter fight, and doom lay on his brow, and weariness.

"And so," he said, "Redlaw'll kill me tomorrow, for I shall be unarmed. I'm tired of killing men. . . . Pass the wine, Bayard. . . ."

And the next day he was dead. . . .

Colonel Sartoris appears also in *The Sound and the Fury*, forming only one of the many family links appearing in Faulkner's novels.

It is, then, from his great-grandfather, the author of *The White Rose of Memphis, The Little Brick Church,* and *Rapid Ramblings in Europe*, that William inherited his name and literary talent. Of the first, 160,000 copies were sold before the thirty-fifth edition of 1909. Aboard a Mississippi side-wheeler, from which the novel takes its name, a *bal masque* is held, the passengers taking the parts of Don Quixote, Sancho Panza, Ivanhoe, the Duke of Wellington, Napoleon, George III, and Mary, Queen of Scots. Hackneyed literary quotations, Portia scenes, a narrow escape from unnatural death by rattlesnake bite, and disembodied spirits provided emotional tremors for the reader of the sensational seventies.

William came as a young child to Oxford, where he was educated in the public schools. Although too small to play ball, he took great interest in school activities and incessantly wrote jests, poetry, and short stories. It must amuse William to know that his teachers now say that they predicted that he would be a writer.

During the War, Faulkner became an officer in the Royal Flying Corps, giving, in his usual ironic way, as his reason for enlistment the fact that he was afraid of being drafted, and that he liked the aviation uniform more than any other. Although he has two enemy planes to his credit and several times barely escaped death, he says, with the customary attempt to scoff at the heroic, that he crashed twice, costing the British government more than four thousand pounds. He is now assembling a plane for private flight.

Upon his return to Mississippi, Faulkner shocked the staid natives of Oxford by walking about the streets barefoot and by sitting on the floor of a local drugstore reading magazines. Because he wore extremely wide army trousers and an overseas cap and stuck a monocle in one eye, he was given the complimentary title of count.

On September 19, 1919, Faulkner was enrolled as a special student at the University of Mississippi, taking a course in French on which he received A for both semesters; a course in Spanish on which he received B for both semesters; and a course in English, on which he received, for the first semester, D, then a failing grade, probably as a result of which he dropped this course during the second semester. In November, 1920, he voluntarily withdrew, probably not wishing to be like Horace in *Sartoris,* who "has spent so much time being educated that he never has learned anything." His conception of education is perhaps best expressed by Dr. Mahon, who, in *Soldiers' Pay,* describes his son Donald: "Education in the bookish sense he had not: the schooling he got was because he wanted to go, the reading he did was because he wanted to read. Least of all did I teach him fortitude. What is fortitude? Emotional atrophy, gangrene. . . ." An attack, more deadly, upon the usual method of teaching sophomore English appears in *Mosquitoes:*

> English literature course whittled Shakespeare down because he wrote...without pointing a moral, and one instructor always insisted that the head devil in *Paradise Lost* was an inspired prophetic portrait of Darwin, and they wouldn't touch Byron with a ten-foot pole, and Swinburne was reduced to his mother and his old standby, the ocean. And I guess they'd have cut this out had they worn one piece bathing suits in those days. But in spite of that I got interested in learning things.

In *Soldiers' Pay,* one of his characters believes that Dr. Gary is thinking of Ella Wilcox or Irene Castle when he mentions

Swinburne: this may well be contrasted with the literary affecta-
tions of the novels of his great-grandfather, whose *filles de joie*
quote Pope. In *The Sound and the Fury*, in which Faulkner
shows that he has no firsthand knowledge of Harvard, the pasture
lands of the idiot Benjy of Maury are sold that Quentin may go to
Harvard, because "Harvard" has a "fine sound." In this novel,
he spells *Harvard, Jew, Jesus* and *I* with small letters. In *Mosquitoes*, however, he says:

> I guess there is a time in the life of every young American of the
> class that wants to go to college or accepts the inevitability of educa-
> tion, when he wants to go to Yale or Harvard. Maybe that's the value
> of Yale and Harvard to our American life: a kind of illusion of an
> intellectual nirvana that makes the ones that can't go there work like
> hell where they do go, so as not to show up so poorly alongside of the
> ones that can go there.
> Still ninety out of a hundred Yale and Harvard turn out are rea-
> sonably bearable to live with, if they ain't anything else. And that's
> something to be said for any manufactory, I guess. But I'd like to have
> gone there....

But Faulkner is not really unsympathetic with any university, even his own; he sees irony in all things, and especially in
teaching, the most ironic of professions. He routs rules and principles and boundaries. He is constantly lamenting the limits of
the English language, which he believes to be too small for adequate expression: as a result, he creates new words, all with
attractive connotation, although frequently an accepted cognate
word appears in the language. His insatiable desire for variety
and originality finds expression in his startling figures of speech,
although his misspellings cannot be accounted for in the same
manner.

Faulkner considers his experience as scoutmaster of the Oxford troop of boy scouts as one of the most pleasant of his life.
His scouts speak glowingly of his war stories told about a camp-
fire, and many of them admit that, because of his solemn adjura-
tion, the weekly bath was replaced by the daily.

While Faulkner was postmaster at the University of Mississippi, he declared that he would write a novel so repulsive that it would be barred from the mails. *Sanctuary*, the most nauseous novel in the language, signally carried out this threat. In 1924, Faulkner says facetiously, he was removed from this position because of reading, while on duty, things other than people's mail, of reluctantly waiting on customers, and of misplacing incoming mail and throwing outgoing mail into piles of refuse.

Faulkner's first published work is a book of verse called *The Marble Faun*. Another collection of poetry called *The Greening Bough*,* not published because of his concentration upon the novel, contains many promising lyrics, of which the following is a specimen:

> Lay me not the rose for lovers,
> Lay me not the bay for fame;
> But something which no symbol covers,
> Some simple shape no sage can name.

Faulkner's apprenticeship in poetry is reflected in all his novels.

While on one of his numerous rambles, Faulkner met in New Orleans Sherwood Anderson, who obtained for him a position as reporter with the *Times-Picayune*. Anderson, somewhat later, suggested that Faulkner write a novel, a suggestion which resulted in *Soldiers' Pay*. This novel, published in 1926, is perhaps the most autobiographic of Faulkner's works; it contains philosophic disenchantment without sordidness. The death of Donald, the young aviator, who is Faulkner, is a bit of masterly description. Because Faulkner gave his heart unstintingly, as one can do only to one's first novel or to one's first-born, this is, in many respects, his best novel.

The next year, 1927, Faulkner published *Mosquitoes*, which contains no endemic characters or scenes.

Sartoris, published in 1929, and dedicated to Sherwood Anderson, is definitely regional. Here, again, Faulkner has placed himself and his ancestors prominently among his characters, and, once more, he introduces the War and its effects.

---

* *A Green Bough*, published 1933. (editors)

In *The Sound and the Fury*, published in 1929, Faulkner has surmounted great psychological difficulties. His reproduction of the thought processes of a thirty-three-year-old idiot—if an idiot may have thought processes—shows his understanding of the subnormal to an almost uncanny degree. Such statements as "I quit crying, but I couldn't stop," and "Caddy smelled like trees in the rain," are simple but eloquent, as is the description of Benjy's burning himself: "My hand jerked back and I put it in my mouth and Dilsey caught me. I could still hear the clock between my voice. Dilsey reached back and hit Luster on the head. My voice was going loud every time." Luster, like the other negroes of this story, is a good portrait of the Mississippi negro, one of whom says of the idiot: "He deef and dumb.... Born looney." The sensitive girl Quentin, another of Faulkner's ladies of sorrow, is an excellent creation, much like the heroine of *Sanctuary*. An interesting study in heredity is offered in Quentin, who, in temperament, is the daughter of her uncle Quentin and her mother Caddy. Much of the dissimulation of the small-town Southerner is found in Jason Compson, the pretended upholder of the ideals of an aristocratic but decadent family.

In 1929, Faulkner married Mrs. Estelle Oldham Franklin, who had, by a past marriage, two children whose ages aggregate thirteen. Mrs. Faulkner thus supplied the title for the recent collection of short stories, entitled *These Thirteen*, by speaking in jest of her thirteen children. University students talk pleasantly of the hospitality of Mrs. Faulkner, who recently entertained a group of them by providing an immense ham—which they consumed—for dinner and by riding backwards on a bicycle; during a part of the afternoon, William excused himself and took a nap, a thing for which William cannot be blamed.

As I Lay Dying, published in 1930 and dedicated to Hal Smith, one of Faulkner's publishers, borders on the grotesque. The building at home of a casket before the death of the one to repose in it (a device used by George Eliot in *Adam Bede*), the sinking of the casket in a swollen stream, and its carriage, with buzzards hovering over it, to the cemetery for burial while Cash, with a broken leg, lies on top of it, and Darl, his brother, suddenly becomes insane, as well as the difficulties of Dewey Dell, the deflowered girl, are evidences of genius gone wild. Darl is finally sent to Jackson, a euphemism which only the Mississippian knowing of the two insane asylums in that city can understand. Anse Bundren, lazy but religious, like many North Mississippi farmers, seems to be taken from life. The local dialect is well revealed by Anse when he says, "I know that Old Marster will care for me as for ere a sparrow that falls." The names of several persons, especially Vardaman and Peabody, are those of buildings on the University of Mississippi campus, as is that of Isom in *Sartoris*. Faulkner uses an interesting method in this novel, in that the chapter heading is the name of the character whose thoughts are recorded within that chapter. Vardaman, who likens the corpse of his mother to a dead fish which he has just dissected, reveals Faulkner's keen knowledge of child psychology. This work is unique among Faulkner's six novels in that, having begun as a tragedy, it ends as a comedy.

Sanctuary, published in 1931, but said to have been written before *As I Lay Dying*, is probably the most local of Faulkner's novels. The heroine, an "Ole Miss" student, and the hero, a University of Virginia graduate, are taken from life, as is Popeye, one of the innumerable base characters, who is undoubtedy Popeye Pumphrey, a Memphis racketeer who recently attempted suicide. The campus of the University of Mississippi is described in detail. This novel, which was evidently written to give America the type of novel that it likes, depicts only the groveling side of college life. In construction and slightly in characterization, it shows advance, but it is unworthy of the talent of Faulkner.

Faulkner's personal appearance varies as much as does his style of writing. Of late he has a mustache, but he is known to have had a Vandyke, and, once upon a time, a smooth face. Frequently he wears an olive drab army shirt with no tie or coat, an old pair of army trousers, and yellow shoes; in this attire, which he gives to some of his characters, he seems most natural. In *Soldiers' Pay*, he says of Donald, "Could you put a faun in formal clothes?" William is not only the aviator, Donald, but also the faun. Sometimes, however, he wears a light grey hat and a modish grey suit, and carries a cane and chamois gloves. William's chief concern seems to be that he may be mistaken for what he really is—a gentleman. He believes that any artificial code, like that of the gentleman, retards progress. In *Soldiers' Pay*, he says that a boy may not be aided by "always letting a gentleman don't do this and a gentleman don't do that interfere." His personal philosophy is not at all that of a lost soul; he views all human conduct with a smiling, satirical tolerance. His sympathies are Southern, but he can poke fun at provincialism, as he does in *The Sound and the Fury*, when he says of Gerald's mother: "She approved of Gerald associating with me because I at least revealed a blundering sense of noblesse oblige by getting myself born below Mason and Dixon." His turn of thought and his tastes are extremely simple; he plays tennis and golf occasionally, and he picks wild flowers with the ecstasy of a child. Not at all is he the unlettered, unsocial person that he would have the world to believe he is. In a dignified old home, fronted with square, white pillars, and surrounded with firs and magnolias, he does most of his dreaming. He writes in a room entirely bare except for a table, a chair, and a typewriter.

Faulkner is a compelling novelist because he has found universality in provincialism. England is supreme in the novel because her authors have reflected the provincial life of every shire in the kingdom. The outstanding American novel is, likewise, regional. Whether, however, American regional literature will live, except as a literary curiosity, cannot now be determined. It is certain, though, that the novel which is to endure must appeal to the intellect as well as to the emotions. Faulkner has yet to write a novel containing great emotional range: when he has equalized the spiritual with the physical he will be truly on the road to permanence. In laying bare sense *nuances*, Faulkner has perhaps surpassed all other American novelists, but he offers little intellectual exaltation and little permanent philosophy with which to perpetuate his name. Faulkner has, however, interpreted his characters with a cosmopolitan insight and a sympathy—the result of his being one of them—which have made them vivid persons. Perhaps he has stirred up too much the dregs of life to which the South has frequently closed her eyes, and perhaps he has too violently snatched the mask from the face of the Southern gentleman, but his method undoubtedly conforms to the elementary psychological principle that every violent action produces an equally violent reaction. He has, on the other hand, given us a new beauty in taking the aristocratic Southerner from a lofty pedestal and placing him close to the earth, where we see on his face not hauteur and arrogance but delicately sculptured kindliness and sorrow. If his characters of this type do not develop, the reason is that there can be no great development in decadent and provincial society, which may be, after all, the highest type of society, provided it does not depart too far from the norm. He has flouted the tender sensibilities of the Old South, and, although his caveman atavism is too marked, his influence may in the end prove salutary. He has, moreover, given feeling and utterance to the downtrodden and inarticulate poor white. He is a master of the stream-of-consciousness method, and, although his consciousness is too physiological, his sense perceptions are so keen that he has made his characters less repulsive than they otherwise would be. At times, he seems to enunciate the doctrine that whatever is, is wrong, but, unfortunately, he offers no solution. Faulkner is essentially tragic, his novels revealing all the sorrows of life. In *Mosquitoes*, he says, "Only an idiot has no grief; only a fool would forget it," but, characteristically, in *Soldiers' Pay*, he says, "Even sorrow is a fake, now." His gods do not either chortle good-humoredly or flash forth their wrath: they smile slightly and ironically out of the sides of their mouths. His social satire is both delicate and axiomatic, and his novels as severely dramatic and as heavy with detail as the modern German drama. Although Life offers combat, the result is a draw. Fate hovers above his characters as it does in Saxon literature, and always "wyrd bi ful araed." (Fate is full inexorable.) In *The Sound and the Fury*, he says, ". . . no battle is ever won. . . . They are not even fought. The field only reveals to man his own folly and despair, and victory is an illusion of philosophers and fools." Man, since the days of classical literature and much before, has been but a bit of clay in the hands of the gods, and so he is in the hands of Faulkner. In *The Sound and the Fury*, he says: "Father was teaching us that all men are just accumulations, dolls stuffed with sawdust swept up from the trash heaps where all previous dolls had been thrown away...." And, in *Sartoris*, he says of Bayard Sartoris, "...he fell to talking of the war. Not of combat, but rather of a life peopled by young men like fallen angels, and of a meteoric violence like that of fallen angels, beyond heaven or hell and partaking of both: doomed immortality and immortal doom." Arnold Bennett said that Faulkner "writes like an angel," but one not really familiar with his novels would be inclined to say, "No; quite the contrary." Faulkner should, however, place a few angels within his novels—just for the sake of contrast! Life in Faulkner's works is as tragic as that of the enduring cypress of the native swamp, with its leaves drooping abjectly toward its roots, alternately exposed to the blistering sun and laved in soft, yellow waters which sluggishly, but steadily, flow to the Mississippi.

II. The Work:

Studies of the Work as a Whole

FAULKNER'S MYTHOLOGY

GEORGE MARION O'DONNELL

WILLIAM FAULKNER is really a traditional moralist, in the best sense. One principle holds together his thirteen books of prose —including his new novel, *The Wild Palms*—giving his work unity and giving it, at times, the significance that belongs to great myth. That principle is the Southern social-economic-ethical tradition which Mr. Faulkner possesses naturally, as a part of his sensibility.

However, Mr. Faulkner is a traditional man in a modern South. All around him the antitraditional forces are at work; and he lives among evidences of their past activity. He could not fail to be aware of them. It is not strange, then, that his novels are, primarily, a series of related myths (or aspects of a single myth) built around the conflict between traditionalism and the antitraditional modern world in which it is immersed.

In a rearrangement of the novels, say for a collected edition, *The Unvanquished* might well stand first; for the action occurs earlier, historically, than in any other of the books, and it objectifies, in the essential terms of Mr. Faulkner's mythology, the central dramatic tension of his work. On one side of the conflict there are the Sartorises, recognizable human beings who act traditionally. Against them the invading Northern armies, and their diversified allies in the reconstruction era, wage open war, aim-

Reprinted with permission from *The Kenyon Review,* Summer, 1939, pp. 285–99.

ing to make the traditional actions of the Sartorises impossible.

The invaders are unable to cope with the Sartorises; but their invasion provides another antagonist with an occasion within which his special anti-Sartoris talent makes him singularly powerful. This antagonist is the landless poor-white horse trader, Ab Snopes; his special talent is his low cunning as an *entrepreneur*. He acts without regard for the legitimacy of his means; he has no ethical code. In the crisis brought about by the war, he is enabled to use a member of the Sartoris family for his own advantage because, for the first time, he can be useful to the Sartorises. Moreover, he is enabled to make this Sartoris (Mrs. Rosa Millard) betray herself into an act of self-interest such as his, and to cause her death while using her as his tool.

The characters and the conflict are particular and credible. But they are also mythological. In Mr. Faulkner's mythology there are two kinds of characters; they are Sartorises or Snopeses, whatever the family names may be. And in the spiritual geography of Mr. Faulkner's work there are two worlds: the Sartoris world and the Snopes world. In all of his successful books, he is exploring the two worlds in detail, dramatizing the inevitable conflict between them.

It is a universal conflict. The Sartorises act traditionally; that is to say, they act always with an ethically responsible will. They represent vital morality, humanism. Being antitraditional, the Snopeses are immoral from the Sartoris point of view. But the Snopeses do not recognize this point of view; acting only for self-interest, they acknowledge no ethical duty. Really, then, they are amoral; they represent naturalism or animalism. And the Sartoris-Snopes conflict is fundamentally a struggle between humanism and naturalism.

As a universal conflict, it is important only philosophically. But it is important artistically, in this instance, because Mr. Faulkner has dramatized it convincingly in the terms of particular history and of actual life in his own part of the South—in the terms of his own tradition.

In *Sartoris,* which was published before *The Unvanquished* but which follows it in historical sequence, the conflict is between young Bayard Sartoris (the grandson of the Bayard Sartoris who was a youth in *The Unvanquished*) and the Snopes world of the 1920's. "General Johnston or General Forrest wouldn't have took a Snopes into his army at all," one of the characters says; but, significantly enough, one Flem Snopes has come, by way of local political usefulness, to be vice-president of old Bayard Sartoris' bank. Young Bayard's brother, John, has been killed in a war; but it is clear that it was a Snopes war and not a Sartoris war. Bayard himself is extremely conscious of his family's doom; he feels cheated because he did not die violently, in the tradition, like his brother; finally, he kills himself, taking up an aeroplane that he knows will crash.

The Snopes world has done more than oppose the Sartorises. It has weakened them internally (as it weakened Rosa Millard) in using them for its advantage; it has made them self-conscious, queer, psychologically tortured. Bayard Sartoris has something of the traditional instinct for noble and disinterested action, under a vital ethical code. But the strength is so warped internally by the psychological effects of the Snopes world upon it, and it is so alien to the habitual actions of that world, that it can only manifest itself in meaningless violence, ending in self-destruction.

The same pattern recurs, varied somewhat and handled in miniature, in the short story about the Sartorises—"There Was a Queen." Here the real conflict centers in Narcissa Benbow, the widow of young Bayard Sartoris, who has given herself to a detective in order to recover from his possession a collection of obscene letters that one of the Snopeses had written to her anonymously and afterwards stolen. The consciousness of Narcissa's deed kills the embodiment of the virile tradition, old Miss Jenny Sartoris (Mrs. DuPré). Narcissa's yielding to the detective is the result of the *formalization* of one aspect of her traditional morality—her pride—through the constant opposition of the Snopes world to it; this formalization allows the Snopes world to betray her into antitraditionalism by creating a situation in which she must make a formalized response. It is a highly significant tactic.

For the moment a tradition begins to be formalized into a code, it commences to lose vitality; when it is entirely formalized, it is dead—it becomes pseudo-tradition.

As early as *Soldiers' Pay* (1926) the same theme is the basis for Mr. Faulkner's organization of experience; and it is the best possible indication of the urgency of the theme with him that it should be central in his first novel. Mahon, the old Episcopal clergyman, conscious of sin, tolerant of human weakness, is still unaware of the vital opponent to his formalized, and so impotent, tradition—the amorality with which history has surrounded him. Donald Mahon, his son, is brought home from the World War, dying; in him, the minister's code has faced antitraditional history. Because Donald is not dead, the conflict must continue; locally, it is between the preacher and Cecily Saunders (Donald's fiancée before he went to war) with her family and associates who are typical of the new Jazz Era. Obviously, Cecily's world of jazz and flappers and sleek-haired jelly-beans represents the same antitraditional historical movement that brought Flem Snopes into Bayard Sartoris' bank. The names and the settings are different; that is all.

In *The Sound and the Fury*, Quentin Compson represents all that is left of the Sartoris tradition. The rest of his family have either succumbed entirely to the Snopes world, like Jason Compson, or else have drugs to isolate them from it—Mr. Compson his fragments of philosophy, Uncle Maury his liquor, Mrs. Compson her religion and her invalidism, Benjy his idiocy. But Quentin's very body is "an empty hall echoing with sonorous defeated names."[1] His world is peopled with "baffled, outraged ghosts"; and although Quentin himself is "still too young to deserve yet to be a ghost," he is one of them. However, it is evident that Quentin's traditionalism is far gone in the direction of formalization, with its concomitant lack of vitality; he is psychologically kin to Bayard Sartoris and to Narcissa Benbow. When he dis-

1. The quotations are from *Absalom, Absalom!*, the other novel in which Quentin appears; but they are necessary for an understanding of his function in *The Sound and the Fury*.

covers that his sister Candace has been giving herself to the town boys of Jefferson, Mississippi, and is pregnant, he attempts to change her situation by telling their father that he has committed incest with her. It is a key incident. Quentin is attempting to transform Candace's yielding to the amorality of the Snopes world into a sin, within the Sartoris morality; but the means he employs are more nearly pseudo-traditional and romantic than traditional; and he fails.

Quentin tells his father: "It was to isolate her out of the loud world so that it would have to flee us of necessity." Precisely. The loud world is the Snopes world, with which the Compson house has become thoroughly infected and to which it is subject. Quentin is really *striving toward the condition of tragedy* for his family; he is trying to transform meaningless degeneracy into significant doom. But because his moral code is no longer vital, he fails and ends in a kind of escapism, breaking his watch to put himself beyond time, finally killing himself to escape consciousness. Only he is aware of the real meaning of his struggle, which sets up the dramatic tension in *The Sound and the Fury.*

In a way, Quentin's struggle is Mr. Faulkner's own struggle as an artist. In *Sartoris*, Mr. Faulkner wrote of the name: "There is death in the sound of it, and a glamorous fatality." Sartoris— all that the name implies—is the tragic hero of his work; it is doomed, like any tragic hero. But the doom toward which the Sartoris world moves should be a noble one. In *Absalom, Absalom!*, although apparently with great difficulty, as if he were wrestling with the Snopes world all the while, Mr. Faulkner finally achieves the presentation of a kind of "glamorous fatality" for the Sartoris world—embodied in Thomas Sutpen and his house.

The book is really a summary of the whole career of the tradition—its rise, its fatal defects, its opponents, its decline, and its destruction. The action is of heroic proportions. The figures are larger than life; but, as Mr. T. S. Eliot has suggested of Tourneur's characters, they are all distorted to scale, so that the whole action has a self-subsistent reality. And the book ends with a

ritualistic purgation of the doomed house, by fire, which is as
nearly a genuine tragic scene as anything in modern fiction.

For the first time, Mr. Faulkner makes explicit here the contrast between traditional (Sartoris) man and modern (Snopes)
man, dissociated into a sequence of animal functions, lacking in
unity under essential morality. One of the characters says of traditional men:

> People too as we are, and victims too as we are, but victims of
> a different circumstance, simpler and therefore, integer for integer,
> larger, more heroic and the figures therefore more heroic too, not
> dwarfed and involved but distinct, uncomplex who had the gift of
> living once or dying once instead of being diffused and scattered
> creatures drawn blindly from a grab bag and assembled.

It was the world of these "diffused and scattered creatures"
in which Quentin Compson lived; and it was the effort not to be
"diffused and scattered"—to transform his own family's doom
into the proportions of the world of Sutpen and Sartoris—that led
to his death. But it is significant that it should be Quentin through
whose gradual understanding the story of Sutpen is told, and that
it should be Quentin who watches the final destruction of Sutpen's
house. For Sutpen's tradition was defective, but it was not formalized as Quentin's was; and his story approaches tragedy.

As I Lay Dying stands a little apart from the rest of Mr.
Faulkner's novels, but it is based upon the philosophical essence
of his Sartoris-Snopes theme—the struggle between humanism
and naturalism. The naïf hill folk who appear in the book are
poor and ungraceful, certainly; they are of low mentality; sex-
ually, they are almost animalistic. But when Anse Bundren promises his dying wife that he will bury her in Jefferson, he sets up
for himself an ethical duty which he recognizes as such—though
not in these terms. It is the fulfillment of this obligation, in spite
of constant temptation to abandon it, and in spite of multiplied
difficulties put in his way by nature itself, that makes up the
action of the novel.

Fundamentally, *As I Lay Dying* is a legend; and the procession of ragged, depraved hillmen, carrying Addie Bundren's body through water and through fire to the cemetery in Jefferson, while people flee from the smell and buzzards circle overhead—this progress is not unlike that of the medieval soul toward redemption. The allegories of Alanus de Insulis and the visions of Sister Hildegard of Bingen would yield a good many parallels. On a less esoteric plane, however, the legend is more instructive for us. Because they are simpler in mind and live more remotely from the Snopes world than the younger Sartorises and Compsons, the Bundrens are able to carry a genuine act of traditional morality through to its end. They are infected with amorality; but it is the amorality of physical nature, not the artificial, self-interested amorality of the Snopeses. More heroism is possible among them than among the inhabitants of Jefferson.

2.

So far I have been concerned mainly with exegesis, aiming to show how fundamental the Sartoris-Snopes conflict is in Mr. Faulkner's novels. To provide such exegesis of the six books that I have discussed, it is necessary to do violence to the fictions themselves, by abstraction. This is the significant point, for criticism; because the necessity for abstraction is evidence that, in these six books, the theme is really informed in the fictions or myths.

The Sartorises and the Sutpens and the Compsons do not represent the tradition in its various degrees of vitality, as x, y, and z may represent a sequence of numbers in mathematics. They are people, in a certain way of life, at a particular time, confronted with real circumstances and with items of history. And their humanity (or their illusion of humanity, on a larger-than-life scale) is not limited, ultimately, by their archetypal significance. Moreover, in each book there is a dramatically credible fiction which remains particular and (sometimes with difficulty) coherent as action, even though the pattern is true, in a larger sense, as myth. In short, Mr. Faulkner's successful work has the same kind, though certainly not the same degree, of general meaning that is to be found in Dante's *Divina Commedia* or in the *Electra*

of Sophocles. The only close parallel in American literature is the
better work of Nathaniel Hawthorne, whom Mr. Faulkner resembles in a great many ways.

However, as I have suggested already, a literary and personal tension arises, for William Faulkner the artist, out of the
same conflict that is central in his work. This tension sets up his
crucial problem as an artist, and his failures result from it. In so
far as he can sustain his inherent tradition, he is enabled to project the central conflict in the valid terms of myth. However, as
a Sartoris artist in a Snopes world, he is constantly subject to
opposition that tends to force him into the same kind of reac-
tionary formalization of tradition that betrayed Narcissa Benbow
as a character. When, because of the opposition and his reaction
to it, Mr. Faulkner writes as *formal* traditionalist rather than as
vital traditionalist, he writes allegory. Allegory might be defined,
indeed, as formalized—and therefore dead—myth.

Sanctuary, which is unfortunately the most widely known
and misunderstood of Mr. Faulkner's novels, is a failure of this
kind. In simple terms, the pattern of the allegory is something
like this: Southern Womanhood Corrupted but Undefiled (Temple Drake), in the company of the Corrupted Tradition (Gowan
Stevens, a professional Virginian), falls into the clutches of
amoral Modernism (Popeye), which is itself impotent, but which
with the aid of its strong ally Natural Lust ("Red") rapes Southern Womanhood unnaturally and then seduces her so satisfactorily that her corruption is total, and she becomes the tacit ally
of Modernism. Meanwhile Pore White Trash (Godwin) has been
accused of the crime which he, with the aid of the Naïf Faithful
(Tawmmy), actually tried to prevent. The Formalized Tradition
(Horace Benbow), perceiving the true state of affairs, tries vainly
to defend Pore White Trash. However, Southern Womanhood is
so hopelessly corrupted that she wilfully sees Pore White Trash
convicted and lynched; she is then carried off by Wealth (Judge
Drake) to meaningless escape in European luxury. Modernism,
carrying in it from birth its own impotence and doom, submits
with masochistic pleasure to its own destruction for the one crime

that it has not yet committed—Revolutionary Destruction of Order (the murder of the Alabama policeman, for which the innocent Popeye is executed).

Here Mr. Faulkner's theme is forced into allegory, not projected as myth. In this sense, the book is a "cheap idea"—as Mr. Faulkner himself calls it in his preface to the Modern Library edition. Its defects are those of allegory in general. The characters are distorted, being more nearly grotesques than human beings; and they are not distorted to scale (Temple is only a type; Benbow is a recognizably human character, and so is Miss Reba, the keeper of the bawdy house); accordingly, the book lacks the "self-subsistent reality" which may be found in a work like *Absalom, Absalom!* It is powerful; and it contains some passages of bawdy folk humor that are of a high order of excellence; but it is fundamentally a caricature.

When *Light in August* appeared in England, an anonymous reviewer for *The Illustrated London News* suggested that it might be a parable of the struggle between good and evil. The notion is not entirely fanciful. But, more specifically, the book might be considered as an allegory based upon Mr. Faulkner's usual theme, with the clergyman, Hightower, standing for the Formalized Tradition. The simple-hearted Byron Bunch corresponds with the naïf traditionalist, Anse Bundren; Christmas, the mulatto, is a Snopes character, as is his partner, Lucas Burch, the seducer of Lena Grove. And the pregnant Lena might represent, vaguely, life itself, which Byron and Hightower are futilely attempting to protect from Lucas Burch and Christmas and their kind.

But the book is not so transparently allegorical as *Sanctuary*; indeed, it is a confused allegory in which realism is present as well. It fails, partly, because of this confusion, which never permits the two sides of the conflict really to join the issue. But it fails, even more clearly, because of the disproportionate emphasis upon Christmas—who ought to be the antagonist but who becomes, like Milton's Satan, the real protagonist in the novel.

This defines the second general type of failure in Mr. Faulkner's work: Mr. Faulkner is unable to sustain his traditional-

ism at all, and the forces of antitraditionalism become the protagonists.

The discussion reaches a dangerous point here. Since the
time of Flaubert, at least, it has been customary to hold the view
that one mark of a novelist's craft is his skill in creating all of his
characters in the round and in maintaining an equal sympathy for
all of them. However, it is not necessary to repudiate this view to
suggest that there is a difference in kind between Flaubert's
studies of human character in the behavior of the French bour-
geois world and Mr. Faulkner's books, which are essentially
myths, built around the conflict of two different worlds, to one of
which Mr. Faulkner belongs as an artist, though he is of physical
necessity a citizen of the other.

When one possesses traditional values of conduct, he has
naturally a kind of hierarchy of sympathy, dependent upon the
values, which makes him more or less sympathetic to characters in
proportion as they are or are not traditional. Mr. Faulkner appears to maintain such a hierarchy in the greater part of his work;
although he projects the characters of the Snopes world as clearly
as he projects those of the Sartoris world, in his better books he
is always seeing them and determining their proportionate stature
from the Sartoris point of view.

But in *Light in August* the proportionate dramatic content
of the characters is the reverse of the norm set up by the other
books; and there is a corollary confusion of the whole scheme of
traditional values. The Sartoris characters, like Hightower, are
vague or typical; Christmas, the Snopes character, dominates
sympathy, and his tortured amorality determines the ethical tone
of the book. In proportion as Christmas becomes the protagonist,
the Snopes world, with its total lack of values, seems to have sup-
planted the Sartoris values *within the artist himself*, although
against his will. And the confused, malproportioned fiction,
wavering between realism and allegory, seems to be the artistic
issue of Mr. Faulkner's violent—but, in this case, unavailing—
effort to maintain the Sartoris point of view in his work.

Mr. Faulkner never gives his whole consent to such a confusion of values. That he is not content to remain within the characters of his protagonists when they are antitraditional, but must go outside them for "purple passages," seems to be evidence of this fact. *Pylon* is a case in point. It is a study of the effect of machinery upon human beings; the aviators who people it are timeless and placeless; they stay drunk most of the time to aggravate their insensitiveness; they have oil in their veins instead of blood; flying is their obsession, and when they are not in the air they do not live at all. In short, they are artifacts of the Snopes world. Against the background of an airport opening and a Mardi-Gras carnival in a Southern city, they move like characters in an animated cartoon, performing incredible antics but never being alive. Unable to speak through them, Mr. Faulkner speaks about them, in an androgynous prose-poetry that is not to be found anywhere else in his work. *Pylon* is his most conspicuous failure; and his imperfect sympathy with, and his inability to control, the protagonists, who should be the antagonists, seem to account for the failure.

Mosquitoes fails for similar reasons. Here, however, the imperfect sympathy issues in satire—of the Snopes-world Bohemia that existed in the Vieux Carré section of New Orleans during the 1920's. Since this is Mr. Faulkner's second novel, and since it was written just after he had lived in the Vieux Carré himself, while he was still under thirty, it offers another clear indication of the centrality of his traditionalism. It shows how great is the distance separating him from many of his contemporaries, such as, let us say, Mr. Ernest Hemingway. For *Mosquitoes* makes it very plain that if Mr. Faulkner is of the "lost generation," it is only of the lost generation of Sartorises. But it shows, too, that Mr. Faulkner is not an Aldous Huxley and should not try to be one. He is primarily a mythmaker; and there can be no such thing as a satiric myth.

3.

William Faulkner's latest novel, *The Wild Palms,* tells two entirely different stories, in alternating sections; but the stories

are complementary in that they both derive from the conflict between humanism and naturalism.

For Harry, the young doctor, and Charlotte, his mistress, all
humanistic morality is equated with the Snopes code of mere
"respectability," into which morality has degenerated. Of that
code, one of the characters says: "If Jesus returned today we
would have to crucify him quick in our own defense, to justify
and preserve the civilization we have worked and suffered and
died...for two thousand years to create and perfect in man's
own image." Charlotte and Harry are attempting to escape from
the code into pure naturalism. Charlotte is natural, or amoral,
Woman; with her, Harry becomes natural, amoral Man. They
are constantly insisting upon the entirely physical nature of their
love—and in no evasive terms. Their fear of any code amounts
to an obsession: when they begin to feel as if they were married,
living and working together in Chicago, they run off to a remote
mining settlement in order to escape respectability. But Harry is
conscious of doom: "So I am afraid. Because They [the forces
of the code] are smart, shrewd, They will have to be; if They
were to let us beat Them, it would be like unchecked murder and
robbery. Of course we can't beat Them; we are doomed, of
course...." The fear is justified; for they are defeated by the very
naturalism to which they have fled: Charlotte dies from the
effects of an abortion that Harry attempts to perform on her.

The other story concerns a nameless convict, adrift in a small
boat on the Mississippi River during the flood of 1927. Like
Harry and Charlotte, the convict exists in a realm of unchecked
natural forces; but unlike them, he has been put there against his
will. With him in the skiff is a pregnant woman whom he has
been sent to rescue. Like Anse Bundren, the convict is capable of
genuine moral action; and his struggle with naturalism is based
upon the ethical urge to return to his prison and to carry back the
woman he has saved. When he is finally captured, he says:
"Yonder's your boat and here's the woman"; with simple-minded
tenacity, he has fulfilled his ethical obligation.

Technically, the book fails; only the complementary themes

connect the two parts, and the connection is not strong enough
for any sort of fictional unity. Indeed, it is a pity that the two
parts are printed together; for the story of Charlotte and Harry
is one of Mr. Faulkner's failures, whereas the story of the convict
is one of his successes.

Charlotte and Harry, fleeing the Snopes world but fleeing all
codes, too, are products of the antitraditional overbalancing in
Mr. Faulkner which yielded *Pylon*. And the failure of their story
derives, like the failure of that book, from the fact that in them
the natural protagonist-antagonist schematism of Mr. Faulkner's
myth is reversed. Sympathy must be given to them reluctantly;
for though they are, as a matter of fact, running away from the
Snopes world, they are running away from the Sartoris world, too;
and, as Harry says, if they were to succeed, it would be like unchecked robbery and murder. In defense of one's own humanism,
one must not yield entire sympathy to human beings who enter
the realm of pure animalism.

But the story of the nameless convict is an heroic legend,
similar to *As I Lay Dying*; it must be counted as one of Mr.
Faulkner's definite achievements. Moreover, it has a quality of
gusty humor (a sense of the outrageously grotesque heroic, related to the humor of the "tall tales" in folk literature) which is
rare in Mr. Faulkner's work but which is always impressive when
it appears. It is to be found in some of the scenes of *Sanctuary*,
notably in the gangster funeral and in the drunken "afternoon
tea" of the middle-aged harlots at Miss Reba's house. It shows
up in some of the short stories—"Spotted Horses," for example.
And it appears in the scenes of the convicts' alligator hunting in
The Wild Palms. However, this quality does not destroy, but
serves rather to strengthen, the heroic legend as a whole.

4.

William Faulkner's myth finds expression in work that is
definitely romantic; when he comes near to tragedy, it is the
tragedy of Webster. His art, like Webster's, is tortured. In form,
each of his novels resembles a late-Elizabethan blank verse line,

where the meter is strained, threatens to break, sometimes breaks, but is always exciting. He is an original craftsman, making his own solutions to his problems of form, often blundering, but occasionally striking upon an effect that no amount of studious craftsmanship could achieve. Consequently, like Dostoievski, or like Miss Djuna Barnes in our own time, he is very special; and his work cannot be imitated except futilely, for he works within no general tradition of craft and hands on no tradition to his successors.

But Mr. Faulkner's difficulties of form derive, in part, from the struggle that he has to make to inform his material. The struggle is manifest, even in the prose itself. Discounting the results of plain carelessness in all of the books, the correlation between the fictions and the quality of the prose in Mr. Faulkner's books is instructive. It appears significant that *The Unvanquished* contains his least tortured and *Pylon* his most tortured prose.

He has worked to project in fiction the conflict between his inherent traditional values and the modern world; and the conflict has affected his fictional projection, so that all of his work is really a *striving toward* the condition of tragedy. He is the Quentin Compson or the Bayard Sartoris of modern fiction. He does not always fail; but when he does, his failure is like theirs—he ends in confused or meaningless violence. And for the same reasons: His heritage is theirs, and it is subject to the same opposition to which they are subject as characters. When he is partially successful, the result is tortured but major romantic art.

Now, in 1939, Mr. Faulkner's work may seem melodramatic. Melodrama differs from tragedy only in the amount of meaning that is subsistent in the pattern of events; and in our time the values of Mr. Faulkner's tradition are available to most men only historically, in the same way that, let us say, medieval values are available. The significance of the work as myth depends, then, upon the willingness of the reader to recover the meaning of the tradition—even historically.

INTRODUCTION TO
THE PORTABLE FAULKNER

MALCOLM COWLEY

WHEN THE WAR WAS OVER—the other war—William Faulkner went back to Oxford, Mississippi. He had served in the Royal Air Force in 1918. Now he was home again and not at home, or at least not able to accept the postwar world. He was writing poems, most of them worthless, and dozens of immature but violent and effective stories, while at the same time he was brooding over his own situation and the decline of the South. Slowly the brooding thoughts arranged themselves into the whole interconnected pattern that would form the substance of his later novels.

This pattern, which almost all his critics have overlooked, was based on what he saw in Oxford or remembered from his childhood; on scraps of family tradition (the Falkners, as they spelled the name, had played their part in the history of the state); on kitchen dialogues between the black cook and her amiable husband; on Saturday-afternoon gossip in Courthouse Square; on stories told by men in overalls squatting on their heels while they passed around a fruit jar full of white corn liquor; on all the sources familiar to a small-town Mississippi boy—but the whole of it was elaborated, transformed, given convulsive life by his emotions; until, by the simple intensity of feeling, the figures in it became a little more than human, became heroic or diabolical, became symbols of the old South, of war and reconstruction, of commerce and machinery destroying the standards of the past. There in Oxford, Faulkner performed a labor of imagination that has not been equaled in our time, and a double labor: first, to invent a Mississippi county that was like a mythical kingdom, but was complete and living in all its details; second, to make his story of Yoknapatawpha County stand as a parable or legend of all the Deep South.

For this double task, Faulkner was better equipped by talent and background than he was by schooling. He was born in New Albany, Mississippi, on September 25, 1897; he was the oldest of four brothers. The family soon moved to Oxford, where he attended the public school, but without being graduated from high school. For a year after the war, he was a student at the University of Mississippi, in Oxford, where veterans could then matriculate without a high-school diploma; but he neglected his classroom work and left without taking a degree. He had less of a formal education than any other good writer of his time, except Hart Crane—less even than Hemingway, who never went to college, but who learned to speak three foreign languages and studied writing in Paris from the best masters. Faulkner taught himself, largely, as he says, by "undirected and uncorrelated reading." Among the authors either mentioned or echoed in his early stories and poems are Keats, Balzac, Flaubert, Swinburne, Mallarmé, Wilde, Housman, Joyce, Eliot, Sherwood Anderson, and E. E. Cummings, with fainter suggestions of Hemingway (in a fishing scene), Dos Passos (in the spelling of compound words), and Scott Fitzgerald. The poems he wrote in those days were wholly derivative, but his prose from the beginning was a form of poetry; and in spite of the echoes it was always his own. He traveled less than any of his writing contemporaries. After a succession of odd jobs in Oxford, there was a brief period when he lived in New Orleans with Sherwood Anderson and met the literary crowd—he even satirized them in a very bad early novel, *Mosquitoes*; then he went to New York, where for a few unhappy months he clerked in a bookstore; in 1925 he took a long walking trip in Europe without settling on the Left Bank. Except for recent visits to Hollywood, the rest of his life has been spent in the town where he grew up, less than forty miles from his birthplace.

Although Oxford, Mississippi, is the seat of a university, it is even less of a literary center than was Salem, Massachusetts, during Hawthorne's early years as a writer; and Faulkner himself has shown an even greater dislike than Hawthorne for literary society. His novels are the books of a man who broods about literature but doesn't often discuss it with his friends; there is no ease about them, no feeling that they come from a background of taste refined by argument and of opinions held in common. They make me think of a passage from Henry James's little book on Hawthorne:

The best things come, as a general thing, from the talents that are members of a group; every man works better when he has companions working in the same line, and yielding to the stimulus of suggestion, comparison, emulation. Great things of course have been done by solitary workers; but they have usually been done with double the pains they would have cost if they had been produced in more genial circumstances. The solitary worker loses the profit of example and discussion; he is apt to make awkward experiments; he is in the nature of the case more or less of an empiric. The empiric may, as I say, be treated by the world as an expert; but the drawbacks and discomforts of empiricism remain to him, and are in fact increased by the suspicion that is mingled with his gratitude, of a want in the public taste of a sense of the proportion of things.

Like Hawthorne, Faulkner is a solitary worker by choice, and he has done great things not only with double the pains to himself that they might have cost if produced in more genial circumstances, but sometimes also with double the pains to the reader. Two or three of his books as a whole and many of them in part are awkward experiments. All of them are full of overblown words like "imponderable," "immortal," "immutable," and "immemorial" that he would have used with more discretion, or not at all, if he had followed Hemingway's example and served an apprenticeship to an older writer. He is a most uncertain judge of his own work, and he has no reason to believe that the world's judgment of it is any more to be trusted; indeed, there is no

American author who would be justified in feeling more suspicion of "a want in the public taste of a sense of the proportion of things." His early novels were overpraised, usually for the wrong reasons; his later and in many ways better novels have been obstinately condemned or simply neglected; and in 1945 all his seventeen books were out of print, with some of them unobtainable in the second-hand bookshops.

Even his warm admirers, of whom there are many—no author has a higher standing among his fellow novelists—have sometimes shown a rather vague idea of what he is trying to do; and Faulkner himself has never explained. He holds a curious attitude toward the public that appears to be lofty indifference (as in the one preface he wrote, for the Modern Library edition of *Sanctuary*), but really comes closer to being a mixture of skittery distrust and pure unconsciousness that the public exists. He doesn't furnish information or correct misstatements about himself (most of the biographical sketches that deal with him are full of preposterous errors). He doesn't care which way his name is spelled in the records, with or without the "u"—"Either way suits me," he said. Once he has finished a book, he is apparently not concerned with the question how it will be presented, to what sort of audience; and sometimes he doesn't bother to keep a private copy of it. He said in a letter, "I think I have written a lot and sent it off to print before I actually realized strangers might read it." Others might say that Faulkner, at least in those early days, was not so much composing stories for the public as telling them to himself—like a lonely child in his imaginary world, but also like a writer of genius.

2.

Faulkner's mythical kingdom is a county in northern Mississippi, on the border between the sand hills covered with scrubby pine and the black earth of the river bottoms. Except for the storekeepers, mechanics, and professional men who live in Jefferson, the county seat, all the inhabitants are farmers or woodsmen. Except for a little lumber, their only product is baled cotton for the Memphis market. A few of them live in big plantation houses, the relics of another age, and more of them in substantial wooden farmhouses; but most of them are tenants, no better housed than slaves on good plantations before the Civil War. Yoknapatawpha County—"William Faulkner, sole owner and proprietor," as he inscribed on one of the maps he drew—has a population of 15,611 persons scattered over 2,400 square miles. It sometimes seems to me that every house or hovel has been described in one of Faulkner's novels; and that all the people of the imaginary county, black and white, townsmen, farmers, and housewives, have played their parts in one connected story.

He has so far written nine books wholly concerned with Yoknapatawpha County and its people, who also appear in parts of three others and in thirty or more uncollected stories. *Sartoris* was the first of the books to be published, in the spring of 1929; it is a romantic and partly unconvincing novel, but with many fine scenes in it, like the hero's visit to a family of independent pine-hill farmers; and it states most of the themes that the author would later develop at length. *The Sound and the Fury* was written before *Sartoris*, but wasn't published until six months later; it describes the fall of the Compson family, and it was the first of Faulkner's novels to be widely discussed. The books that followed, in the Yoknapatawpha series, are *As I Lay Dying* (1930), about the death and burial of Addie Bundren; *Sanctuary* (1931), always the most popular of his novels; *Light in August* (1932), in many ways the best; *Absalom, Absalom!* (1936), about Colonel Sutpen and his ambition to found a family; *The Unvanquished* (1938), a book of interrelated stories about the Sartoris dynasty; *The Wild Palms* (1939), half of which deals with a convict from back in the pine hills; *The Hamlet* (1940), a novel about the Snopes clan; and *Go Down, Moses* (1942), in which Faulkner's theme is the Negroes. There are also many Yoknapatawpha stories in *These Thirteen* (1931) and *Dr. Martino* (1934), besides other stories privately printed (like "Miss Zilphia Gant") or published in magazines and still to be collected or used as episodes in novels.

Just as Balzac, who seems to have inspired the series, divided his *Comédie Humaine* into "Scenes of Parisian Life," "Scenes of Provincial Life," "Scenes of Private Life," so Faulkner might divide his work into a number of cycles: one about the planters and their descendants, one about the townspeople of Jefferson, one about the poor whites, one about the Indians (consisting of stories already written but never brought together), and one about the Negroes. Or again, if he adopted a division by families, there would be the Compson-Sartoris saga, the still unfinished Snopes saga, the McCaslin saga, dealing with the white and black descendants of Carothers McCaslin, and the Ratliff-Bundren saga, devoted to the backwoods farmers of Frenchman's Bend. All the cycles or sagas are closely interconnected; it is as if each new book was a chord or segment of a total situation always existing in the author's mind. Sometimes a short story is the sequel to an earlier novel. For example, we read in *Sartoris* that Byron Snopes stole a packet of letters from Narcissa Benbow; and in "There Was a Queen," a story published five years later, we learn how Narcissa got the letters back again. Sometimes, on the other hand, a novel contains the sequel to a story; and we discover from an incidental reference in *The Sound and the Fury* that the Negro woman whose terror of death was described in "That Evening Sun" had later been murdered by her husband, who left her body in a ditch for the vultures. Sometimes an episode has a more complicated history. Thus, in the first chapter of *Sanctuary*, we hear about the Old Frenchman place, a ruined mansion near which the people of the neighborhood had been "digging with secret and sporadic optimism for gold which the builder was reputed to have buried somewhere about the place when Grant came through the country on his Vicksburg campaign." Later this digging for gold served as the subject of a story published in the *Saturday Evening Post*: "Lizards in Jamshyd's Courtyard." Still later the story was completely rewritten and became the last chapter of *The Hamlet*.

As one book leads into another, Faulkner sometimes falls into inconsistencies of detail. There is a sewing-machine agent named V.K. Suratt who appears in *Sartoris* and some of the later stories. By the time we reach *The Hamlet*, his name has changed to Ratliff, although his character remains the same (and his age, too, for all the twenty years that separate the backgrounds of the two novels). Henry Armstid is a likable figure in *As I Lay Dying* and *Light in August*; in *The Hamlet* he is mean and half-demented. His wife, whose character remains consistent, is called Lula in one book and Martha in another; in the third she is nameless. There is an Indian chief named Doom who appears in several stories; he starts as the father of Issetibeha and ends as his grandson. The mansion called Sutpen's Hundred was built of brick at the beginning of *Absalom, Absalom!* but at the end of the novel it is all wood and inflammable except for the chimneys. But these errors are comparatively few and inconsequential, considering the scope of Faulkner's series; and I should judge that most of them are afterthoughts rather than oversights.

All his books in the Yoknapatawpha saga are part of the same living pattern. It is this pattern, and not the printed volumes in which part of it is recorded, that is Faulkner's real achievement. Its existence helps to explain one feature of his work: that each novel, each long or short story, seems to reveal more than it states explicitly and to have a subject bigger than itself. All the separate works are like blocks of marble from the same quarry: they show the veins and faults of the mother rock. Or else—to use a rather strained figure—they are like wooden planks that were cut not from a log, but from a still living tree. The planks are planed and chiseled into their final shapes, but the tree itself heals over the wound and continues to grow. Faulkner is incapable of telling the same story twice without adding new details. In the present volume I wanted to use part of *The Sound and the Fury*, the novel that deals with the fall of the Compson family. I thought that the last part of the book would be most effective as a separate episode, but still it depended too much on what had gone before. Faulkner offered to write a very brief introduction that would explain the relations of the characters. What he finally sent me is the much longer passage here printed as an appendix: a genealogy of the Compsons from their first arrival in this country. Whereas the novel is confined to a period of eighteen years ending in 1928, the genealogy goes back to the battle of Culloden in 1745, and forward to the year 1945, when Jason, last of the Compson males, has sold the family mansion, and Sister Caddy has last been heard of as the mistress of a German general. The novel that Faulkner wrote about the Compsons had long ago been given its final shape; but the pattern or body of legend behind the novel—and behind all his other books—was still developing.

Although the pattern is presented in terms of a single Mississippi county, it can be extended to the Deep South as a whole; and Faulkner always seems conscious of its wider application. He might have been thinking of his own novels when he described the ledgers in the commissary of the McCaslin plantation, in *Go Down, Moses*. They recorded, he said, "that slow trickle of molasses and meal and meat, of shoes and straw hats and overalls, of plowlines and collars and heelbolts and clevises, which returned each fall as cotton"—in a sense they were local and limited; but they were also "the continuation of that record which two hundred years had not been enough to complete and another hundred would not be enough to discharge; that chronicle which was a whole land in miniature, which multiplied and compounded was the entire South."

3.

"Tell about the South," says Quentin Compson's roommate at Harvard, a Canadian named Shreve McCannon who is curious about the unknown region beyond the Ohio. "What's it like there?" he asks. "What do they do there? Why do they live there? Why do they live at all?" And Quentin, whose background is a little like that of Faulkner himself and who sometimes seems to speak for him—Quentin answers, "You can't understand it.

You would have to be born there." Nevertheless, he tells a long and violent story that he regards as the essence of the Deep South, which is not so much a mere region as it is, in Quentin's mind, an incomplete and frustrated nation trying to relive its legendary past.

The story he tells—I am trying to summarize the plot of *Absalom, Absalom!*—is that of a mountain boy named Thomas Sutpen whose family drifted into the Virginia lowlands, where his father found odd jobs on a plantation. One day the father sent him with a message to the big house, but he was turned away at the door by a black man in livery. Puzzled and humiliated, the mountain boy was seized upon by the lifelong ambition to which he would afterward refer as "the design." He too would own a plantation with slaves and a liveried butler; he would build a mansion as big as any of those in the Tidewater; and he would have a son to inherit his wealth.

A dozen years later, Sutpen appeared in the frontier town of Jefferson, where he managed to obtain a hundred square miles of land from the Chickasaws. With the help of twenty wild Negroes from the jungle and a French architect, he set about building the largest house in northern Mississippi, using timbers from the forest and bricks that his Negroes molded and baked on the spot; it was as if his mansion, Sutpen's Hundred, had been literally torn from the soil. Only one man in Jefferson—he was Quentin's grandfather, General Compson—ever learned how and where Sutpen had acquired his slaves. He had shipped to Haiti from Virginia, worked as overseer on a sugar plantation and married the rich planter's daughter, who had borne him a son. Then, finding that his wife had Negro blood, he had simply put her away, with her child and her fortune, while keeping the twenty slaves as a sort of indemnity.

In Jefferson, Sutpen married again. This time his wife belonged to a pious family of the neighborhood, and she bore him two children, Henry and Judith. He became the biggest cotton planter in Yoknapatawpha County, and it seemed that his "design" had already been fulfilled. At this moment, however,

Henry came home from the University of Mississippi with an older and worldlier new friend, Charles Bon, who was in reality Sutpen's son by his first marriage. Charles became engaged to Judith. Sutpen learned his identity and, without making a sign of recognition, ordered him from the house. Henry, who refused to believe that Charles was his half-brother, renounced his birthright and followed him to New Orleans. In 1861, all the male Sutpens went off to war, and all of them survived four years of fighting. Then, in the spring of 1865, Charles suddenly decided to marry Judith, even though he was certain by now that she was his half-sister. Henry rode beside him all the way back to Sutpen's Hundred, but tried to stop him at the gate, killed him when he insisted on going ahead with his plan, told Judith what he had done, and disappeared.

But Quentin's story of the Deep South does not end with the war. Colonel Sutpen came home, he says, to find his wife dead, his son a fugitive, his slaves dispersed (they had run away even before they were freed by the Union army), and most of his land about to be seized for debt. Still determined to carry out "the design," he did not even pause for breath before undertaking to restore his house and plantation to what they had been. The effort failed and Sutpen was reduced to keeping a crossroads store. Now in his sixties, he tried again to beget a son; but his wife's younger sister, Miss Rosa Coldfield, was outraged by his proposal ("Let's try it," he had said, "and if it's a boy we'll get married"); and later poor Milly Jones, with whom he had an affair, gave birth to a baby girl. At that Sutpen abandoned hope and provoked Milly's grandfather into killing him. Judith survived her father for a time, as did the half-caste son of Charles Bon by a New Orleans octoroon. After the death of these two by yellow fever, the great house was haunted rather than inhabited by an ancient mulatto woman, Sutpen's daughter by one of his slaves. The fugitive Henry Sutpen came home to die; the townspeople heard of his illness and sent an ambulance after him; but old Clytie thought they were arresting him for murder and set fire to Sutpen's Hundred. The only survival of the conflagration was Jim Bond, a halfwitted creature who was Charles Bon's grandson.

"Now I want you to tell me just one thing more," Shreve McCannon says after hearing the story. "Why do you hate the South?"—"I dont hate it," Quentin says quickly, at once. "I dont hate it," he repeats, speaking for the author as well as himself. *I dont hate it,* he thinks, panting in the cold air, the iron New England dark; *I dont. I dont hate it! I dont hate it!*

The reader cannot help wondering why this somber and, at moments, plainly incredible story had so seized upon Quentin's mind that he trembled with excitement when telling it and felt it revealed the essence of the Deep South. It seems to belong in the realm of Gothic romances, with Sutpen's Hundred taking the place of the haunted castle on the Rhine, with Colonel Sutpen as Faust and Charles Bon as Manfred. Then slowly it dawns on you that most of the characters and incidents have a double meaning; that besides their place in the story, they also serve as symbols or metaphors with a general application. Sutpen's great design, the land he stole from the Indians, the French architect who built his house with the help of wild Negroes from the jungle, the woman of mixed blood whom he married and disowned, the unacknowledged son who ruined him, the poor white whom he wronged and who killed him in anger, the final destruction of the mansion like the downfall of a social order: all these might belong to a tragic fable of Southern history. With a little cleverness, the whole novel might be explained as a connected and logical allegory, but this, I think, would be going far beyond the author's intention. First of all he was writing a story, and one that affected him deeply, but he was also brooding over a social situation. More or less unconsciously, the incidents in the story came to represent the forces and elements in the social situation, since the mind naturally works in terms of symbols and parallels. In Faulkner's case, this form of parallelism is not confined to *Absalom, Absalom!* It can be found in the whole fictional framework that he has been elaborating in novel after novel, until his work has become a myth or legend of the South.

I call it a legend because it is obviously no more intended as a historical account of the country south of the Ohio than *The Scarlet Letter* was intended as a history of Massachusetts or *Paradise Lost* as a factual description of the Fall. Briefly stated, the legend might run something like this: The Deep South was settled partly by aristocrats like the Sartoris clan and partly by new men like Colonel Sutpen. Both types of planters were determined to establish a lasting social order on the land they had seized from the Indians (that is, to leave sons behind them). They had the virtue of living single-mindedly by a fixed code; but there was also an inherent guilt in their "design," their way of life; it was slavery that put a curse on the land and brought about the Civil War. After the War was lost, partly as a result of their own mad heroism (for who else but men as brave as Jackson and Stuart could have frightened the Yankees into standing together and fighting back?) they tried to restore "the design" by other methods. But they no longer had the strength to achieve more than a partial success, even after they had freed their land from the carpetbaggers who followed the Northern armies. As time passed, moreover, the men of the old order found that they had Southern enemies too: they had to fight against a new exploiting class descended from the landless whites of slavery days. In this struggle between the clan of Sartoris and the unscrupulous tribe of Snopes, the Sartorises were defeated in advance by a traditional code that kept them from using the weapons of the enemy. As a price of victory, however, the Snopeses had to serve the mechanized civilization of the North, which was morally impotent in itself, but which, with the aid of its Southern retainers, ended by corrupting the Southern nation.

Faulkner's novels of contemporary Southern life continue the legend into a period that he regards as one of moral confusion and social decay. He is continually seeking in them for violent images to convey his sense of despair. *Sanctuary* is the most violent of all his novels; it is also the most popular and by no means the least important (in spite of Faulkner's comment that it was "a cheap idea . . . deliberately conceived to make money").

The story of Popeye and Temple Drake has more meaning than appears on a first hasty reading—the only reading that most of the critics have been willing to grant it. Popeye himself is one of several characters in Faulkner's novels who represent the mechanical civilization that has invaded and partly conquered the South. He is always described in mechanical terms: his eyes "looked like rubber knobs"; his face "just went awry, like the face of a wax doll set too near a hot fire and forgotten"; his tight suit and stiff hat were "all angles, like a modernistic lampshade"; and in general he had "that vicious depthless quality of stamped tin." Popeye was the son of a professional strikebreaker, from whom he had inherited syphilis, and the grandson of a pyromaniac. Like two other villains in Faulkner's novels, Joe Christmas and Januarius Jones, he had spent most of his childhood in an institution. He was the man "who made money and had nothing he could do with it, spend it for, since he knew that alcohol would kill him like poison, who had no friends and had never known a woman"—in other words, he was the compendium of all the hateful qualities that Faulkner assigns to finance capitalism. *Sanctuary* is not a connected allegory, as one critic explained it, but neither is it a mere accumulation of pointless horrors. It is an example of the Freudian method turned backward, being full of sexual nightmares that are in reality social symbols. It is somehow connected in the author's mind with what he regards as the rape and corruption of the South.

In all his novels dealing with the present, Faulkner makes it clear that the descendants of the old ruling caste have the wish but not the courage or the strength to prevent this new disaster. They are defeated by Popeye (like Horace Benbow), or they run away from him (like Gowan Stevens, who had gone to school at Virginia and learned to drink like a gentleman, but not to fight for his principles), or they are robbed and replaced in their positions of influence by the Snopeses (like old Bayard Sartoris, the president of the bank), or they drug themselves with eloquence and alcohol (like Quentin Compson's father), or they retire into the illusion of being inviolable Southern ladies (like

Mrs. Compson, who says, "It can't be simply to flout and hurt me. Whoever God is, He would not permit that. I'm a lady."), or they dwell so much on the past that they are incapable of facing the present (like Reverend Hightower of *Light in August*), or they run from danger to danger (like young Bayard Sartoris) frantically seeking their own destruction. Faulkner's novels are full of well-meaning and even admirable persons, not only the grandsons of the cotton aristocracy, but also pine-hill farmers and storekeepers and sewing-machine agents and Negro cooks and sharecroppers; but they are almost all of them defeated by circumstances and they carry with them a sense of their own doom.

They also carry, whether heroes or villains, a curious sense of submission to their fate. "There is not one of Faulkner's characters," says André Gide in his dialogue on "The New American Novelists," "who properly speaking, has a soul"; and I think he means that not one of them exercises the faculty of conscious choice between good and evil. They are haunted, obsessed, driven forward by some inner necessity. Like Miss Rosa Coldfield, in *Absalom, Absalom!* they exist in "that dream state in which you run without moving from a terror in which you cannot believe, toward a safety in which you have no faith." Or, like the slaves freed by General Sherman's army, in *The Unvanquished*, they blindly follow the roads toward any river, believing that it will be their Jordan:

They were singing, walking along the road singing, not even looking to either side. The dust didn't even settle for two days, because all that night they still passed; we sat up listening to them, and the next morning every few yards along the road would be the old ones who couldn't keep up any more, sitting or lying down and even crawling along, calling to the others to help them; and the others—the young ones—not stopping, not even looking at them. "Going to Jordan," they told me. "Going to cross Jordan."

All Faulkner's characters, black and white, are a little like that. They dig for gold frenziedly after they have lost their hope of finding it (like Henry Armstid in *The Hamlet* and Lucas Beauchamp in *Go Down, Moses*); or they battle against and survive a Mississippi flood for the one privilege of returning to the state prison farm (like the tall convict in "Old Man"); or, a whole family together, they carry a body through flood and fire and corruption to bury it in the cemetery at Jefferson (like the Bundrens in *As I Lay Dying*); or they tramp the roads week after week in search of men who had promised but never intended to marry them (like Lena Grove, the pregnant woman of *Light in August*); or, pursued by a mob, they turn at the end to meet and accept death (like Joe Christmas in the same novel). Even when they seem to be guided by a conscious purpose, like Colonel Sutpen, it is not something they have chosen by an act of will, but something that has taken possession of them: Sutpen's great design was "not what he wanted to do but what he just had to do, had to do it whether he wanted to or not, because if he did not do it he knew that he could never live with himself for the rest of his life." In the same way, Faulkner himself writes not what he wants to, but what he just has to write whether he wants to or not.

4.

He is not primarily a novelist: that is, his stories do not occur to him in book-length units of 70,000 to 150,000 words. Almost all his novels have some weakness in structure. Some of them combine two or more themes having little relation to each other, like *Light in August*, while others, like *The Hamlet*, tend to resolve themselves into a series of episodes resembling beads on a string. In *The Sound and the Fury*, which is superb as a whole, we can't be sure that the four sections of the novel are presented in the most effective order; at any rate, we can't fully understand and perhaps can't even read the first section until we have read the other three. *Absalom, Absalom!* though pitched in too high a key, is structurally the soundest of all the novels in the Yoknapatawpha series; but even here the author's attention shifts halfway through the book from the principal theme of Colonel Sutpen's ambition to the secondary theme of incest and miscegenation.

Faulkner is best and most nearly himself either in long

stories like "The Bear," in *Go Down, Moses,* and "Old Man,"
which was published as half of *The Wild Palms,* and "Spotted
Horses," which was first printed separately, then greatly expanded
and fitted into the loose framework of *The Hamlet*—all three
stories are included in this volume; or else in the Yoknapatawpha
saga as a whole. That is, he is most effective in dealing with the
total situation that is always present in his mind as a pattern of
the South; or else in shorter units that can be conceived and written in a single burst of creative effort. It is by his best that we
should judge him, like every other author; and Faulkner at his
best—even sometimes at his worst—has a power, a richness of
life, an intensity to be found in no other American novelist of
our time. He has—once more I am quoting from Henry James's
essay on Hawthorne—"the element of simple genius, the quality
of imagination."

Moreover, he has a brooding love for the land where he was
born and reared and where, unlike other writers of his generation,
he has chosen to spend his life. It is "...this land, this South, for
which God has done so much, with woods for game and streams
for fish and deep rich soil for seed and lush springs to sprout it
and long summers to mature it and serene falls to harvest it
and short mild winters for men and animals." So far as Faulkner's
country includes the Delta, it is also (in the words of old Ike
McCaslin)

This land which man has deswamped and denuded and derivered
in two generations so that white men can own plantations and com-
mute every night to Memphis and black men own plantations and ride
in jim crow cars to Chicago and live in millionaires' mansions on Lake
Shore Drive, where white men rent farms and live like niggers and
niggers crop on shares and live like animals, where cotton is planted
and grows man-tall in the very cracks of the sidewalks, and usury and
mortgage and bankruptcy and measureless wealth, Chinese and Afri-
can and Aryan and Jew, all breed and spawn together.

Here are the two sides of Faulkner's feeling for the South: on the
one side, an admiring and possessive love; on the other, a com-

pulsive fear lest what he loves should be destroyed by the ignorance of its native serfs and the greed of traders and absentee
landlords.

No other American writer takes such delight in the weather.
He speaks in various novels of "the hot still pinewiney silence of
the August afternoon"; of "the moonless September dust, the
trees along the road not rising soaring as trees should but squatting like huge fowl"; of "the tranquil sunset of October mazy with
windless wood-smoke"; of the "slow drizzle of November rain
just above the ice point"; of "those windless Mississippi December days which are a sort of Indian summer's Indian summer"; of
January and February when there is "no movement anywhere
save the low constant smoke... and no sound save the chopping
of axes and the lonely whistle of the daily trains." Spring in
Faulkner's country is a hurried season, "all coming at once, pell
mell and disordered, fruit and bloom and leaf, pied meadow and
blossoming wood and the long fields shearing dark out of winter's
slumber, to the shearing plow." Summer is dust-choked and blaz-
ing, and it lasts far into what should be autumn. "That's the one
trouble with this country," he says in *As I Lay Dying*. "Everything, weather, all, hangs on too long. Like our rivers, our land:
opaque, slow, violent; shaping and creating the life of man in its
implacable and brooding image."

And Faulkner loves these people created in the image of the
land. After a second reading of his novels, you continue to be
impressed by his villains, Popeye and Jason and Joe Christmas
and Flem Snopes; but this time you find more place in your memory for other figures standing a little in the background yet presented by the author with quiet affection: old ladies like Miss
Jenny DuPré, with their sharp-tongued benevolence; shrewd but
kindly bargainers like Ratliff, the sewing-machine agent, and Will
Varner, with his cotton gin and general store; long-suffering farm
wives like Mrs. Henry Armstid (whether her name is Lula or
Martha); and backwoods patriarchs like Pappy MacCullum, with
his six middle-aged but unmarried sons named after the generals
of Lee's army. You remember the big plantation houses that

collapse in flames as if a whole civilization were dying, but you also remember men in patched and faded but quite clean overalls sitting on the gallery—here in the North we should call it the porch—of a crossroads store that is covered with posters advertising soft drinks and patent medicines; and you remember the stories they tell while chewing tobacco until the suption is out of it (everything in their world is reduced to anecdote, and every anecdote is based on character). You remember Quentin Compson not in his despairing moments, but riding with his father behind the dogs as they quarter a sedge-grown hillside after quail; and not listening to his father's story, but still knowing every word of it, because, as he thought to himself, "You had learned, absorbed it already without the medium of speech somehow from having been born and living beside it, with it, as children will and do: so that what your father was saying did not tell you anything so much as it struck, word by word, the resonant strings of remembering."

Faulkner's novels have the quality of being lived, absorbed, remembered rather than merely observed. And they have what is rare in the novels of our time, a warmth of family affection, brother for brother and sister, the father for his children—a love so warm and proud that it tries to shut out the rest of the world. Compared with that affection, married love is presented as something calculating, and illicit love as a consuming fire. And because the blood relationship is central in his novels, Faulkner finds it hard to create sympathetic characters between the ages of twenty and forty. He is better with children, Negro and white, and incomparably good with older people who preserve the standards that have come down to them "out of the old time, the old days."

In his later books, which have attracted so little attention that they seem to have gone unread, there is a quality not exactly new to Faulkner—it had appeared already in passages of *Sartoris* and *Sanctuary*—but now much stronger and no longer overshadowed by violence and horror. It is a sort of homely and sober-sided frontier humor that is seldom achieved in contemporary writing (except by Erskine Caldwell, another Southerner). The horse-trading episodes in *The Hamlet*, and especially the long story of the spotted ponies from Texas, might have been inspired by the Davy Crockett almanacs. "Old Man," the story of the convict who surmounted the greatest of all the Mississippi floods, might almost be a continuation of *Huckleberry Finn*. It is as if some older friend of Huck's had taken the raft and drifted on from Aunt Sally Phelps's farm into wilder adventures, described in a wilder style, among Chinese and Cajuns and bayous crawling with alligators. In a curious way, Faulkner combines two of the principal traditions in American letters: the tradition of psychological horror, often close to symbolism, that begins with Charles Brockden Brown, our first professional novelist, and extends through Poe, Melville, Henry James (in his later stories), Stephen Crane, and Hemingway; and the other tradition of frontier humor and realism, beginning with Augustus Longstreet's *Georgia Scenes* and having Mark Twain as its best example.

But the American author he most resembles is Hawthorne, for all their polar differences. They stand to each other as July to December, as heat to cold, as swamp to mountain, as the luxuriant to the meager but perfect, as planter to Puritan; and yet Hawthorne had much the same attitude toward New England that Faulkner has toward the South, together with a strong sense of regional particularity. The Civil War made Hawthorne feel that "the North and the South were two distinct nations in opinions and habits, and had better not try to live under the same institutions." In the spring of 1861, he wrote to his Bowdoin classmate Horatio Bridge, "We were never one people and never really had a country."—"New England," he said a little later, "is quite as large a lump of earth as my heart can really take in." But it was more than a lump of earth for him; it was a lump of history and a permanent state of consciousness. Like Faulkner in the South, he applied himself to creating its moral fables and elaborating its legends, which existed, as it were, in his solitary heart. Pacing the hillside behind his house in Concord, he listened for a voice; you might say that he lay in wait for it, passively but expectantly, like a hunter behind a rock; then, when it had spoken, he transcribed its words—more slowly and carefully than Faulkner, it is true; with more form and less fire, but with the same essential fidelity. If the voice was silent, he had nothing to write. "I have an instinct that I had better keep quiet," he said in a letter to his publisher. "Perhaps I shall have a new spirit of vigor if I wait quietly for it; perhaps not." Faulkner is another author who has to wait for the spirit and the voice. Essentially he is not a novelist, in the sense of not being a writer who sets out to observe actions and characters, then fits them into the architectural framework of a story. For all the weakness of his own poems, he is an epic or bardic poet in prose, a creator of myths that he weaves together into a legend of the South.

WILLIAM FAULKNER

ROBERT PENN WARREN

MALCOLM COWLEY'S editing of *The Portable Faulkner*[1] is remarkable on two counts. First, the selection from Faulkner's work is made not merely to give a cross section or a group of good examples but to demonstrate one of the principles of integration in the work. Second, the introductory essay is one of the few things ever written on Faulkner which is not hagridden by prejudice or preconception and which really sheds some light on the subject.

The selections here are made to describe the place, Yoknapatawpha County, Mississippi, which is, as Cowley puts it, "Faulkner's mythical kingdom," and to give the history of that kingdom.

Reprinted with permission from *The New Republic*, August 12, 1946, pp. 176–80, and August 26, 1946, pp. 234–37.
1. *The Portable Faulkner*, edited by Malcolm Cowley. New York: Viking Press.

The place is the locale of most of Faulkner's work. Its 2,400 square miles lie between the hills of north Mississippi and the rich, black bottom lands. It has a population of 15,611 persons, composing a society with characters as different as the Bundrens, the Snopeses, Ike McCaslin, Percy Grimm, Temple Drake, the Compsons, Christmas, Dilsey, and the tall convict of *The Wild Palms*. No land in all fiction lives more vividly in its physical presence than this mythical county—the "pine-winey" afternoons, the nights with "a thin sickle of moon like the heel print of a boot in wet sand," the tremendous reach of the big river in flood, "yellow and sleepy in the afternoon," and the "little piddling creeks, that run backward one day and forward the next and come busting down on a man full of dead mules and hen houses," the ruined plantation which was Popeye's hangout, the swamps and fields and hot, dusty roads of the Frenchman's Bend section, and the remnants of the great original forests, "green with gloom" in summer, "if anything actually dimmer than they had been in November's gray dissolution, where even at noon the sun fell only in windless dappling upon the earth which never completely dried."

And no land in all fiction is more painstakingly analyzed from the sociological standpoint. The descendants of the old families, the descendants of bushwhackers and carpetbaggers, the swamp rats, the Negro cooks and farm hands, bootleggers and gangsters, peddlers, college boys, tenant farmers, country store-keepers, county-seat lawyers are all here. The marks of class, occupation, and history are fully rendered and we know completely their speech, dress, food, houses, manners, and attitudes. Nature and sociology, geography and human geography, are scrupulously though effortlessly presented in Faulkner's work, and their significance for his work is very great; but the significance is of a conditioning order. They are, as it were, aspects of man's "doom"— a word of which Faulkner is very fond—but his manhood in the face of that doom is what is important.

Cowley's selections are made to give the description of the mythical kingdom, but more important, they are made to give its

history. Most critics, even those who have most naïvely or deliberately misread the meaning of the fact, have been aware that the
sense of the past is crucial in Faulkner's work. Cowley has here
set up selections running in date of action from 1820 to 1940.
The first, "A Justice," is a story about Ikkemotubbe, the nephew
of a Chickasaw chief who went to New Orleans, where he received the name of *du Homme*, which became Doom; who came
back to the tribe to poison his way to the Man-ship; and who, in
the end (in Faulkner's "history" though not in "A Justice" itself),
swaps a mile square of "virgin north Mississippi dirt" for a racing
mare owned by Jason Lycurgus Compson, the founder of the
Compson family in Mississippi. The last selection, "Delta Autumn," shows us Isaac McCaslin, the man who brings the best
of the old order, philosopher, aristocrat, woodsman, into the
modern world and who gives the silver-mounted horn which General Compson had left him to a mulatto woman for her bastard
son by a relative of McCaslin's. In between "A Justice" and
"Delta Autumn" fall such pieces as the magnificent "Red Leaves,"
the profoundly symbolic story called "The Bear," the Civil War
and Reconstruction stories, "Rain" (from *The Unvanquished*)
and "Wash," "Old Man" (the story of the tall convict from *The
Wild Palms*), and the often anthologized "That Evening Sun"
and "A Rose for Emily," and the brilliant episode of "Percy
Grimm" (from *Light in August*). There are other pieces included, but these are the best, and the best for showing high
points in the history of Yoknapatawpha County.

Cowley's introduction undertakes to define the significance
of place and history in Faulkner's work, that "labor of imagination that has not been equaled in our time." That labor is, as he
points out, a double labor: "first, to invent a Mississippi county
that was like a mythical kingdom, but was complete and living in
all its details; second, to make his story of Yoknapatawpha
County stand as a parable or legend of all the Deep South." The
legend—called a legend "because it is obviously no more intended
as a historical account of the country south of the Ohio than *The*

Scarlet Letter was intended as a history of Massachusetts"—is, as Cowley defines it, this:

The South was settled by Sartorises (aristocrats) and Sutpens (nameless, ambitious men) who, seizing the land from the Indians, were determined to found an enduring and stable order. But despite their strength and integrity their project was, to use Faulkner's word, "accursed" by slavery, which, with the Civil War as instrument, frustrated their design. Their attempt to rebuild according to the old plan and old values was defeated by a combination of forces—the carpetbaggers and Snopeses ("a new exploiting class descended from the landless whites"). Most of the descendants of the old order are in various ways incompetent: They are prevented by their code from competing with the codeless Snopeses, they cling to the letter and forget the spirit of their tradition, they lose contact with the realities of the present and escape into a dream world of alcohol or rhetoric or gentility or madness, they fall in love with defeat or death, they lose nerve and become cowards, or they, like the last Jason in *The Sound and the Fury*, adopt Snopesism and become worse than any Snopes. Figures like Popeye (eyes like "rubber knobs," a creature having "that vicious depthless quality of stamped tin," the man "who made money and had nothing he could do with it, spend it for, since he knew that alcohol would kill him like poison, who had no friends and had never known a woman") are in their dehumanized quality symbols of modernism, for the society of finance capitalism. The violence of some of Faulkner's work is, according to Cowley, "an example of the Freudian method turned backward, being full of sexual nightmares that are in reality social symbols. It is somehow connected in the author's mind with what he regards as the rape and corruption of the South."

This is, in brief, Cowley's interpretation of the legend, and it provides an excellent way into Faulkner; it exactly serves the purpose which an introduction should serve. The interpretation is indebted, no doubt, to that of George Marion O'Donnell (the first and still an indispensable study of Faulkner's theme), but it modifies O'Donnell's tendency to read Faulkner with an allegorical rigidity and with a kind of doctrinal single-mindedness.

It is possible that the present view, however, should be somewhat modified, at least in emphasis. Although no writer is more deeply committed to a locality than Faulkner, the emphasis on the Southern elements may blind us to other elements, or at least other applications, of deep significance. And this is especially true in so far as the work is interpreted merely as Southern apologetics or, as it is by Maxwell Geismar, as the "extreme hallucinations" of a "cultural psychosis."

It is important, I think, that Faulkner's work be regarded not in terms of the South against the North, but in terms of issues which are common to our modern world. The legend is not merely a legend of the South, but is also a legend of our general plight and problem. The modern world is in moral confusion. It does suffer from a lack of discipline, of sanctions, of community of values, of a sense of a mission. It is a world in which self-interest, workableness, success, provide the standards. It is a world which is the victim of abstraction and of mechanism, or at least, at moments, feels itself to be. It can look back nostalgically upon the old world of traditional values and feel loss and perhaps despair—upon the world in which, as one of Faulkner's characters puts it, men "had the gift of living once or dying once instead of being diffused and scattered creatures drawn blindly from a grab bag and assembled"—a world in which men were, "integer for integer," more simple and complete.

If it be objected that Faulkner's view is unrealistic, that had the old order satisfied human needs it would have survived, and that it is sentimental to hold that it was killed from the outside, the answer is clear in the work: the old order did not satisfy human needs—the Southern old order or any other—for it, not being founded on justice, was "accursed" and held the seeds of its own ruin in itself. But even in terms of the curse the old order, as opposed to the new order (in so far as the new is to be equated with Snopesism), allowed the traditional man to define himself as human by setting up codes, concepts of virtue, obligations, and by accepting the risks of his humanity. Within the traditional order was a notion of truth, even if man in the flow of things did not succeed in realizing that truth. Take, for instance, the passage from "The Bear":

"All right," he said. "Listen," and read again, but only one stanza this time and closed the book and laid it on the table. "She cannot fade, though thou hast not thy bliss," McCaslin said: "Forever wilt thou love, and she be fair."

"He's talking about a girl," he said.

"He had to talk about something," McCaslin said. Then he said, "He was talking about truth. Truth is one. It doesn't change. It covers all things which touch the heart—honor and pride and pity and justice and courage and love. Do you see now?"

The human effort is what is important, the capacity to make the effort to rise above the mechanical process of life, the pride to endure, for in endurance there is a kind of self-conquest.

When it is said, as it is often said, that Faulkner's work is "backward-looking," the answer is that the constant ethical center is to be found in the glorification of the human effort and of human endurance, which are not in time, even though in modernity they seem to persist most surely among the despised and rejected. It is true that Faulkner's work contains a savage attack on modernity, but it is to be remembered that Elizabethan tragedy, for instance, contained just such an attack on its own special "modernity." (Ambition is the most constant tragic crime, and ambition is the attitude special to an opening society; all villains are rationalists and appeal to "nature" beyond traditional morality for justification, and rationalism is, in the sense implied here, the attitude special to the rise of a secular and scientific order before a new morality can be formulated.)

It is not ultimately important whether the traditional order (Southern or other) as depicted by Faulkner fits exactly the picture which critical historical method provides. Let it be granted, for the sake of discussion, that Faulkner does oversimplify the matter. What is ultimately important, both ethically and artistically, is the symbolic function of that order in relation to the world which is set in opposition to it. The opposition between the old order and the new does not, however, exhaust the picture. What of the order to come? "We will have to wait," old Ike McCaslin says to the mulatto girl who is in love with a white man. A curse may work itself out in time; and in such glimpses, which occur now and then, we get the notion of a grudging meliorism, a practical supplement to the idealism, like Ike McCaslin's, which finds compensation in the human effort and the contemplation of "truth."

The discussion, even at a larger scope and with more satisfactory analysis, of the central theme of Faulkner would not exhaust the interest of his work. In fact, the discussion of this question always runs the risk of making his work appear too schematic, too dry and too complacent when in actual fact it is full of rich detail, of shadings and complexities of attitude, of ironies and ambivalences. Cowley's introduction cautions the reader on this point and suggests various fruitful topics for investigation and thought. But I shall make bold—and in the general barrenness of criticism on Faulkner it does not require excessive boldness—to list and comment on certain topics which seem to me to demand further critical study.

Nature. The vividness of the natural background is one of the impressive features of Faulkner's work. It is accurately observed, but observation only provides the stuff from which the characteristic effects are gained. It is the atmosphere which counts, the poetry, the infusion of feeling, the symbolic weight. Nature provides a backdrop—of lyric beauty (the meadow in the cow episode of *The Hamlet*), of homely charm (the trial scene of the "Spotted Horses" story from the same book), of sinister, brooding force (the river in "Old Man" from *The Wild Palms*), of massive dignity (the forest in "The Bear")—for the human action and passion. The indestructible beauty is there: "God created man," Ike McCaslin says in "Delta Autumn," "and He created the world for him to live in and I reckon He created the kind of world He would have wanted to live in if He had been a man."

Ideally, if man were like God, as Ike McCaslin puts it, man's attitude toward nature would be one of pure contemplation, pure participation in its great forms and appearances; the appropriate attitude is love, for with Ike McCaslin the moment of love is equated with godhood. But since man "wasn't quite God himself," since he lives in the world of flesh, he must be a hunter, user, and violator. To return to McCaslin: God "put them both here: man and the game he would follow and kill, foreknowing it. I believe He said, 'So be it.' I reckon He even foreknew the end. But He said, 'I will give him his chance. I will give him warning and foreknowledge too, along with the desire to follow and the power to slay. The woods and the fields he ravages and the game he devastates will be the consequence and signature of his crime and guilt, and his punishment.' "

There is, then, a contamination implicit in the human condition—a kind of Original Sin, as it were—but it is possible, even in the contaminating act, the violation, for man to achieve some measure of redemption, a redemption through love. For instance, in "The Bear," the great legendary beast which is pursued for years to the death is also an object of love and veneration, and the symbol of virtue, and the deer hunt of "Delta Autumn" is for Ike McCaslin a ritual of renewal. Those who have learned the right relationship to nature—"the pride and humility" which young Ike McCaslin learns from the half-Negro, half-Indian Sam Fathers—are set over against those who have not. In "The Bear," General Compson speaks up to Cass McCaslin to defend the wish of the boy Ike McCaslin to stay an extra week in the woods: "You got one foot straddled into a farm and the other foot straddled into a bank; you ain't even got a good hand-hold where this boy was already an old man long before you damned Sartorises and Edmondses invented farms and banks to keep yourselves from having to find out what this boy was born knowing and fearing too maybe, but without being afraid, that could go ten miles on a compass because he wanted to look at a bear none of us had ever got near enough to put a bullet in and looked at the bear and came the ten miles back on the compass in the dark; maybe by God that's the why and the wherefore of farms and banks."

Those who have the wrong attitude toward nature are the pure exploiters, the apostles of abstractionism, the truly evil men. For instance, the very opening of *Sanctuary* presents a distinction on this ground between Benbow and Popeye. While the threat of Popeye keeps Benbow crouching by the spring, he hears a Carolina wren sing, and even under these circumstances tries to recall the local name for it. And he says to Popeye: "And of course you don't know the name of it. I don't suppose you'd know a bird at all, without it was singing in a cage in a hotel lounge, or cost four dollars on a plate." Popeye, as we may remember, spits in the spring (he hates nature and must foul it), is afraid to go through the woods ("Through all them trees?" he demands when Benbow points out the short cut), and when an owl whisks past them in the twilight, claws at Benbow's coat with almost hysterical fear ("It's just an owl," Benbow says. "It's nothing but an owl.")

The pure exploiters, though they may gain ownership and use of a thing, never really have it; like Popeye, they are impotent. For instance, Flem Snopes, the central character and villain of *The Hamlet*, who brings the exploiter's mentality to Frenchman's Bend, finally marries Eula Varner, a kind of fertility goddess or earth goddess; but his ownership is meaningless, for she always refers to him as "that man" (she does not even have a name for him), and he has only got her after she has given herself willingly to one of the bold, hotblooded boys of the neighborhood. In fact, nature can't, in one sense, be "owned." Ike Mc-Caslin, in "The Bear," says of the land which has come down to him: "It was never Father's and Uncle Buddy's to bequeath me to repudiate, because it was never Grandfather's to bequeath them to bequeath me to repudiate, because it was never old Ikkemotubbe's to sell to Grandfather for bequeathment and repudiation. Because it was never Ikkemotubbe's father's father's to bequeath Ikkemotubbe to sell to Grandfather or any man because on the instant when Ikkemotubbe discovered, realized, that he could sell it for money, on that instant it ceased ever to have been his forever, father to father, to father, and the man who bought it bought nothing."

The right attitude toward nature is, as a matter of fact, associated with the right attitude toward man, and the mere lust for power over nature is associated with the lust for power over other men, for God gave the earth to man, we read in "The Bear," not "to hold for himself and his descendants inviolable title forever, generation after generation, to the oblongs and squares of the earth, but to hold the earth mutual and intact in the communal anonymity of brotherhood, and all the fee He asked was pity and humility and sufferance and endurance and the sweat of his face for bread." It is the failure of this pity which curses the earth (the land in Faulkner's particular country is "accursed" by chattel slavery, but slavery is simply one of the possible forms of the failure). But the rape of nature and the crime against man are always avenged. The rape of nature, the mere exploitation of it without love, is always avenged because the attitude which commits that crime also commits the crime against men which in turn exacts vengeance, so that man finally punishes himself. It is only by this line of reasoning that one can, I think, read the last page of "Delta Autumn":

> This land which man has deswamped and denuded and derivered in two generations so that white men can own plantations and commute every night to Memphis and black men own plantations and ride in jim crow cars to Chicago to live in millionaires' mansions on Lake Shore Drive; where white men rent farms and live like niggers and niggers crop on shares and live like animals; where cotton is planted and grows man-tall in the very cracks of the sidewalks, and usury and mortgage and bankruptcy and measureless wealth, Chinese and African and Aryan and Jew, all breed and spawn together until no man has time to say which one is which nor cares....No wonder the ruined woods I used to know don't cry for retribution! he thought: The people who have destroyed it will accomplish its revenge.

The attitude toward nature in Faulkner's work, however, does not involve a sinking into nature. In Faulkner's mythology man has "suzerainty over the earth," he is not of the earth, and it is the human virtues which count—"pity and humility and sufferance and endurance." If we take even the extreme case of the idiot Snopes and his fixation on the cow in *The Hamlet* (a scene whose function in the total order of the book is to show that even the idiot pervert is superior to Flem), a scene which shows the human being as close as possible to the "natural" level, we find that the scene is the most lyrical in Faulkner's work: even the idiot is human and not animal, for only human desires, not animal, clothe themselves in poetry. I think that George Marion O'Donnell is right in pointing to the humanism-naturalism opposition in Faulkner's work, and over and over again we find that the point of some novel or story has to do with the human effort to find or create values in the mechanical round of experience— "not just to eat and evacuate and sleep warm," as Charlotte Rittenmeyer says in *The Wild Palms*, "so we can get up and eat and evacuate in order to sleep warm again," or not just to raise cotton to buy niggers to raise cotton to buy niggers, as it is put in another place. Even when a character seems to be caught in the iron ring of some compulsion, of some mechanical process (the hunted Negro of "Red Leaves," the tall convict of *The Wild Palms*, Christmas of *Light in August*), the effort may be discernible. And in Quentin's attempt, in *The Sound and the Fury*, to persuade his sister Caddy, who is pregnant by one of the boys of Jefferson, to confess that she has committed incest with him, we find among other things the idea that "the horror" and "the clean flame" would be preferable to the meaninglessness of the "loud world."

Humor. One of the most important remarks in Cowley's introduction is that concerning humor. There is, especially in the later books, "a sort of homely and sober-sided frontier humor that is seldom achieved in contemporary writing." Cowley continues: "In a curious way, Faulkner combines two of the principal traditions in American letters: the tradition of psychological horror, often close to symbolism, that begins with Charles Brockden Brown, our first professional novelist, and extends through Poe, Melville, Henry James (in his later stories), Stephen Crane and Hemingway; and the other tradition of frontier humor and realism, beginning with Augustus Longstreet's *Georgia Scenes* and having Mark Twain as its best example." The observation is an acute one, for the distortions of humor and the distortions of horror in Faulkner's work are closely akin and frequently, in a given instance, can scarcely be disentangled.

It is true that the most important strain of humor in Faulkner's work is derived from the tradition of frontier humor (though it is probable that he got it from the porches of country stores and the courthouse yards of county-seat towns and not from any book), and it is true that the most spectacular displays of Faulkner's humor are of this order—for example, the "Spotted Horses" episode from *The Hamlet* or the story "Was." But there are other strains which might be distinguished and investigated. For example, there is a kind of Dickensian humor; the scene in the Memphis brothel from *Sanctuary*, which is reprinted here under the title "Uncle Bud and the Three Madams," is certainly more Dickensian than frontier. There is a subdued humor, sometimes shading into pathos, in the treatment of some of the Negro characters and in their dialogue. And there is an irony ranging from that in the scene in *Sanctuary* where Miss Reba, the madam, in offended decency keeps telling Temple, "Lie down and cover up your nekkidness," while the girl talks with Benbow, to that in the magnificently sustained monologue of Jason at the end of *The Sound and the Fury*.

In any case, humor in Faulkner's work is never exploited for its own sake. It is regularly used as an index, as a lead, to other effects. The humor in itself may be striking, but Faulkner is not a humorist in the sense, say, that Mark Twain is. His humor is but one perspective on the material and it is never a final perspective, as we can see from such an example as the episode of "Spotted Horses." Nothing could be more wide of the point than the remark in Maxwell Geismar's essay on Faulkner to the effect that Faulkner in *The Hamlet* "seems now to accept the antics of his provincial morons, to enjoy the chronicle of their low-grade behavior; he submerges himself in their clownish degradation." All the critic seems to find in Mink Snopes' victim with his life-long devotion to the memory of his dead wife, and in Ratliff with his good heart and ironical mind and quiet wisdom, is comic "descendants of the gangling and giggling Wash Jones."

The Poor White. The above remark leads us to the not un-common misconception about the role of the poor white in Faulkner's work. It is true that the Snopeses are poor whites, descendants of bushwhackers (and therefore outside society, as the bushwhacker was outside society, had no "side" in the Civil War but tried to make a good thing of it), and it is true that Snopesism represents a special kind of villainy and degradation, the form that the pure doctrine of exploitation and degradation takes in the society of which Faulkner writes, but any careful reader realizes that a Snopes is not to be equated with a poor white. For instance, the book most fully about the poor white, *As I Lay Dying*, is full of sympathy and poetry. There are a hundred touches like that in Cash's soliloquy about the phono-graph: "I reckon it's a good thing we ain't got ere a one of them. I reckon I wouldn't never get no work done a-tall for listening to it. I don't know if a little music ain't about the nicest thing a fellow can have. Seems like when he comes in tired of a night, it ain't nothing could rest him like having a little music played and him resting." Or like the long section toward the middle of the book devoted to Addie Bundren, a section which is full of eloquence like that of this paragraph: "And then he died. He did not know he was dead. I would lie by him in the dark, hearing the dark land talking of God's love and His beauty and His sin; hearing the dark voicelessness in which the words are the deeds, and the other words that are not deeds, that are just the gaps in people's lacks, coming down like the cries of geese out of the wild darkness in the old terrible nights, fumbling at the deeds like orphans to whom are pointed out in a crowd two faces and told, That is your father, your mother." Do these passages indicate a relish in the "antics of his provincial morons"?

The whole *As I Lay Dying* is based on the heroic effort of the Bundren family to fulfill the promise to the dead mother, to take her body to Jefferson; and the fact that Anse Bundren, after the heroic effort has been completed, immediately gets him a new wife, the "duck-shaped woman" with the "hard-looking pop-eyes," does not negate the heroism of the effort nor the poetry and feeling which give flesh to the book. We are told by one critic that "what should have been the drama of the Bundrens thus becomes in the end a sort of brutal farce," and that we are "unable to feel the tragedy because the author has refused to accept the Bundrens, as he did accept the Compsons, as tragic." Rather, I should say, the Bundrens may come off a little better than the latter-day Compsons, the whining mother, the promiscuous Caddy, the ineffectual Quentin, and the rest. The Bundrens, at least, are capable of the heroic effort, and the promise is fulfilled. What the conclusion indicates is that even such a fellow as Anse Bundren (who is not typical of his family, by the way), in the grip of an idea, in terms of promise or code, is capable of rising out of his ordinary level; Anse falls back at the end, but only after the prop of the idea and obligation have been removed. And we may recall that even the "gangling and giggling Wash Jones" has always been capable of some kind of obscure dream and aspiration (his very attachment to Sutpen indicates that), and that in the end he achieves dignity and manhood.

The final and incontrovertible evidence that Snopes is not to be equated with poor white comes in *The Hamlet* (though actually most of the characters in the book, though they may be poor, are not, strictly speaking, "poor whites" at all, but rather what uninstructed reviewers choose to call by that label). The point of the book is the assault made on a solid community of plain, hard-working small farmers by Snopeses and Snopesism. Ratliff is not rich, but he is not Flem Snopes. And if the corruption of Snopesism does penetrate into the community, there is no one here who can be compared in degradation and vileness to Jason of *The Sound and the Fury*, the Compson who has embraced Snopesism. In fact, Popeye and Flem, Faulkner's best advertised villains, cannot, for vileness and ultimate meanness, touch Jason.

The Negro. In one of Faulkner's books it is said that every white child is born crucified on a black cross. Remarks like this have led to a gross misconception of the place of the Negro in Faulkner's work, to the notion that Faulkner "hates" Negroes. For instance, we find Maxwell Geismar exclaiming what a "strange inversion" it is to take the Negro, who is the "tragic consequence," and to exhibit him as the "evil cause" of the failure of the old order in the South.

This is a misreading of the text. It is slavery, not the Negro, which is defined, quite flatly, as the curse, over and over again, and the Negro is the black cross in so far as he is the embodiment of the curse, the reminder of the guilt, the incarnation of the problem. That is the basic point. But now and then, as a kind of tangential irony, we have the notion, not of the burden of the white on the black, but of the burden of the black on the white, the weight of obligation, inefficiency, and so on, as well as the weight of guilt (the notion we find in the old story of the plantation mistress who, after the Civil War, said: "Mr. Lincoln thought he was emancipating those slaves, but he was really emancipating me").

For instance, we get hints of this notion in "Red Leaves": one of the Indians, sweating in the chase of the runaway Negro who is to be killed for the Man's funeral, says, "Damn that Negro," and the other Indian replies, "Yao. When have they ever been anything but a trial and a care to us?" But the black cross is, fundamentally, the weight of the white man's guilt, the white man who now sells salves and potions to "bleach the pigment and straighten the hair of negroes that they might resemble the very race which for two hundred years had held them in bondage and from which for another hundred years not even a bloody civil war would have set them completely free." The curse is still operative, as the crime is still compounded.

The actual role of the Negro in Faulkner's fiction is consistently one of pathos or heroism. It is not merely, as has been suggested more than once, that Faulkner condescends to the good and faithful servant, the "white folks' nigger." There are figures like Dilsey, but they are not as impressive as the Negro in "Red Leaves" or Sam Fathers, who, with the bear, is the hero of "The Bear." The fugitive, who gains in the course of the former story a shadowy symbolic significance, is told in the end by one of the Indians who overtake him, "You ran well. Do not be ashamed," and when he walks among the Indians, he is "the tallest there, his high, close, mud-caked head looming above them all." And Sam Fathers is the fountainhead of wisdom which Ike McCaslin finally gains, and the repository of the virtues which are central for Faulkner—"an old man, son of a Negro slave and an Indian king, inheritor on the one hand of the long chronicle of a people who had learned humility through suffering and learned pride through the endurance which survived suffering, and on the other side the chronicle of a people even longer in the land than the first, yet who now existed there only in the solitary brotherhood of an old and childless Negro's alien blood and the wild and invincible spirit of an old bear."

Even Christmas, in *Light in August*, though he is sometimes spoken of as a villain, is a mixture of heroism and pathos. He is the lost, suffering, enduring creature (the figure like Sam Fathers, the tall convict of *The Wild Palms*, or Dilsey in *The Sound and the Fury*), and even the murder he commits at the end is a fumbling attempt to define his manhood, is an attempt to break out of the iron ring of mechanism, to lift himself out of "nature," for the woman whom he kills has become a figure of the horror of the human which has surrendered the human attributes. (We may compare Christmas to Mink Snopes in *The Hamlet* in this respect: Mink, mean and vicious as he is, kills out of a kind of warped and confused pride, and by this affirmation is set off against his kinsman Flem, whose only values are those of pure Snopesism.)

Even such a brief comment on the Negro in Faulkner's
work cannot close without this passage from "The Bear":

"Because they will endure. They are better than we are. Stronger
than we are. Their vices are vices aped from white men or that white
men and bondage have taught them: improvidence and intemperance
and evasion—not laziness: evasion: of what white men had set them
to, not for their aggrandizement or even comfort but his own—" and
McCaslin

"All right. Go on: Promiscuity. Violence. Instability and lack of
control. Inability to distinguish between mine and thine—" and he

"How distinguish when for two hundred years mine did not even
exist for them?" and McCaslin

"All right. Go on. And their virtues—" and he

"Yes. Their own. Endurance—" and McCaslin

"So have mules:" and he

"—and pity and tolerance and forbearance and fidelity and love
of children—" and McCaslin

"So have dogs:" and he

"—whether their own or not or black or not. And more: what
they got not only from white people but not even despite white people
because they had it already from the old free fathers a longer time
free than us because we have never been free—"

And there is the single comment under Dilsey's name in the
annotated genealogy of the Compsons which Faulkner has prepared for the present volume: "They endured."

Technique. There are excellent comments on this subject
by Cowley, Conrad Aiken, Warren Beck, Joseph Warren Beach,
and Alfred Kazin, but the subject has not been fully explored. One
difficulty is that Faulkner is an incorrigible and restless experi-
menter, is peculiarly sensitive to the expressive possibilities of
shifts in technique and has not developed (like Hemingway or
Katherine Anne Porter—lyric rather than dramatic writers, artists
with a great deal of self-certainty) in a straight line.

Provisionally, we may distinguish in Faulkner's work three
basic methods of handling a narrative. One is best typified in
Sanctuary, where there is a tightly organized plot, a crisp, laconic

style, an objective presentation of character—an impersonal method. Another is best typified by *As I Lay Dying* or *The Sound and the Fury*, where each character unfolds in his own language or flow of being before us—a dramatic method in that the author does not obtrude, but a method which makes the subjective reference of character the medium of presentation. Another is best typified by "Was," "The Bear," or the story of the tall convict in *The Wild Palms*, where the organization of the narrative is episodic and the sense of a voice, a narrator's presence (though not necessarily a narrator in the formal sense), is almost constantly felt—a method in which the medium is ultimately a "voice" as index to sensibility. The assumptions underlying these methods, and the relations among them, would provide a study.

Cowley's emphasis on the unity of Faulkner's work, the fact that all the novels and stories are to be taken as aspects of a single, large design, is very important. It is important, for one thing, in regard to the handling of character. A character, Sutpen, for instance, may appear in various perspectives, so that from book to book we move toward a final definition much as in actual life we move toward the definition of a person. The same principle applies to event, as Conrad Aiken has pointed out, the principle of the spiral method which takes the reader over and over the same event from a different altitude, as it were, and a different angle. In relation to both character and event this method, once it is understood by the reader, makes for a kind of realism and a kind of suspense (in the formal not the factual sense) not common in fiction.

The emphasis on the unity of Faulkner's work may, however, lead to an underrating of the degree of organization within individual works. Cowley is right in pointing out the structural defect in *Light in August*, but he may be putting too much emphasis on the over-all unity and not enough on the organization of the individual work when he says that *The Hamlet* tends to resolve into a "series of episodes resembling beads on a string." I think that in that novel we have a type of organization in which the thematic rather than the narrative emphasis is the basic principle, and once we grasp that fact the unity of the individual work may come clear. In fact, the whole subject of the principle of thematic organization in the novels and long stories, "The Bear," for instance, needs investigation. In pieces which seem disjointed, or which seem to have the mere tale-teller's improvisations, we may sometimes discover the true unity if we think of the line of meaning, the symbolic ordering, and surrender ourselves to the tale-teller's "voice." And it may be useful at times to recall the distinction between the formal, forensic realism of Ibsen as opposed to the fluid, suggestive realism of Chekhov.

Symbol and Image. Cowley and O'Donnell have given acute readings of the main symbolic outline of Faulkner's fiction, but no one has yet devoted himself to the study of symbolic motifs which, though not major, are nevertheless extremely instructive. For instance, the images of the hunt, the flight, the pursuit, such as we have in "Red Leaves," *The Wild Palms*, the episode of "Percy Grimm" in *Light in August*, "The Bear," "Delta Autumn," "Was," and (especially in the hordes of moving Negroes) in *The Unvanquished*. Or there is the important symbolic relationship between man and earth. Or there is the contrast between images of compulsion and images of will or freedom. Or there is the device of what we might call the frozen moment, the arrested action which becomes symbolic, as in the moment when, in "An Odor of Verbena" (from *The Unvanquished*), Drusilla offers the pistols to the hero.

Polarity. To what extent does Faulkner work in terms of polarities, oppositions, paradoxes, inversions of roles? How much does he employ a line of concealed (or open) dialectic progression as a principle for his fiction? The study of these questions may lead to the discovery of principles of organization in his work not yet defined by criticism.

The study of Faulkner is the most challenging single task in contemporary American literature for criticism to undertake. Here is a novelist who, in mass of work, in scope of material, in range of effect, in reportorial accuracy and symbolic subtlety, in philosophical weight can be put beside the masters of our own past literature. Yet this accomplishment has been effected in what almost amounts to critical isolation and silence, and when the silence has been broken it has usually been broken by someone (sometimes one of our better critics) whose reading has been hasty, whose analysis unscholarly and whose judgments superficial. The picture of Faulkner presented to the public by such criticism is a combination of Thomas Nelson Page, a fascist and a psychopath, gnawing his nails. Of course, this picture is usually accompanied by a grudging remark about genius.

Cowley's book, for its intelligence, sensitivity, and sobriety in the introduction, and for the ingenuity and judgment exhibited in the selections, would be valuable at any time. But it is especially valuable at this time. Perhaps it can mark a turning point in Faulkner's reputation. That will be of slight service to Faulkner, who, as much as any writer of our place and time, can rest in confidence. He can afford to wait. But can we?

RITUAL AND HUMOR IN THE WRITING OF WILLIAM FAULKNER

JOHN ARTHOS

FAULKNER seems to think of writing as a kind of consecration. And he seems to consider the characters in his stories as if they were performing a ritual, enthralled by the same sense of dedication as his own. The writer in relating the ritual is taking part in it, in a religious effort to justify the sense of consecration.

Given such an attitude, the narrative itself ought to be the sufficiently pure embodiment of things as they are, of truth. But Faulkner's intense belief in the value of dedication forcing him into lyricism also forces him to comment on the story. Just as the

Reprinted with permission from *Accent*, Autumn, 1948, pp. 17–30.

sophisticated readers of myths require allegorical explanations that were once, we suppose, unneeded, so Faulkner is driven to interpret the stories his characters enact. It is not enough merely to describe the performance of the ritual. The mystery itself must be divulged—divulged and exhausted in the revelation of the narrator's own interests and feelings. The story-teller gives in to the romantic poet, and we are asked to attend not only the action of the story but the way it appeared to the actors in it, of whom their creator is one. We see not merely men and women, but men and women who sense that they are symbols, and in their midst the character of the author himself, their observer and companion. All come to be described as ghosts, demonic animals, children of the passionate parentage of sun and earth, and as the writer's brothers and sisters.

In *Mosquitoes*, Faulkner's second novel, one of the characters is talking about literature:

"Genius." He spoke slowly, distinctly, staring into the sky. "People confuse it so, you see. They have got it now to where it signifies only an active state of the mind in which a picture is painted or a poem is written. When it is not that at all. It is that Passion Week of the heart, that first instant of timeless beatitude which some never know, which some, I suppose, gain at will, which others gain through an outside agency like alcohol, like to-night—that passive state of the heart with which the mind, the brain, has nothing to do at all, in which the hackneyed accidents which make up this world—love and life and death and sex and sorrow—brought together by chance in perfect proportions, take on a kind of splendid and timeless beauty. Like Yseult of the White Hands and her Tristan with that clean, highhearted dullness of his; like that young Lady Something that some government executed, asking permission and touching with a kind of sober wonder the edge of the knife that was to cut her head off; like a redhaired girl, an idiot, turning in a white dress beneath a wisteria covered trellis on a late sunny afternoon in May."

The rest of his writing is proof enough that this is an expression of Faulkner's own belief, even the cardinal article. And the idea of dedication is not merely the controlling idea of an artist. It is the principle that governs all human beings who wish to mature. In understanding and obeying this principle one grows to decency and manhood. But in order to understand and obey, one must relate oneself to the past. One does so by means of rituals.

In one of Faulkner's latest stories ("The Bear") we find a boy growing up in the South, living excitedly for those times when he goes hunting with his elders, and with the great Negro-Indian hunter, Sam Fathers. Everyone knows that through proper conduct in hunting the boy will become a man.

There are various preliminary trials before the boy meets the bear, the ultimate prize, and these preliminary trials are the means of assimilating a mysterious quality. In one of the trials (in the story called "Delta Autumn") a buck is the boy's antagonist and his measure. When the boy kills the buck, Sam Fathers dips his hands in the animal's blood, and marks the boy's face in order to signify what the boy felt but was himself unable to express: "I slew you; my bearing must not shame your quitting life. My conduct forever onward must become your death." The animal is sacred, the hunt is a ritual, the hunter is consecrated.

In the crucial time when the boy finds the bear, and is aiming to shoot, he lowers his gun. He saw or sensed something that prevented his killing the bear. And this, we are given to understand, was proper: he ought not to have killed him. His cousin, who is one of the hunting party, explains to the boy that the bear represented something eternal, something the boy instinctively understood he could not harm, something he needed only to see and remember. In explaining this to the boy he recalls what he says is the meaning of the "Ode on a Grecian Urn": "Courage and honor and pride, and pity and love of justice and of liberty. They all touch the heart, and what the heart holds to becomes truth, as far as we know truth." The boy has seen a vision, and visions are not to be touched.

These two ideas—of life consecrated by the blood of the nobly slain, and of the holiness of the heart's affections—may be regarded as amplifications of the remark in *Mosquitoes*, that

genius is the Passion Week of the heart. They are the ideas in
which the figures and devices of almost all Faulkner's writing are
conceived.

In another story ("The Fire and the Hearth") the idea of
chastity belongs to the same conception. Hunting, killing, blood
baptism, and the rest are the necessary ceremonies through which
"a young boy's high and selfless innocence" is transformed into
the manliness of such people as Sam Fathers and Major de Spain.
Here, innocence (which means, I think, selfless devotion and the
disinterested imagination) is inducted into the violence of life
and transformed into something which is also admirable. Sam
Fathers represents the strength and enduringness of the primeval
American continent, persistent in all the generations of men,
and Major de Spain is the father of a civilized family. The boy
is joining their company.

And so it is with Faulkner in the life of his imagination,
always himself a character in his stories, always ceremoniously
preparing himself for a life among men, and especially the god-
like and legendary figures who belong to the history of the South.
This sense of a holy process linking him to history seems always
to return to its initial impulse, the reader enthralled by the poem
on the Grecian urn. However deeply Faulkner searches the life
of the South for the characters that will support his imagination,
the charity or passion in which he conceives of them is always
determined by the perceptions and ideas fostered by reading
Keats. In a note printed in 1925 Faulkner wrote:

I read "Thou still unravished bride of quietness" and found a still
water withal strong and potent, quiet with its own strength, and
satisfying as bread. That beautiful awareness, so sure of its own power
that it is not necessary to create the illusion of force by frenzy and
motion. Take the odes to a Nightingale, to a Grecian urn, "Music to
hear," etc.; here is the spiritual beauty which the moderns strive vainly
for with trickery, and yet beneath it one knows are entrails, mas-
culinity.

The Passion Week ends in peace, peace which now and then
survives the hackneyed accidents of the world. History, which is

the sum of so many accidents, is the source of our strength and the substance of our holy passion. It is what has been and what is, it is the record nature itself has made, once alive and still generating itself within us, and through history, or nature (there is little difference), we are linked to death as well as to life.

Whatever may have absorbed Keats in his effort to achieve serenity, for Faulkner the chief preoccupation was violence. This preoccupation appears to rise in part from his experience and interest in the first World War; but his interest in the issues of that war soon merged with his thinking about the South. His home country had been living with the effects of violence for nearly three quarters of a century, and the ravishment was continuing into his own life-time. Injuries so deep bring pain that cries for a divine explanation. As Faulkner says again and again, the survivors think of themselves as ghosts, the living wreckage of a perennially violated world. As with ghosts their suffering is rigidly controlled, and the pattern of their lives is like a ritual because each movement is determined by the germinal pain of the past. The ritual means that there is no justification for pain and death, and yet that each man needs to dedicate his life before he meets with the inevitable violation.

Soldiers' Pay, Faulkner's first novel, is about a young lieutenant who was shot down in France in the first World War. He is blind and seems to have nothing in his mind but the pain of some uncertain need. Casual acquaintances, a young war widow and a discharged sergeant, take charge of him on the train, and they continue to care for him at the house of his father. The young widow stays on in order to will herself into a state of fidelity; she reproaches herself for not missing her husband of so brief a period, and she hopes to gain some stability in life by devotedly serving this nearly unconscious man. By his very unconsciousness he is a symbol for her of a marriage that never had time to become part of her living, and a symbol of the object of any love. She needs to be faithful to it.

In this novel Faulkner hit upon the great image that was to dominate so many of his stories, the voiceless pain of an idiot.

Elsewhere it takes the form of babbling, of the desire to murder, of self-torment, but always some form of a mind disarranged by pain and terribly unable to find the words that justify pain. The past had loosed its forces, and the lieutenant, who had once given himself to a cause, is now an inarticulate actor in a story signifying nothing.

From contemplating the results of violence upon the mind of one individual, as in this story, Faulkner went on to consider its results in the conflicts of races and social classes, in rivers flooding valleys and breaking jails, and in animals. The violence of war was merely an event in the normal violence of the world, the world understood as history. After the first novels, his stories turn mostly towards the past, towards the Civil War, towards the Indians, and even towards Africa. In his own community of the South this history still lived and still continued to destroy. And in the stories of the people there, the living captives of the past, Faulkner was determined to discover if some saving meaning could be found. Writing about the South, he was dedicated, as Sartre finely expressed it, to *"cette foi, mi-sincère mi-rêvée, dans le pouvoir magique des histoires."*

And yet in *Soldiers' Pay*, alongside this intense preoccupation, there are passages of a most delightfully humorous kind, and the plot itself has a wry quality. Even at the beginning Faulkner exploited some of the humorous implications of his zeal. The humor was something to be cherished. In an essay published in 1926 he wrote:

We have one priceless universal trait, we Americans. That trait is our humor. What a pity it is that it is not more prevalent in our art. This characteristic alone, being national and indigenous, could, by concentrating our emotional forces inward upon themselves, do for us what England's insularity did for English art during the reign of Elizabeth. One trouble with us American artists is that we take our art and ourselves too seriously. And perhaps seeing ourselves in the eyes of our fellow artists, will enable those who have strayed to establish anew a sound contact with the fountainhead of our American life.

It is difficult to preserve humor when the writer considers his work a kind of Passion Week. The strain of inventing rituals and the peculiarly modern difficulties in the way of consecration obscure the perceptions which need to be so finely adjusted in comedy. But to obscure humor is not to kill it, and in much of Faulkner's writing one sees the continuing struggle for comedy. In *The Wild Palms* (where one story is a joke about a convict who returns to jail in order to escape a woman) the humor almost controlled the troubled excitement that elsewhere supports his romanticism. Only in *The Hamlet*, I think, in the characterization of Ratliff and in the incident of the toy cow, do comedy and its lovely reasoning win out.

The curious conflict is apparent in such an elaborately serious work as *The Sound and the Fury*. The story is told in sections presenting the thoughts of four people at certain times over a period of years, when they are thinking mostly about the events of one day, and the effect of that day upon their lives. The central subject of their thought is the seduction of a young girl and its consequences, but the chief interest of the book lies in the description of her brother's attitude towards the catastrophe. He is extremely fond of her, and her situation thrusts upon him a burden of responsibility he accepts as a man who has been brought up in pride of family and delicacy of character. He comes to believe that his own love has failed her, and in something like adolescent self-torment he thinks his guilt is equivalent to the betrayal itself. He extends his torment to the point where it is as if he himself had betrayed her through incest. This straining for guilt places such a burden upon his consciousness that he is unequal to it, and finally he kills himself.

The problem appears ridiculous (the comic writer turning in his sleep), but it is not intrinsically so. If the brother's concern is justified, as it certainly is, we are tempted to mock him because he is only flirting with despair. As his father tells him (they have been talking of death): "you seem to regard it merely as an experience that will whiten your hair overnight so to speak without altering your appearance at all." The brother tries to understand what sin is, but he cannot; and yet he thinks he must assume his sister's guilt. His confusion drives him mad. He wants to believe in original sin, he wants to make himself into a symbol of it, and he finds himself unable to through some defect of insight and understanding. Accordingly, the plot of the novel is resolved through an explicit demonstration of the meaninglessness of an historic doctrine. A generous man, dedicated to something without meaning, finds his end in absurdity and madness. The absurdity is obvious, but not obvious enough to be presented comically. The author's sympathy prevents the detachment necessary for comedy, and even the meaning of the calamity is blurred. No meaningful comment is offered to present a larger view than Quentin Compson's own, no more than is found in a poem called "Visions in Spring," where the author speaks of himself as one

> who toiled through corridors of harsh laughter,
> Who sought for light in dark reserves of pain....

On the other hand, the idiot brother, Benjy, the most vivid character in the book, achieves symbolic significance. His mind is like a shattered mirror, and he understands very little of what goes on about him. But the fragments of his mind reflect everything, not merely a single evil, and everything that he sees is transformed, as it were, purely and without distortion, into a continuous moan. Benjy is the embodiment of disintegration, the mind shattered by the pain of evil, and Faulkner implies that the sound he makes is the music of the spheres. As such its disharmony is the mingling of the cries rising into the minds of all the characters in the story and in the world. Evil is thus represented as the world's invasion of the individual soul, where once it was merely a bullet, fired at some time in the past, and still wounding a lieutenant.

The painful mind of this idiot is Faulkner's first sustained effort to create a single symbolic figure to represent the minds of all people whose ideals and lives have been violated. The lives of the two brothers seem to show that sin cannot be a symbol in

Faulkner's world, and that only evil, in its meaninglessness, can provide a satisfactory image.

In *Soldiers' Pay* and in *The Sound and the Fury* the initial evil is an event in the past, and the author treats the story through what we might call an historical method, and the past itself becomes increasingly the very substance of his thought. So, here and there in all his books Faulkner picked up the subject he first emphasized in *Sartoris*, the condition of the ravaged South, the remainder of a civilization living in the memory of "the wild bugles and the clashing sabres and the dying thunder of hooves." The thoughtful educated men and women—like Horace Benbow in *Sanctuary*, Miss Jenny in *Sartoris*, and many another— are living in the past. It was with them as with the central figure of *Absalom, Absalom!*—"Quentin Compson preparing for Harvard in the South, the deep South dead since 1865 and peopled with garrulous outraged baffled ghosts, listening, having to listen . . . the Quentin Compson who was still too young to deserve yet to be a ghost, but nevertheless having to be one for all that, since he was born and bred in the deep South. . . ." To whatever degree this is the condition of the South, ghosts became a preoccupation of Faulkner's, if we take ghosts to be what haunt the mind and memory with vague and inescapable compulsions, representing the power of the past and the dead over the living. The references are innumerable and the conception clear. "In the wide, empty, shadow-brooded street he looked like a phantom, a spirit, strayed out of its own world, and lost." "He sees himself a shadowy figure among shadows . . . (*Light in August*)." "Not only a man never outlives his father but not even his friends and acquaintances do" (*Absalom, Absalom!*). "And as he talked about those old times and those dead and vanished men of another race [the Indians] from either that the boy knew, gradually to the boy those old times would cease to be old times and would become a part of the boy's present, not only as if they had happened yesterday but as if they were still happening, the men who walked through them actually walking in breath and air and casting an actual shadow on the earth they had not quitted (*Go*

Down, Moses)." The lieutenant in *Soldiers' Pay* is half ghost, and the central figure of *Pylon* at least that.

This idea, we must believe, is natural to any defeated nation, but it is not necessarily important to all Southerners writing about the South. In Faulkner it is important partly because he thinks of himself as a lyrical recorder present in each scene he describes. In *Mosquitoes* he once introduced himself among his characters by a name similar to his own (the humor is crude), but by means of his personal style he introduced himself in the later books as a kind of presence. The sense of his own brooding mind as a person on the scene is intensified elsewhere in the stories carried along by the recording of the stream of consciousness. For all his magnificent skill in presenting the thoughts of various minds, his sympathy with what he describes creates another character, his own, for he is attempting to identify his needs and the needs of all his people. In what I take to be his own essay in a recent issue of *Furioso*, he calls himself a "ghost writer."

Ghosts are important to him because they are that which is on the way to being completely destroyed and are ready to join the past. Their value is further strengthened by Faulkner's occasional determinism. As Malraux saw it, *"il y a un Destin dressé, unique, derrière tous ces êtres différents et semblables, comme la mort derrière une salle d'incurables."* Just as in *Sanctuary* we recognize the pessimism, the sense of the irremediable in Faulkner's acceptance of individuals as the symptoms of disease in society, in all his works except *As I Lay Dying* and *The Hamlet* we learn how men are inextricably controlled by the past, the charmed circle: "I have never got outside that circle. I have never broken out of the ring of what I have already done and cannot ever undo. . . ." It is the necessary condition of ghosts to be bound by the laws of hell, or, as Faulkner would have it, by the prolific evil of the past.

In *Light in August* Faulkner made his most ambitious effort to raise questions about the meaning of a life controlled by pain, tracing one individual's life to its farthest origins in history, in Judea and in Africa. The central character is a man, Joe

Christmas, who comes to believe he has Negro blood. In his
pride, and while he is doubtful of his origin, he refuses to pass as
a white man. He murders his benefactress because his pride cannot endure her pity, but he discovers that the added burden of
that crime, even when he thinks of it as a sin, does not entitle
him to the depth of pain the knowledge of his birth has brought
him. Even the threat of damnation cannot move him to humility,
to a state of mind in which he can bring himself to ask for relief.
He needs some myth to explain his situation, and to liberate him
from his torment. And the characters in the story, who are vari-
ously pursuing or protecting him, are involved in the same search
for a clarifying myth. A lawyer in the community summarized
what was in the minds of all the characters:

"But there was too much running with him, stride for stride with
him. Not pursuers: but himself: years, acts, deeds, omitted and committed, keeping pace with him, stride for stride, breath for breath,
thud for thud of the heart, using a single heart. It was not alone all
those thirty years which she did not know, but all those successions of
thirty years before that which had put that stain either on his white
blood or his black blood, whichever you will, and which killed him.
But he must have run with believing for a while; anyway, with hope.
But his blood would not be quiet, let him save it. It would not be
either one or the other and let his body save itself. Because the black
blood drove him first to the negro cabin. And then the white blood
drove him out of there, as it was the black blood which snatched up
the pistol and the white blood which would not let him fire it. And
it was the white blood which sent him to the minister, which rising in
him for the last and final time, sent him against all reason and all
reality, into the embrace of a chimera, a blind faith in something read
in a printed Book. Then I believe that the white blood deserted him
for the moment. Just a second, a flicker, allowing the black to rise in
its final moment and make him turn upon that on which he had
postulated his hope of salvation. It was the black blood which swept
him by his own desire beyond the aid of any man, swept him up into
that ecstasy out of a black jungle where life has already ceased before
the heart stops and death is desire and fulfillment. And then the black
blood failed him again, as it must have in crises all his life. He did not

kill the minister. He merely struck him with the pistol and ran on and crouched behind the table and defied the black blood for the last time, as he had been defying it for thirty years. He crouched behind that overturned table and let them shoot him to death, with that loaded and unfired pistol in his hand."

The point is that Faulkner knows of no way in which a civilized mind can accept any myths, of race, or sin, or salvation, that will justify this half-breed's confusion. Joe Christmas can only welcome destruction, overcome in life by a world the author conceives to be controlled by demons, all the hackneyed accidents rising out of the centuries to deprive him of peace. History made him run and made the others pursue him, and Joe Christmas, caught in flight as in some formal intoxication, hoped still to propitiate the past, to find his father, Christ, who long ago gave him his name and his hopes.

Along with this deeply serious story there is another interwoven, and in this one humor has its chance. A young, ignorant country girl, who has been seduced, starts out alone from her home in Alabama to find the father of the baby she is soon to have. She has the inexorable strength of the people in *As I Lay Dying*. Her apparently senseless journey, on foot, sometimes picked up on wagons, ignorant of her destination, and meanwhile growing heavier in her pregnancy, is first of all heroic, and finally comic. Somewhere on her journey an older man falls in love with her, and his affection is full of the sense of her worthiness. At the end of the book he is accompanying her to Tennessee, and a man who has given them a ride in his truck sees that she has just been taken up with the joy of travelling. She had forgotten all about her misery.

Two strange pilgrimages are thus contrasted: Joe Christmas seeks salvation and finds death; the ignorant little girl seeks justice and finds pleasure. It is her story that begins and ends the book, but the comic contrast fails. Faulkner was not quite prepared to view the search for salvation humorously.

In these stories it is possible to see a certain development in Faulkner's ideas. In all there were the usual assumptions: we are the products of the past, and as the defeated survivors of a war we are oppressed by memories of a struggle that is still costing us our assurance. Since we are thus cursed, we need to understand the cause for this evil's being let loose among us; there must have been some initial evil, some original deviation from our nature.

As Faulkner approaches the idea of original sin, progressing beyond the conception of universal evil, he becomes vague. He has no philosophy to support his imagination in conceiving of incest as the symbol of the original evil. Remaining true to his imagination he had no recourse but to deal with imagined incest. The cry of protest that comes from Quentin and the others rises when they cannot find the cause of evil. And Faulkner seems to be conscious that, in the absence of theology, he has been constructing a pseudo-demonology. He has exploited the myths of a romantic anthropology and of aristocracy, dreams in the blood, racial memory, and all the seductive paraphernalia waiting for the man who believes that the meaning of life is to be found in suffering, and yet one who is still committed to thinking of life as a form of dedication.

There is an impasse, then, an intolerable one, and the only resolution or escape that Faulkner knew was to be found in something like comedy, that humor that has always kept him company. Once or twice, I think, in his long work, *The Hamlet,* he found a use for humor that exploited all his faculties and feelings, and the result was what I believe to be his most remarkable writing.

The Hamlet is a long novel describing the rise of the Snopes family to power in a small, rural community. The book falls into at least four separate stories, each primarily developed for its own sake. Though the characters are common to each, and the rise of an ignorant, avaricious family is the theme of the book, there is no real unity.

The great achievement of the work is the characterization of Ratliff, the sewing-machine salesman, shrewd, witty, disinterested, the civilized commentator on the progress to power of the ambitious and unworthy. He is all but free from the passions that enslave his community. For the first time Faulkner sets up a rational man as the central figure of a story. The gain is enormous, considering that the characters and pictures have lost neither intensity nor vividness. The picture of the stooped man in the blue cotton shirt, sitting on the porch of the store, whittling, seeing everything while appearing to see nothing, matching wits with all, is memorable to the point that it is exactly as if one saw him there. For art of this kind there can be no useful comment.

In the end, avarice infected Ratliff and made a fool of him, but as long as his reason is in command he is a great figure, and his worsting of the Snopes family in the first part of the book seems to me one of the best really comic stories in American literature.

In a long section of this work Faulkner treats a myth in a new way for him. This is the story of an idiot boy given to the pursuit of a cow. We see some of the workings of the idiot's mind, but we construct much of our idea of him from his acts and from what others say of him. The technique now is partly that of the stream of consciousness, and partly reportorial and objective. His family and the neighbors who know of his bestiality endeavor to prevent it, but they have no means of communicating their desires to his consciousness. Locking up is ineffectual. There is a particular cow the idiot is in love with: ". . . the bright thin horns of morning, of sun, would blow the mist away and reveal her, planted, blond, dew-pearled, standing in the parted water of the ford, blowing into the water the thick, warm, heavy, milk-laden breath. . . ." Finally someone gives the idiot a small toy cow, and his pursuit is ended. The metamorphosis of the goddess into a toy seems to me a myth considered rationally, brilliantly explaining the nature of idiocy, and for the first time the symbol includes a fully satisfactory judgment. For the first time Faulkner achieved the balance between comedy and horror. For once the story spoke for itself, and the ghosts departed.

Most of Faulkner's work reveals some mythical pretension, though nowhere else are his myths treated wittily. And it is curious to observe that in the two novels which seem to be the best constructed (*As I Lay Dying* and *Sanctuary*) the mythical and religious interests are subdued and there is comparatively little emphasis upon history. The point I wish to make is that, though humor gives a remarkable grace to *The Hamlet*, the form of two of his works is strictly controlled by other attitudes, one by a kind of decent respect for people, the other by hatred. And yet in these, also, humor or comedy (I am not sure which) provides something significant and necessary.

As I Lay Dying is the story of the death and burial of Addy Bundren, wife of Anse Bundren, a poor-white farmer, and the mother of his four children. The story is told through the reporting of streams of consciousness. The thoughts of each character are recorded in short chapters as the coffin is built before the mother dies, and as her family carry her to the burial place she has chosen, some miles away.

The subject of the novel is kinship. The people are "poor whites," with all the strength and tenacity that permit them to survive in spite of their pride and ignorance. Their unquestioning observance of the mother's request could only have been maintained by a primitive sense of blood-loyalty. The problems that face them are elementary—making a coffin, obtaining horses to draw the wagon, finding a place to cross the river when bridge after bridge has been washed out. No obstacle can prevent the burial, nor is there anything in their characters to weaken or even question their purpose. For them the burial according to the wish of the dead person is an enjoinder having all the authority of whatever has granted them existence in the first place. There is little thought of naming the authority—God or the church or honor—and it overrides inertia, family differences, and the protests of neighbors. It takes many days before the family is able to bury the mother as delay after delay holds up the wagon. Her body rots, and as the funeral party passes through villages the smell of the dead woman excites the inhabitants, and they complain of a menace to health. A bridge collapses, the mules drown, but all that nature or men can oppose is overcome.

The narrative increases steadily in interest and awe. The story is heroic. The passions that govern the characters are intensified by the absence of interests distracting to members of more self-conscious classes of society. The family relationships, the burial, the seduction of the daughter, are given the full range of human passion by people who have no other means of spending it.

Several incidents are ugly and bitter, but they are not meant to be merely horrible. They are incidents which appear to the participants simply as the commonplaces of existence, and to the extent that Faulkner makes this clear to us his treatment of them may be said to be that of a heroic joke. But these events are too fierce and tense to allow for humor; we understand that what might have been ridiculous is indeed serious because the absurd actors are human, and great. These men and women are struggling against a universe which opposes them with fire and floods, and against the limitations of their own natures, all in order to fulfill the obligations of kinship. The horror of the novel is that men and women are playing parts in a joke. But because they feel the need of loyalty so deeply, their story becomes decent.

Faulkner said that he wrote *Sanctuary* in order to revile a public that had been insensitive to the quality of his previous work. It was originally meant to be a shocker, though later Faulkner revised it to avoid, I suppose, the imputation of cheapness. But the conception of the book as a joke continued to control it in one important respect. It is the nature of a joke that it have a contemporary subject, viewed without historical perspective. It follows that ghosts can have no place in *Sanctuary*.

This is the story of an underworld in Memphis and the neighboring country, created by the favored as well as the depressed classes. The chief figure, Popeye, is the product of a criminal environment and poverty, and towards the end of the book he is rather prosaically treated as a case study. He may be considered to be congenitally deformed, though it is clear that Faulkner means us to recognize that a certain kind of corrupt society spawned, brought up, and favored him.

Temple Drake and her college friends were the spoiled children of a class of people with pretensions to superiority, a class that had become morally bankrupt through accepting the superficial standards of a suburban civilization. They understood neither social nor individual responsibility. Though Temple had been given the privileges of a lady and had been allowed the arrogance of a coquette by a society still gasping after the aristocratic dream, she drifted easily into the underworld because her parents and her society had done nothing to make anything but thrills meaningful. Nor had her society, in contrast with that of the Bundrens, allowed her to preserve even the rudiments of passion. When Popeye carried her off, she accepted the gangster world as a satisfactory environment.

I believe that Wyndham Lewis's characterization of *Sanctuary* as a satire conceived in pessimism is only partly correct. The moral of the story is that when the immature and irresponsible have power they understand none of its uses except violence. The impotent Popeye, raping Temple by proxy, offers the bitterest of comments on the nature of violence. But as I understand it, satire is conceived more in indignation than in pessimism, and in this book the controlling impulse is still something else. Malraux's analysis seems to me more satisfactory:

C'est, soit d'une impuissance d'esclave pleinement ressentie...soit de l'absurde irrémédiable...que jaillit chez Faulkner l'exaltation tendue qui fait sa force, et c'est l'absurdité qui donne à ses personnages secondaires, presque comiques...une intensité comparable à celle de Chtchédrine. Je ne dirai pas de Dickens; car, même autour de tels personnages, rôde le sentiment qui fait la valeur de l'oeuvre de Faulkner: la haine.

The phrase recurs, "presque comique." But just as respect transformed the horrible absurdities of *As I Lay Dying*, so hatred in *Sanctuary* ruthlessly vivifies the emptiness of the immoral. The hatred is the hatred of a man who sees a part of his society clearly, and that clarity, like objectivity, is almost comic. Viewed comically, there is no need to blame the evil in these characters upon the past.

It appears that the union of outrage and humor is not an easy one. It seems that if this holy zeal and this humor of Faulkner's were balanced differently, many of the long stories would have been better integrated in the form they seem to seek, a comic form. As it is, each long work, for the most part, is a mixture of fine or wild rhetoric and religiously passionate investigations into the meaning of things, together with the brightest kind of comic comment. The passionate seeker after truth is the dominant personality in every work. But occasionally the comic writer holds his ground, at one time to mock, at another to illuminate the story with something more like reason than religion. Then the horrible stories seem like jokes, or even like comedies. At such times, happily enough, the strained religion deviates into sense. And at times, as in *As I Lay Dying*, there is a balance where the writing is merely simply true.

FAULKNER AND THE EXILED GENERATION

RABI

THE BIRTH OF THE WORD. Through the treacherous darkness of Faulkner's work, occasionally pierced by light, his characters finally escape from their slow and solitary groping for thought and stop amazed before the dazzling light of consciousness. Then their own truth appears, free of all ambiguity. One of these truths is declared by young Bayard, son of Colonel Sartoris, the progenitor of the whole Sartoris dynasty. It illuminates all of Faulkner's desperate attempt to comprehend the

Reprinted with permission from *Esprit*, no. 175 (January, 1951), 47-65. Translated by Martine Darmon, with the assistance of the editors.

universe in its three dimensions. Bayard has just reached his twentieth year when he discovers an incestuous attraction for Drusilla, his stepmother. Influenced by his adolescent reading, he thinks of the woman of thirty as the symbol of the ancient and eternal serpent: "And I realized then the immitigable chasm between all life and all print—that those who can, do, those who cannot and suffer enough because they can't, write about it." This sentence, written in the first person, is typical of *The Un-vanquished*; it is like the donor's portrait in the right hand corner of the canvases of primitive painters.

For Faulkner the purpose of art is not "to translate the perishable into the imperishable" (Goethe); such an attempt is doomed to failure in advance, so elusive is man, like water that a child tries to hold in his clenched hands. Through his intuition and full use of tone, the artist can sometimes succeed, not in translating but simply in making the individual reader feel the terrible complexity of the world, charged with myths and signs and broken into fragments, in its past, present and future.

We are still as we were in the first days of the world, in the moment when God created man, when this thing that yesterday was mud and today is still black mold, painfully emerges from the darkness of eternal night. It gropes about with its blind hands, broods painfully over unformed thoughts, and discovers humble everyday words. But words are at the same time a means of communication and an instrument of misunderstanding. I make an effort to translate my thought with these words, and at the very moment when my mouth pronounces them I know that they do not reproduce what I meant to say, that the person who hears them will understand them in a way different from that in which I said and thought them. Thus they necessarily suffer a twofold betrayal. Communication between persons seems quite impossible. One must go even further to underline the basic difficulty involved in language. It translates and betrays at the same time. All of Faulkner's characters, with the exception of the Witnesses, whose mission is to give a final meaning to the tragedy, say very little. Yet, they give the reader a sense of primeval life. Not long

ago, I was mere clay and I will again be clay tomorrow—
after my face has assumed the belated mask of truth for a fugitive
instant before my Judge.

In that admirable novel, *As I Lay Dying,* the difficulty of
language and the supreme vanity of all expression appear with
maximum force. In that story Faulkner gives us the most striking
image of man in the first days of the world, and the unbearable
impression of his final doom. Here, the word painfully traverses
the darkness of the simple mind. Man is still mud, and God has
just given him breath. He moves slowly out of this state of inor-
ganic matter. I am the seed buried in the deepest part of the dark
earth, and I walk with a stubborn gait towards the light.

On her bed of agony, Addie Bundren lies dying, hiding her
lonely pride and her torn heart. She is happy to go. With her head
raised, she looks through the window at her son Cash, who is
making the coffin in which she will sleep for eternity. During all
these days of anguish, the only sign of life is the noise of the saw
and the adze which her oldest son is using. For Faulkner, one's
act has reality only when it is registered in the consciousness of
another. But each of us has, and can only have, a fragmentary
view of the event. At the beginning, each of the characters
describes the sufferings of Addie and the making of the coffin.
Thus we are able to see Faulkner's intention, which is to gather
the fragments of the broken mirror and to reconstruct out of
them a total vision of the world.

Then follows the heroic tale of the long funeral journey con-
ducted by Anse, the husband, and by the children. They have to
face numerous difficulties: the rain, the collapse of bridges, the
perilous crossing of the river, Cash's wound, the loss of the mules,
the fire, and the sight of buzzards attracted by the stench of the
body. They overcome all perils, and finally arrive in Jefferson,
where, according to her wish, they bury Addie.

Sometimes, through the stammering of the sentence that
comes out of the sleeping earth, the image of truth appears in a
furtive and violent flash. Dewey Dell carries the fruit of her sin
and feels life stirring in her: "I feel my body, my bones and flesh

beginning to part and open upon the alone." The youngest child Vardaman screams when they close the box: "Are you going to nail her up in it, Cash? Cash? Cash? . . . Are you going to nail it shut, Cash? Nail it? *Nail* it?" Cash, the conscientious and skillful carpenter, offers thirteen carefully deduced reasons for his particular method of constructing the coffin. Darl, the seer, the only lucid one of all these lost beings (who will, for this reason, sink into madness), feels in himself the encroachment of the frenzied world: "I don't know what I am. I don't know if I am or not. Jewel knows he is, because he does not know that he does not know whether he is or not." Finally Anse, the sordid and greedy father, mutters hypocritically, "God's will be done. . . . Now I can get them teeth"—the teeth that will finally help him to eat God's victuals "as a man should," and that he will buy in Jefferson once the dead woman is buried.

But Addie reaches far beyond those who survive her, with all of the authority that death suddenly provides. Carted for days in this box, which Vardaman has pierced with holes so that she can breathe, she speaks a last time. She defines her fault, explains the nature of her pride and describes the meeting with her lover, clothed in the garments of sin, doubly guilty because the adultery mocks his ministerial garb. "That was when I learned that words are no good; that words don't ever fit even what they are trying to say at. . . . He [Anse] had a word, too. Love, he called it. But I had been used to words for a long time. I knew that that word was like the others: just a shape to fill a lack. . . . I would think how words go straight up in a thin line, quick and harmless, and how terribly doing goes along the earth, clinging to it."

Thus the Faulkner hero moves, Oedipus-like, silently, blindly, his hands extended. Painfully he tries to unravel the drama, while the horrified chorus begs and prophesies. In Faulkner, the word is first the stammer of an awakening man, still numbed by the darkness. But sometimes, miraculously, it comes as a pure flash, a black diamond scintillating with a cold light— like the obsessive fixation of the sick person, or like the insomniac who, while everyone else is asleep, isolates his suffering and

makes it more acute. In fact, it is almost necessary to stay awake
during those hours, lost by a futile and discontented humanity.
Out of Adam's body, formed from the earth, in the heart of night,
the word was born. Faulkner portrays his heroes at the moment
of slow awakening, before man is completely aware, while he is
crude and unformed. At that moment he feels hunger, thirst,
terror; he suffers intolerable pain caused by the memory of his
original sin, and unbearable anguish from the memory of his lost
paradise.

For Faulkner it is impossible to grasp the great complexity
of man or to communicate it to the reader. It is useless to attempt
an explanation of the world, because the writer usually appeals
only to the logic of his reader. But through this apparently disordered narrative, through a conscious disarrangement of chronology, through the use of innocents and idiots as witnesses and
as consciousnesses—all of which result in ambiguity—Faulkner
forces the reader to recreate the work for himself. Faulkner
always tries to do the impossible, and he succeeds admirably.
"Fatal immortality and immortal fatality." We stop short of the
Word; the sleeper, scarcely awake, stammers his awful and incomprehensible message.

THE FAULKNER GEOGRAPHY. C. E. Magny, in *L'Age du roman
americain,* has perceived with her usual clarity, in Faulkner's
work as in Balzac's, the technique of recurring characters.* But
is this really a "technique"? I rather believe that in Faulkner,
the creature escapes his creator as soon as he is created, and that
he then enjoys an independent life. In Balzac this method effectively provides a coherent system which allows him to give a
sociological vision of the world; for Faulkner, on the other hand,
its use only reveals once more his conviction that it is impossible
to express the universe in its totality.

The ultimate purpose of the author is to free himself through
his work of art. In Faulkner, however, the liberation is never
complete, and his characters live by a passion that is extinguished

* *Retour des personnages.*

only when the body is destroyed. Faulkner often seems unable to conclude his work. This sense of incompleteness affects the form of *Light in August,* for example. The theme of Lena's search for her forgetful lover is linked with that of Christmas, the child of sin with one drop of black blood; and this second theme occupies the greater part of the work and becomes central. Linked with these, there are many secondary themes. Just as the reader expects the novel to end, Faulkner begins a parenthetical short story: "In the town on that day lived a young man named Percy Grimm." *Sanctuary* employs a similar method. Though everything has apparently been told, Faulkner seems unwilling to stop. He adds things, and finally, in a few rapid and nervous pages, writes a postscript to the work, describing, in a series of flashes, the birth of Popeye, his miserable childhood and his burdensome heredity.

Faulkner abhors the reasonable mind which neatly constructs and resolves its work. His universe is caught up in the ebb and flow of passions, where the human mind stammers in panic, for there is too much to say. Faulkner's hero, once created, lives with all the violence of his being, which carries him beyond the limits of the book.

Since he cannot free himself entirely of his familiar world, Faulkner tries to recreate it in his imagination. We can therefore think of a Faulknerian geography and a Faulknerian climate, a fixed element in which his people move. Jefferson appears persistently at the center of his map. It is the main town in this rural region, where men cultivate wheat, corn and cotton; the flat countryside is marked occasionally by slight hills. The long and straight roads are traversed by the slow step of mules, which, as the legend moves toward the present, slowly give way to automobiles. But most often, men travel in wagons. The rich houses of the whites and the isolated farms are seen here and there, surrounded by arable fields, pastures, forests well-stocked with game, and great areas of fallow land. Clear brooks and a wide river cross this country. Near the huge plantations are the cabins of the Negroes in which the whites sought refuge during the

Civil War, when their own houses had burned down. Finally, some distance from Jefferson there is a tiny village, made up of a store, a sawmill and five shacks.

Over all this country burns a relentless sun, the perfect symbol of Noon, and an ideal dividing line between thought and act. The drama always takes place in the clearest part of the day, and in the heart of summer (June, July and August, or dry September), at that instant when the light is most glaring. One can't help thinking that Faulkner's choice of this moment has the quality of sacrificial symbolism. One can never escape the light of the day. The long night has known gestation, but God hands down his judgment and executes it in the great shadowless light under a placid noon sky. There are no stones on which you can rest your head. There is no burrow in which you can hide.

In *Light in August* the action develops without pause under a motionless sky. The same climate is found in *Sanctuary*. The murder and rape would normally have been committed during the night. This is not what happens. The night spent by Temple in the bootlegger's shack is only a period of preparation for the sacrifice. It is a night of "comparative inviolation," as she herself says, in which things do happen, but only gradually, until her cowardly companion deserts her. Tommy is killed and Temple raped after the night has passed.

Jefferson is situated at the center of the map; here live the fallen representatives of these great old families of the South, the Sartorises and the Compsons. They live in their proud solitude, their minds turned backwards in contemplation of their former grandeur, surrounded by Negroes who serve their masters with dumb loyalty.

The men of the older generation still remember the paving of the streets, until that time dusty and shaded; they remember the Negro women, balancing bundles of laundry on their turbaned heads. At the same time, they recall that the telephone and power companies cut the trees, thus depriving them of shade and comfort. Since that time, the town has become modern, though it still retains its old-fashioned provincial character: its post office;

its tavern, where the initiates drink moonshine in the back room; the soda counter; the sawmill; the Sartoris bank; the loan company, where Jason ruins himself, maddened by his passion for money; the barbershop in which Hawkshaw cuts little girls' hair and thinks of a certain color, "not blonde and not brunette"; finally, the Negro district, whose inhabitants awaken slowly to the hope of escape from their somber life, "gloomy and outraged."

In the heart of the Faulkner world, at the center of Jefferson, there is the courthouse, with its distinctive odor: the musty tobacco smells, the rank sweat, earth, "that musty odor of spent lusts and greeds and bickerings and bitterness and withal a certain clumsy stability in lieu of anything better." The courthouse exists both before and after the drama. One after the other, the actors in Faulkner's world come to this absurd but necessary symbol of man's justice. On the square of the courthouse, the crowd sometimes gathers, suddenly passionate, hysterical, erotic, drunk with blood, honor and lust. Relentlessly the clock of the courthouse measures out time in imperious terms of work and days.

In the heart of the courthouse there is a prison, with thick walls, solid and stable, the doors padlocked and a window that opens on the streets of the town. Blake once said that prisons were made with the stones of laws, and brothels with the stones of religions. Like all the prisons of the world, that in Jefferson is not only the symbol of punishment, but also by virtue of its fixed location in space and time, the best place of refuge. The Negro murderer leans his forehead against the barred window of his cell. He sings a sad and quiet song, and his dark brothers down in the street join him in singing it. In the same jail, Goodwin's mistress finds a refuge for the night, after she has been driven from her hotel by the "Christian" women of the town.

There are two other towns on this map. First, Mottson, the town through which people only pass, the purgatory where Doc Hines stays (*Light in August*), awaiting the day appointed by the Lord when he will again meet Joe Christmas, the black-blooded child of sin. Further on, Memphis, the swarming city which had already in the past been tainted by the corruption of its slavetraders, now sweats with the abomination and the lust of its brothels, its dubious hotels, its questionable bars, its shady politicians. Memphis, reeking of sin, of pride and of money.

I don't know if, as Malcolm Cowley says, the true subject of Faulkner is the "downfall of a social order," following the Civil War, the military occupation and the development of financial capitalism. I am not sure that the author of the great Legend of the South was capable of such a strict sociological view. I believe that he had his own insights into this legend, and that he was inclined to feel rather than to reason about the decline of Southern society. His greatest interest is in the resurrection of myths and in the revival of a sense of tragedy. The Faulkner geography and climate provide the spatial element in which the heroes move; and more precisely, the framework within which we find his version of the myth.

The North American tradition was founded not so much on the capture of Indian land, nor on the settling of the first pioneers in virgin territories, but rather on the memory of the violent Civil War, which tore the country for four bloody years. Out of two hundred years of American history Faulkner's characters remember only the Civil War: the heroism and the suffering of the valiant Southerners; the women, whose greatest glory was to dress in mourning, as "the bride-widow of a lost cause" (*The Unvanquished*); the tricks used to beat the boorish Yankees; the many cases of violence and destruction; and finally, the bitterness of defeat. What was left for them, then, besides this unending and unchanging contemplation of the past? What of these original virtues could be called upon, to face the new reality? The only thing that emerged was a verbal puritanism, made of conventions, of signs, of idiosyncrasies and prejudices, and a petty notion of honor which finally concealed their inability to face the new situation. Throughout Faulkner's work we find this puritanism, which is actually a form of the eternal aspiration to innocence and the eternal inability to reach it by human means.

The disgust felt for the sexual act, which the author often associates with vomiting, illustrates further the nature of this clash with the living world. What meaning can acts have, when they are only empty manifestations, deprived of any real link with concrete reality? It is an unreal world: Caddy's mother, for example, put on black veils, cried and declared with sobs that Caddy was dead because Caddy (at that time fifteen years old at most) was caught kissing a boy (*The Sound and the Fury*). If words are always lies, acts must often seem ambiguous; God alone knows the truth, and is able to see into our secret hearts.

Finally, surrounding the whites, living in the closest union with them, there is the black world, the cause and the object of the fighting in the Civil War. Faulkner makes the Negroes live for us in *The Unvanquished*; just before their liberation, suddenly obeying a very obscure but a very strong feeling, they begin their journey, and for days and days the dust raised by their passing does not settle, because they push ahead night and day. While they walk, gazing intently ahead, they chant in their monotonous voices: "Hit's Jordan we coming to. . . . Jesus gonter see me that far. God's own angel proclamated me free and gonter general me to Jordan. I don't belong to John Sartoris now; I belongs to me and God."

Faulkner's attitude towards the Negroes is rather ambiguous. If he implicitly accepts their liberation, it is because it is hardly possible to do otherwise. This attitude explains and justifies the censure of the American Communist critics on this point. How are we to explain the comments of Miss Burden (*Light in August*), who, though a friend of the Negroes, repeats her father's words concerning the black race, which was created by God as the condemnation and the curse of the white race: "I thought of all the children coming forever and ever into the world, white, with the black shadow already falling upon them before they drew breath. . . . And I seemed to see the black shadow in the shape of a cross. And it seemed like the white babies were struggling, even before they drew breath, to escape from the shadow that was not only upon them but beneath them too, flung out like their arms were flung out, as if they were nailed to the cross."

THE POWER OF MYTH. Everyone is born in pain and dies in pain. We know that the supreme mission of the artist is to look into the abyss of suffering and the darkness with which we are obsessed, in order to free himself and to deliver us. In Greek tragedy, says Nietzsche, "one could sense at the end that metaphysical consolation, without which delight in tragedy cannot be explained at all." In this sense, although Faulkner's work does not have the proper form, it is essentially a true tragedy: in its themes, in its evocation of ancient myths, and even in its internal composition. Faulkner is attracted to myth because it is often tragic, and because myth, a striking epitome of human life and accessible to new interpretation from generation to generation, has a miraculous power of evocation; finally, because of his instinctive distrust of thought and of the word, the vehicle of thought. For the word is degraded by usage and deprived of all its initial magic and affective power; in this respect it becomes an instrument of betrayal rather than a vehicle of tradition.

Perhaps nowhere else do we find repeated with so much insistence such terms as "fatality," "tragic," "doom." Thus Faulkner speaks of "the blind tragedy of human destinies," "the tragic and inevitable land," and "the ancient and tragic womb of the world." Again and again, the Faulkner hero relives both his paradise and his expulsion, the first innocence and the fall, without hope and without a redeemer. Faulkner is quite at home in the world of myth, born in the collective consciousness of humanity and subsisting in its ancient memory.

Nothing would save *As I Lay Dying* from being a dull novel of peasant cupidity, were it not for the epic tone of that extraordinary funeral journey. After the coffin has been made (its construction supervised in every detail by the dying woman), the misadventures of the long return trip begin; they recall the distant tribulations of folklore, where we see the dead painfully reaching the kingdom of souls after a journey full of terrible events; crossing rivers and bridges, passing through mountains, and fighting with brigands. In ancient Egypt, the dead had to reach the sacred oasis of Jupiter Ammon, west of the Nile, over the six hundred kilometers of the Lybian desert. Not very long ago, long caravans of camels led the dead to the Shiite sanctuaries of Mesopotamia. Even today, holy cities like Mecca and Kairouan and the lamaseries of Tibet are the goal of unending processions which, in Mongolia, represent a year-long voyage. Finally we know that each year whole shipments of coffins reach Shanghai and Canton; they are the bodies of coolies which come back to their native land, thanks to an explicit clause in their work contract. In his work, Faulkner suggests immediately the idea of a sacred tie between man and his land. Man expects the land to give him both food and protection, and he finds in the land the security he needs. Foreign lands represent an unknown danger, his own, a familiar danger.

Another theme has to do with time. It is found in the conscious reordering of events, in the fragments that the reader himself has to rearrange, both illustrated by *The Sound and the Fury*. We see it also in the continual flashbacks which help us to understand the present and explain its constant interruption —as well as in the appearance of those breathless Witnesses who report and comment, messengers whose purpose is to sharpen and intensify the meaning of the Legend for the particular moment of the narrative.

The Sound and the Fury illustrates this theme particularly well. Let us reread Quentin's superb and terrifying soliloquy, at the end of which he is to destroy himself. On June 2nd, 1910, he gets up as the shadow of the sash appears on the curtains. He hears the ticking of the large watch lying on his dresser, and whether he wishes it or not, finds himself again in the real

world of responsibilities. His grandfather had once given him
the watch, so that he could remember time, as well as forget
it. Quentin goes towards the dresser and puts the watch face
down. Then, though he can no longer see the motion of the
hands, he still hears the ticking, which is methodically marking
off time: "I went to the dresser and took up the watch, with the
face still down. I tapped the crystal on the corner of the dresser
and caught the fragments of glass in my hand and put them into
the ashtray and twisted the hands off and put them in the tray.
The watch ticked on." When Quentin goes out, he still hears
the broken watch in his pocket. And he remembers one of his
father's remarks: "Only when the clock stops does time come
to life."

Before man's fall, in the golden age, the notion of innocence
was linked with that of eternity. The divine was outside time,
but after the fall man found himself inexorably in time, with
its succession of seasons and of rites paralleling the measured
recurrence of work and worship. To remember their rhythm
man created the week, the month, the year—in short, the limits
of time. Slowly, man came to realize his responsibility to events,
and the imperative necessity of choice, though only after much
experience and much pain. When Quentin breaks the watch, he
secretly hopes to stop time, to flee the world of unbearable
duties, to seek refuge in the world of divinity, innocence and
eternity. But the broken watch continues its ticking during
Quentin's last walk, just as the clock of the courthouse in
Jefferson continues to count the hours of day and night. Faulkner thus shows that man cannot escape, however much he might
wish to. He notes the bitter mockery of human freedom. The
watch will continue, until the day of death, to eat away time,
with its persistent ticking, and to remind man of his obligation
to live, to struggle and to choose.

Faulkner's almost obsessive concern with incest gives it
an importance similar to that of the myth of time and of
eternity. They are identical modes of escaping from a world
which seems always to demand an act and a choice. To return

to Quentin's soliloquy: in the following passage he forces to their limits both his dominating wish and his shame: "Then you will have only me then only me then the two of us amid the pointing and the horror beyond the clean flame." Such really is the incentive for incest: the desire to be with those we know, in a land we know well, where it is easier to fight against evil, where it is simpler to find shelter, and where we need not face the terrifying world of men and things. Quentin relives in his memory the time when Benjy, screaming, pulled and shoved Caddy by her dress, and led her to the bathroom to wash away her misconduct and her sin. Is not Jason's hatred for Caddy, and later for her daughter Quentin, another example of this furious instinct which forces the cursed brothers of this unfortunate family upon their accursed sister? "You wanted to sublimate a piece of natural human folly into a horror and then exorcise it with truth," Quentin's father had once told him. Quentin answers, and then everything is clear and precise: "It was to isolate her out of the loud world. . . . Then the world would roar away. . . ." He broods over sin which he will never commit, but which has fascinated him since childhood. Incest is associated with the joys of childhood, the innocence of the first days, the flight beyond the boundaries of time, and the escape from the world of suffering. At the end of his painful experience of reliving his past, nothing can keep Quentin from destroying himself. Everything that happened has led inevitably to suicide. The innocent Benjy, with his enfeebled mind, will be castrated and punished for a fault of which he is not aware. Throughout Faulkner's world we find the same dismal fate. It is a massacre of the Innocents: Quentin drowns himself, Benjy is castrated, Goodwin is lynched, Christmas is murdered and castrated, Miss Burden is decapitated and Bayard Sartoris kills himself, while Darl becomes mad at the very point of self-knowledge. Funereal drumming. Muffled drums. Flags at half-mast. It is always the same dramatic progress. "Death—that Roman holiday," says Bayard Sartoris (*The Unvanquished*). Fate pursues each of the actors, a fate like an ancient curse that might be warded off if only men knew how.

Fatal Immortality and Immortal Fatality. Fatality is a continuous thread in all of Faulkner's work. Each man has his own destiny. But this destiny never becomes what he has planned, decided or striven for; it is never the sum of his earthly life, with its hopes and decisions. His destiny is always inevitable, in the sense that man is predetermined. The Faulknerian tragedy is a tragedy where the hero has no access to freedom, no matter how small. "Fatality," we read in *Sartoris*, is "the augury of a man's destiny peeping out at him from the roadside hedge, if he but recognize it. . . ."

Similarly, Christmas knows that he is going to commit a murder before he has decided anything. The razor is suddenly in his hand. He realizes it only when he notices the fright of the passers-by. "Something is going to happen. Something is going to happen to me," he says to himself; and, a moment later, already speaking in the past, he adds, even though he has not committed the act: "I had to do it . . . I had to do it." What, after all, is the point of heeding signs and warnings? It is possible to foresee, but it is never possible to force the course of events.

Goodwin, who tries to prevent a tragedy, advises Temple to escape from the bootleggers' shack. But she remains there, motionless, frozen, fascinated by the rape that is to happen, that she has been awaiting for years, and that she deserves because of her wilful conduct—this rape that all signs had foreshadowed, even the obscene inscription in the lavatories of the University. "Now I can stand anything," she says at the end of her night of ordeal. Then, when the sacrifice has been made, she screams: "I told you it was! . . . I told you! I told you all the time!" and thus gives voice to her desire, and brings to an end her expectation of this monstrous act.

Because we can see the "dark shadow of fatality and doom" on his forehead, we know, before he does, that Colonel John Sartoris will be murdered the next day, when he goes to town

for the first time without any weapons. We also know that his
son Bayard will refuse to shoot his father's murderer—or, rather,
that he will be unable to shoot him. Bayard is at college and his
faithful Ringo has come to tell him of the murder. Then the
struggle begins: "At least this will be my chance to find out if
I am what I think I am or if I just hope; if I am going to do
what I have taught myself is right or if I am just going to wish
I were." He travels, on horseback, the long distance to Jefferson,
which seems very short to him today. He enters and faces Aunt
Jenny, Drusilla, and his father's former soldiers, all waiting to
see how he will act. Uncertain himself, since the announcement
of the murder, he too is anxious to know his reaction. Then
Drusilla speaks. Putting the gun into his right hand, she tells
him that he is beautiful, because, so young, he has the chance
to kill and to pick up the fire that Lucifer cast down from heaven.
But suddenly she understands and laughs hysterically. For she
has seen that he will not kill. And we also know, because of
the questions that Bayard asks himself, that he will not kill:
"But what good will that do? I said. What good will that do?"
Everyone else, in silent chorus, observes him hesitate. On the
next day, they know, when he meets Ben Richmond, he will not
shoot. For the first time in Faulkner's work, we seem to see
the circle broken and the irremediable defied. But the struggle
has never actually been decisive. Instead, for the first time since
the bloody Civil War we observe a moment of hesitation and of
failure.

Each of Faulkner's heroes is led inexorably to the fulfillment of his own fate. Each finally realizes the irremediable:
Temple, her rape; Quentin, his suicide; Caddy, her seduction;
Christmas, his murder; Shumann, his death; Miss Burden, like
Nancy, her murder. And each one suffers his fate without re-
belling. The fate of Christmas is typical. At no time does he
think of resisting. He is the battleground in the struggle between
his white and black blood. He absorbed black smells, black
thoughts and the very essence of the Negro; the black tide
coursed through him, and it was black as death. At other times

he felt his white blood; he lived like a white man and knew the terrible hardness of the Whites. But it never occurred to him to find out the truth, to determine once and for all whether he had that drop of black blood. Thanks to an ambiguity that Faulkner is careful not to clear up, we remain uncertain about the point until the end, and even after the book is finished. The drama then concerns not so much a refusal to struggle as the futility of struggle. In Faulkner's world the struggle is intrinsically absurd, because the universe itself is absurd. Always the same tale, told by an idiot, full of sound and fury.

To understand this absurdity, one must also know the design of the Player in the game he plays with his pawns (*Sanctuary*). The plans of the Player, however, remain hidden from us. He alone starts the pawns moving and brings the tragedy to an end (*Light in August*). But one day the Player will grow weary. The following sentence reminds us of another phrase, "fatal immortality and immortal fatality." "For there is death in the sound of it, and a glamorous fatality, like silver pennons downrushing at sunset, or a dying fall of horns along the road to Roncevaux."

It is better to suffer than to attempt understanding. The man who tries to get too near to truth ends in madness, like poor Darl, who was subdued, bound, and placed on a train for Jackson (*As I Lay Dying*). Man's effort to understand this universe, to give it a meaning and to influence its course, continues to be futile and ludicrous. Justice in Jefferson always ends in absurdity. Horace Benbow's struggle to save Goodwin is a dismal failure (*Sanctuary*). After his mad flight in pursuit of Quentin, Jason humbly returns home. There, everything is known and the disorder of things is in itself a kind of certitude, "a familiar order."

THE EXILED GENERATION. Faulkner's work reminds one forcibly of Greek tragedy, in the sense that man appears less the agent of action than the instrument of the gods and their playground. Although some critics may disagree, Greek tragedy is a tragedy of fate. Let us look again at the exact moment in the Aeschylean legend when Orestes has just killed Aegisthus. Suddenly he faces his mother. He dashes toward her, his sword raised. Clytemnestra falls at his knees and tears at her garments. "Stop, oh my son," she screams. Orestes lets his sword fall. "Pylades, what shall I do?" he says. "Can I kill my mother?" And Pylades answers: "And what would become then of Apollo's oracles, of the advice given at Pytho, and our sworn promises? Believe me, it is better to have all men against you than the gods."

We find this attitude throughout Faulkner's work, except that for him the gods are never defined; they remain in the background, all the more redoubtable because they are left vague. Greek tragedy still permitted some hope, because man could explain the gods' actions in terms of a strict conception of justice. Nietzsche was right in emphasizing the metaphysical consolation that tragedy finally communicates to the spectator. In spite of the underlying theme of Fate, Greek tragedy knows a Prometheus who deliberately assumed the burden of crime to create the race of men, and an Antigone who symbolized the eternal law before the written law. Let us imagine for a moment what Greek tragedy would be if all its heroes were like Prometheus or Antigone. We would be faced, not with the tragedy of Fate, but with a tragedy of Freedom.

In Faulkner, there is no hope. Though the Redeemer has come, he has left no traces. He has given us only a sense of the irremediable, and the painful memory of our lost Paradise. The Faulknerian tragedy is a tragedy of exile.

In those of Faulkner's works that are conventionally called novels, we find the most authentic elements of tragedy. I am not, of course, referring to the "content"; in terms of form, however, the similarities are striking. It is scarcely necessary to note the places where Faulkner uses the technical terms of the theater: as in *The Unvanquished*, when Bayard explicitly speaks of his *entrance* on the *scene* of his rôle and of Drusilla's, while in the background his father's soldiers act as a *chorus*. The conclusion of this work is typically dramatic, the action sharply delineated, the antagonists posed in extreme states of tension, in such a way that the atmosphere of ambiguity is resolved finally, at the moment of highest tension, into a situation free of all doubt. The choice is clear-cut. The reader is held fascinated, as an audience might be, by the hero, to the point of forgetting that the fate enacted is not really his.

Malraux justly noticed in his preface to *Sanctuary* that Faulkner must have conceived his scenes before imagining his characters. We are still more convinced of this assertion because of the intervention of Witnesses, chorus, coryphaes, and excited messengers with important news. At every moment we see them appearing, wonderfully lyrical, giving a meaning to what is otherwise silence and disorder. While he acts, the hero is silent, because he has nothing to say and is absorbed by the act, or because the violence of his curses paralyzes him. The spectator hears only meaningless sounds.* Dramatic convention requires that the hero be confined to the center of the action. But nothing limits the Witness. He has seen extraordinary events, and he tells what he has seen and what he has heard. In *Pylon*, the role of the chorus is given to the Reporter; we are not given his name, but that does not matter since the Witness is part of an unknown and nameless world. It is the Witness who suddenly endows the characters with stature, and the story with its epic character. When the Reporter, fascinated by the pilots, does take part in the action, he becomes silent. In *Light in August,* the act always takes place away from the stage; it is observed, interpreted and often disclosed by the Witnesses, who see it from more than one perspective.

Oedipus himself, when the catastrophe befell him, tried to understand and to illuminate the darkness around him. He followed the thread which led him back to his initial sin. Not one of Faulkner's heroes makes this effort. His world is not irrational, but beyond our comprehension. It has its internal order, but this order remains secret. As to the "tragic flaw," it

* *Onomatopées incompréhensibles.*

is so distant in time, so indefinite, that it merges with man's original sin. At one time, long ago, man was given a choice. He chose evil and malediction. Since then, he has blindly sought the return of innocence and the lost Paradise. Faulkner wishes to ignore the fact that the same choice is presented again to each generation, to every man, and that this choice, which everyone must make, implies that he himself determines his future. One can imagine the golden age in the past or in the future. If we think of it as in the future, it is a phenomenon not only of grace but of active faith, of free will and decision. The Messiah will come one day, but he will come only if men deserve and win Him. This means that the Messiah is my will, my strength, my act. That is why Jewish humanism maintains that the universe rests on the sanctity of every living being. If we imagine the golden age as in the past, then all human existence is only a vain contemplation of vanished glory, a future of suffering and an exile without hope. But this is Faulkner's world. I can see in it a communion of sinners, but I do not see a communion of saints. The frequent use of idiots, of Negroes, and of children in his fiction is just another way of expressing regret for a lost past.

The Negroes provide a fluid setting in which the whites act. But children also appear, at many points of the legend. Laverne's child in *Pylon*; Bayard Sartoris in *The Unvanquished*, talking in the first person and recalling the Civil War, as he has remembered it from his youth; the little Belle in *Sartoris*, witness of her mother's adultery; Vardaman in *As I Lay Dying*, who pierces his mother's coffin so that she can breathe; young Christmas in *Light in August*, living his first years in a white orphanage, then in a black orphanage, and knowing hatred while he is still a child; in *Sanctuary*, young Popeye, whose pitiful childhood and dreadful heredity are revealed at the end. Finally, in *The Sound and the Fury* we have the Compson children, Jason, Benjy, Quentin, Caddy; and we know from further information given by the author that his primary purpose was to describe the burial of the grandmother as seen by the children. Undoubtedly it is these children, reminders of a hope not yet entirely destroyed, who save Faulkner's world from being altogether cursed.

We know that for Faulkner it is better to live fully than to write. But if one can only write, then at every opportunity he must take the lead in the struggle, fighting alone, and attempt to transcend the boundaries of life. "You wanted to sublimate a piece of natural human folly into a horror and then exorcise it with truth," says Quentin's father. Faulkner leads us beyond the familiar levels of experience and forces us to look unflinchingly into the darkness.

Among the numerous references to the Bible in Faulkner's work which contribute to its legendary tone, there is no mention of the crossing of the desert. Such an allusion is, however, essential. The crossing of the desert lasted forty years, and these forty years of austere preparation shaped and formed the people of the Old Testament. When Moses spoke to them before they entered the land of Canaan, he gave them many recommendations, commandments and warnings, and ended by saying: "See, I have set before thee this day life and good, death and evil."

We must go one step beyond Faulkner, to the inevitable battle, for only struggle will deliver the exiled generation from terror and from death.

III. The Work:

Studies of Method and Language

WILLIAM FAULKNER: THE NOVEL
AS FORM

CONRAD AIKEN

THE FAMOUS REMARK MADE TO MACAULAY—"Young man, the more I consider the less can I conceive where you picked up that style"—might with advantage have been saved for Mr. William Faulkner. For if one thing is more outstanding than another about Mr. Faulkner—some readers find it so outstanding, indeed, that they never get beyond it—it is the uncompromising and almost hypnotic zeal with which he insists upon having a style, and, especially of late, the very peculiar style which he insists upon having. Perhaps to that one should add that he insists *when he remembers*—he can write straightforwardly enough when he wants to; he does so often in the best of his short stories (and they are brilliant), often enough, too, in the novels. But that *style* is what he really wants to get back to; and get back to it he invariably does.

And what a style it is, to be sure! The exuberant and tropical luxuriance of sound which Jim Europe's jazz band used to exhale, like a jungle of rank creepers and ferocious blooms taking shape before one's eyes,—magnificently and endlessly intervolved, glisteningly and ophidianly in motion, coil sliding over coil, and leaf and flower forever magically interchanging,—was scarcely more bewildering, in its sheer inexhaustible fecundity, than Mr.

Reprinted with permission from *The Atlantic Monthly,* November, 1939, pp. 650–654.

Faulkner's style. Small wonder if even the most passionate of Mr. Faulkner's admirers—among whom the present writer honors himself by enlisting—must find, with each new novel, that the first fifty pages are always the hardest, that each time one must learn all over again *how* to read this strangely fluid and slippery and heavily mannered prose, and that one is even, like a kind of Laocoön, sometimes tempted to give it up.

Wrestle, for example, with two very short (for Mr. Faulkner!) sentences, taken from an early page of *Absalom, Absalom!*

Meanwhile, as though in inverse ratio to the vanishing voice, the invoked ghost of the man whom she could neither forgive nor revenge herself upon began to assume a quality almost of solidity, permanence. Itself circumambient and enclosed by its effluvium of hell, its aura of unregeneration, it mused (mused, thought, seemed to possess sentience as if, though dispossessed of the peace—who was impervious anyhow to fatigue—which she declined to give it, it was still irrevocably outside the scope of her hurt or harm) with that quality peaceful and now harmless and not even very attentive—the ogre-shape which, as Miss Coldfield's voice went on, resolved out of itself before Quentin's eyes the two half-ogre children, the three of them forming a shadowy background for the fourth one.

Well, it may be reasonably questioned whether, on page thirteen of a novel, that little cordite bolus of suppressed reference isn't a thumping aesthetic mistake. Returned to, when one has finished the book, it may be as simple as daylight; but encountered for the first time, and no matter how often reread, it guards its enigma with the stony impassivity of the Sphinx.

Or take again from the very first page of *The Wild Palms*— Mr. Faulkner's latest novel, and certainly one of his finest—this little specimen of "exposition": "Because he had been born here, on this coast though not in this house but in the other, the residence in town, and had lived here all his life, including the four years at the State University's medical school and the two years as an intern in New Orleans where (a thick man even when young, with thick soft woman's hands, who should never have been a doctor at all, who even after the six more or less metro-

politan years looked out from a provincial and insulated amazement at his classmates and fellows: the lean young men swagger-
ing in the drill jackets on which—to him—they wore the myriad
anonymous faces of the probationer nurses with a ruthless and
assured braggadocio like decorations, like flower trophies) he
had sickened for it." What is one to say of that—or of a sentence
only a little lower on the same page which runs for thirty-three
lines? Is this, somehow perverted, the influence of the later
Henry James—James the Old Pretender?

In short, Mr. Faulkner's style, though often brilliant and
always interesting, is all too frequently downright bad; and it has
inevitably offered an all-too-easy mark for the sharpshooting of
such alert critics as Mr. Wyndham Lewis. But if it is easy enough
to make fun of Mr. Faulkner's obsessions for particular words, or
his indifference and violence to them, or the parrotlike mechanical mytacism (for it is really like a stammer) with which he will
go on endlessly repeating such favorites as "myriad, sourceless,
impalpable, outrageous, risible, profound," there is nevertheless
something more to be said for his passion for overelaborate
sentence structure.

Overelaborate they certainly are, baroque and involuted in
the extreme, these sentences: trailing clauses, one after another,
shadowily in apposition, or perhaps not even with so much connection as that; parenthesis after parenthesis, the parenthesis itself
often containing one or more parentheses—they remind one of
those brightly colored Chinese eggs of one's childhood, which
when opened disclosed egg after egg, each smaller and subtler
than the last. It is as if Mr. Faulkner, in a sort of hurried despair,
had decided to try to tell us everything, absolutely everything,
every last origin or source or quality or qualification, and every
possible future or permutation as well, in one terrifically concentrated effort: each sentence to be, as it were, a microcosm. And it
must be admitted that the practice is annoying and distracting.

It is annoying, at the end of a sentence, to find that one does
not know in the least what was the subject of the verb that
dangles *in vacuo*—it is distracting to have to go back and sort

out the meaning, track down the structure from clause to clause, then only to find that after all it doesn't much matter, and that the obscurity was perhaps neither subtle nor important. And to the extent that one *is* annoyed and distracted, and *does* thus go back and work it out, it may be at once added that Mr. Faulkner has defeated his own ends. One has had, of course, to emerge from the stream, and to step away from it, in order properly to see it; and as Mr. Faulkner works precisely by a process of *immersion*, of hypnotizing his reader into *remaining immersed* in his stream, this occasional blunder produces irritation and failure.

Nevertheless, despite the blunders, and despite the bad habits and the willful bad writing (and willful it obviously is), the style as a whole is extraordinarily effective; the reader *does* remain immersed, *wants* to remain immersed, and it is interesting to look into the reasons for this. And at once, if one considers these queer sentences not simply by themselves, as monsters of grammar or awkwardness, but in their relation to the book as a whole, one sees a functional reason and necessity for their being as they are. They parallel in a curious and perhaps inevitable way, and not without aesthetic justification, the whole elaborate method of *deliberately withheld meaning*, of progressive and partial and delayed disclosure, which so often gives the characteristic shape to the novels themselves. It is a persistent offering of obstacles, a calculated system of screens and obtrusions, of confusions and ambiguous interpolations and delays, with one express purpose; and that purpose is simply to keep the form—and the idea—fluid and unfinished, still in motion, as it were, and unknown, until the dropping into place of the very last syllable.

What Mr. Faulkner is after, in a sense, is a *continuum*. He wants a medium without stops or pauses, a medium which is always *of the moment*, and of which the passage from moment to moment is as fluid and undetectable as in the life itself which he is purporting to give. It is all inside and underneath, or as seen from within and below; the reader must therefore be steadily *drawn in*; he must be powerfully and unremittingly hypnotized inward and downward to that image-stream; and this suggests, perhaps, a reason not only for the length and elaborateness of the sentence structure, but for the repetitiveness as well. The repetitiveness, and the steady iterative emphasis—like a kind of chanting or invocation—on certain relatively abstract words ("sonorous, latin, *vaguely* eloquent"), have the effect at last of producing, for Mr. Faulkner, a special language, a conglomerate of his own, which he uses with an astonishing virtuosity, and which, although in detailed analysis it may look shoddy, is actually for his purpose a life stream of almost miraculous adaptability. At the one extreme it is abstract, cerebral, time-and-space-obsessed, tortured and twisted, but nevertheless always with a living *pulse* in it; and at the other it can be as overwhelming in its simple vividness, its richness in the actual, as the flood scenes in *The Wild Palms*.

Obviously, such a style, especially when allied with such a *concern* for method, must make difficulties for the reader; and it must be admitted that Mr. Faulkner does little or nothing as a rule to make his highly complex "situation" easily available or perceptible. The reader must simply make up his mind to go to work, and in a sense to cooperate; his reward being that there *is* a situation to be given shape, a meaning to be extracted, and that half the fun is precisely in watching the queer, difficult, and often so laborious evolution of Mr. Faulkner's idea. And not so much idea, either, as form. For, like the great predecessor whom at least in this regard he so oddly resembles, Mr. Faulkner could say with Henry James that it is practically impossible to make any real distinction between theme and form. What immoderately delights him, alike in *Sanctuary, The Sound and the Fury, As I Lay Dying, Light in August, Pylon, Absalom, Absalom!* and now again in *The Wild Palms*, and what sets him above—shall we say it firmly—all his American contemporaries, is his continuous preoccupation with the novel *as form*, his passionate concern with it, and a degree of success with it which would clearly have commanded the interest and respect of Henry James himself. The novel as revelation, the novel as slice-of-life, the novel as mere story, do not interest him: these he would say, like James again, "are the circumstances of the interest," but not the interest itself. The interest itself will be the use to which these circumstances are put, the degree to which they can be organized.

From this point of view, he is not in the least to be considered as a mere "Southern" writer: the "Southernness" of his scenes and characters is of little concern to him, just as little as the question whether they are pleasant or unpleasant, true or untrue. Verisimilitude—or, at any rate, *degree* of verisimilitude—he will cheerfully abandon, where necessary, if the compensating advantages of plan or tone are a sufficient inducement. The famous scene in *Sanctuary* of Miss Reba and Uncle Bud in which a "madam" and her cronies hold a wake for a dead gangster, while the small boy gets drunk, is quite false, taken out of its context; it is not endowed with the same *kind* of actuality which permeates the greater part of the book at all. Mr. Faulkner was cunning enough to see that a two-dimensional cartoon-like statement, at this juncture, would supply him with the effect of a chorus, and without in the least being perceived as a change in the temperature of truthfulness.

That particular kind of dilution, or adulteration, of verisimilitude was both practised and praised by James: as when he blandly admitted of *In the Cage* that his central character was "too ardent a focus of divination" to be quite credible. It was defensible simply because it made possible the coherence of the whole, and was itself absorbed back into the luminous texture. It was for him a device for organization, just as the careful cherishing of "viewpoint" was a device, whether simply or in counterpoint. Of Mr. Faulkner's devices, of this sort, aimed at the achievement of complex "form," the two most constant are the manipulation of viewpoint and the use of the flashback, or sudden shift of time-scene, forward or backward.

In *Sanctuary*, where the alternation of viewpoint is a little lawless, the complexity is given, perhaps a shade disingenuously, by violent shifts in time; a deliberate disarrangement of an otherwise straightforward story. Technically, there is no doubt that the novel, despite its fame, rattles a little; and Mr. Faulkner him-

self takes pains to disclaim it. But, even done with the left hand,
it betrays a genius for form, quite apart from its wonderful virtuosity in other respects. *Light in August*, published a year after
Sanctuary, repeats the same technique, that of a dislocation of
time, and more elaborately; the time-shifts alternate with shifts
in the viewpoint; and if the book is a failure it is perhaps because
Mr. Faulkner's tendency to what is almost a hypertrophy of form
is not here, as well as in the other novels, matched with the
characters and the theme. Neither the person nor the story of
Joe Christmas is seen fiercely enough—by its creator—to carry
off that immense machinery of narrative; it would have needed
another Popeye, or another Jiggs and Shumann, another Temple
Drake, and for once Mr. Faulkner's inexhaustible inventiveness
seems to have been at fault. Consequently what we see is an extraordinary power for form functioning relatively *in vacuo*, and
existing only to sustain itself.

In the best of the novels, however,—and it is difficult to
choose between *The Sound and the Fury* and *The Wild Palms*,
with *Absalom, Absalom!* a very close third,—this tendency to
hypertrophy of form has been sufficiently curbed; and it is interesting, too, to notice that in all these three (and in that remarkable *tour de force, As I Lay Dying*, as well), while there is still
a considerable reliance on time-shift, the effect of richness and
complexity is chiefly obtained by a very skillful fugue-like alternation of viewpoint. Fugue-like in *The Wild Palms*—and fugue-like
especially, of course, in *As I Lay Dying*, where the shift is kalei-
doscopically rapid, and where, despite an astonishing violence to
plausibility (in the reflections, and *language* of reflection, of the
characters) an effect of the utmost reality and immediateness is
nevertheless produced. Fugue-like, again, in *Absalom, Absalom!*
where indeed one may say the form is really circular—there is
no beginning and no ending properly speaking, and therefore no
logical point of entrance: we must just submit, and follow the
circling of the author's interest, which turns a light inward towards the centre, but every moment from a new angle, a new
point of view. The story unfolds, therefore, now in one color of

light, now in another, with references backward and forward: those that refer forward being necessarily, for the moment, blind. What is complete in Mr. Faulkner's pattern, *a priori*, must nevertheless remain incomplete for us until the very last stone is in place; what is "real," therefore, at one stage of the unfolding, or from one point of view, turns out to be "unreal" from another; and we find that one among other things with which we are engaged is the fascinating sport of trying to separate truth from legend, watching the growth of legend from truth, and finally reaching the conclusion that the distinction is itself false.

Something of the same sort is true also of *The Sound and the Fury*—and this, with its massive four-part symphonic structure, is perhaps the most beautifully *wrought* of the whole series, and an indubitable masterpiece of what James loved to call the "fictive art." The joinery is flawless in its intricacy; it is a novelist's novel—a whole textbook on the craft of fiction in itself, comparable in its way to *What Maisie Knew* or *The Golden Bowl*.

But if it is important, for the moment, to emphasize Mr. Faulkner's genius for form, and his continued exploration of its possibilities, as against the usual concern with the violence and dreadfulness of his themes—though we might pause to remind carpers on this score of the fact that the best of Henry James is precisely that group of last novels which so completely concerned themselves with moral depravity—it is also well to keep in mind his genius for invention, whether of character or episode. The inventiveness is of the richest possible sort—a headlong and tumultuous abundance, an exuberant generosity and vitality, which makes most other contemporary fiction look very pale and chaste indeed. It is an unforgettable gallery of portraits, whether character or caricature, and all of them endowed with a violent and immediate vitality.

"He is at once"—to quote once more from James—"one of the most corrupt of writers and one of the most naïf, the most mechanical and pedantic, and the fullest of *bonhomie* and natural impulse. He is one of the finest of artists and one of the coarsest. Viewed in one way, his novels are ponderous, shapeless, overloaded; his touch is graceless, violent, barbarous. Viewed in another, his tales have more color, more composition, more grasp of the reader's attention than any others. [His] style would demand a chapter apart. It is the least simple style, probably, that was ever written; it bristles, it cracks, it swells and swaggers; but it is a perfect expression of the man's genius. Like his genius, it contains a certain quantity of everything, from immaculate gold to flagrant dross. He was a very bad writer, and yet unquestionably he was a very great writer. We may say briefly, that in so far as his method was an instinct it was successful, and that in so far as it was a theory it was a failure. But both in instinct and in theory he had the aid of an immense force of conviction. His imagination warmed to its work so intensely that there was nothing his volition could not impose upon it. Hallucination settled upon him, and he believed anything that was necessary in the circumstances."

That passage, from Henry James's essay on Balzac, is almost word for word, with scarcely a reservation, applicable to Mr. Faulkner. All that is lacking is Balzac's greater *range* of understanding and tenderness, his greater freedom from special preoccupations. For this, one would hazard the guess that Mr. Faulkner has the gifts—and time is still before him.

WILLIAM FAULKNER'S STYLE

WARREN BECK

No OTHER contemporary American novelist of comparable stature has been as frequently or as severely criticized for his style as has William Faulkner. Yet he is a brilliantly original and

Reprinted with permission from *American Prefaces,* Spring, 1941, pp. 195–211.

versatile stylist. The condemnations of his way of writing have been in part just; all but the most idolatrous of Faulkner's admirers must have wished he had blotted a thousand infelicities. However, an enumeration of his faults in style would leave still unsaid the most important things about his style. There is need here for a reapportionment of negative and positive criticism.

It is true that the preponderant excellences of Faulkner's prose, when recognized, make his faults all the more conspicuous and irritating. And under criticism Faulkner has not only remained guilty of occasional carelessness, especially in sentence construction, but seems to have persisted in mannerisms. On the other hand, his progress as a stylist has been steady and rapid; his third novel, *Sartoris*, while still experimenting toward a technique, was a notable advance over his first two in style as well as in theme and narrative structure, and in his fourth novel, *The Sound and the Fury*, style is what it has continued to be in all his subsequent work, a significant factor, masterfully controlled. This growth has been made largely without the aid of appreciative criticism, and in the face of some misunderstanding and abuse of the most dynamic qualities in his writing. It is quite possible that Faulkner would have paid more attention to the critics' valid objections if these had not been so frequently interlarded with misconceptions of his stylistic method, or indeed complete insensitivity to it.

Repetition of words, for instance, has often seemed an obvious fault. At times, however, Faulkner's repetitions may be a not unjustifiable by-product of his thematic composition. Some of his favorites in *Absalom, Absalom!*—not just Miss Rosa's "demon," which may be charged off to her own mania, nor "indolent" applied to Bon, but such recurrent terms as effluvium, outrage, grim, indomitable, ruthless, fury, fatality—seem to intend adumbration of the tale's whole significance and tone. Nor is the reiteration as frequent or as obvious here as in earlier books; perhaps Faulkner has been making an experiment over which he is increasingly gaining control.

Faulkner often piles up words in a way that brings the

charge of prolixity. He has Wilbourne say of his life with Charlotte in Chicago,

it was the mausoleum of love, it was the stinking catafalque of the dead corpse borne between the olfactoryless walking shapes of the immortal unsentient demanding ancient meat.

However, these word-series, while conspicuous at times, may have a place in a style as minutely analytical as Faulkner's. In their typical form they are not redundant, however elaborate, and sometimes their cumulative effect is undeniable—for example, the "long still hot weary dead September afternoon" when Quentin listens to Miss Rosa's story. Colonel Feinman, the wealthy exploiter of impecunious aviators, had as secretary "a young man, sleek, in horn rim glasses," who spoke "with a kind of silken insolence, like the pampered intelligent hateridden eunuchmountebank of an eastern despot," and here the amplification redounds to the significance of the whole scene. Quite often, too, these series of words, while seemingly extravagant, are a remarkably compressed rendering, as in the phrase "passionate tragic ephemeral loves of adolescence."

In fairness it must be noted too that Faulkner's later work never drops to the level of fantastic verbosity found in the thematic paragraph introducing his second novel, *Mosquitoes*. Nor does he any longer break the continuum of his narrative with rhapsodies like the notable description of the mule in *Sartoris*, a sort of cadenza obviously done out of exuberance. In the later books profuseness of language is always knit into the thematic structure. Thus the elaborate lyrical descriptions of the sunrise and of a spring rain in book three of *The Hamlet* furnish by their imagery and mood a sharp, artistically serviceable contrast to the perversion of the idiot Ike Snopes, and as such they deepen the melancholy perspective from which this episode is observed.

Faulkner's studied use of a full style and his sense of its place in the architectonics of an extended and affecting narrative is well displayed in the last chapters of *Light in August*, chapter nineteen closing with the first climax, of Joe Christmas' death, poetically expressed; chapter twenty closing similarly in the second and more comprehensive climax of Hightower's final vision; and then chapter twenty-one, which completes the book, furnishing a modulation to detached calm through the simply prosaic, somewhat humorous account, by a new and neutral spokesman, of the exodus of Lena and Byron into Tennessee. Indeed, one of the best indexes to the degree of Faulkner's control of eloquence is in a comparison of the novels' conclusions—some of them in a full descriptive style, as in *Soldiers' Pay, Sartoris, Sanctuary*, and to a degree in *The Sound and the Fury* and *The Unvanquished*; more of the novels closing with a meaningful but plainly stated utterance or gesture of a character, as in *Mosquitoes, As I Lay Dying, Pylon, Absalom, Absalom!, The Wild Palms*, and *The Hamlet*—(the last that wonderful "Snopes turned his head and spat over the wagon wheel. He jerked the reins slightly. 'Come up,' he said.") This ratio suggests that while Faulkner does not avoid elaboration, neither is he its slave.

Faulkner's diction, charged and proliferate though it may be, usually displays a nice precision, and this is especially evident in its direct imagery. An example is in the glimpse of Cash, after he has worked all night in the rain, finishing his mother's coffin:

In the lantern light his face is calm, musing; slowly he strokes his hands on his raincoated thighs in a gesture deliberate, final and composed.

Frequently, however, Faulkner proceeds in descriptive style beyond epithet and abstract definition to figurative language. Having written,

It is just dawn, daylight: that gray and lonely suspension filled with the peaceful and tentative waking of birds.

he goes on in the next sentence to a simile:

The air, inbreathed, is like spring water.

The novels abound in examples of his talent for imaginative comparisons; for instance, the hard-boiled flier Shumann, dressed up:

He wore a new gray homburg hat, not raked like in the department store cuts but set square on the back of his head so that (not tall, with blue eyes in a square thin profoundly sober face) he looked out not from beneath it but from within it with open and fatal humorlessness, like an early Briton who has been assured that the Roman governor will not receive him unless he wear the borrowed centurion's helmet.

There is nothing unique, however, in Faulkner's use of direct and forceful diction or fine figurative image. What is most individual in his style is its persistent lyrical embroidery and coloring, in extended passages, of the narrative theme. In this sense Faulkner is one of the most subjective of writers, his brooding temperament constantly probing and interpreting his subject matter. Thus his full style is comprehensive in its intention. He may often be unfashionably rhapsodic, but he seldom falls into the preciosity that lingers over a passage for its own sweet sake. Definition of his story as a whole and the enhancement of its immediate appeals to the imagination are his constant aims.

The latest of Faulkner's novels demonstrates the grasp he has developed upon all the devices of his style. *The Hamlet* is a sort of prose fantasia; the various episodes employ colloquial tall stories, poetic description, folk humor, deliberate reflective narration, swift cryptic drama, and even a grotesque allegory, of Snopes in hell. Differing in tone from the elegiac brooding of *Light in August*, or the exasperated volubility of *Pylon*, the modulant intricacy and fusion of *Absalom, Absalom!*, the tender directness of *The Unvanquished*, or the eloquent turbulence of *The Wild Palms*, *The Hamlet* seems an extravaganza improvised more freely in a more detached mood, the author apparently delighting in the realizations of varied subject-matters through the flexibilities of his multiform style.

A number of passages in *The Hamlet* give precise indications of Faulkner's purpose as a stylist, inasmuch as they are reworkings of material released as short stories in magazines from four to nine years before the novel's publication. "Spotted Horses," which appeared in *Scribner's* for June, 1931, contains in germ Flem Snopes' whole career in *The Hamlet*. The story is in first person; Ratliff is the reciter, but he is not quite the shrewd and benevolent spectator he becomes under the touches of Faulkner's own descriptions in the third-person narrative of the novel. The short story moves faster, of course, sketching the drama more broadly and making no pause for brooding lyrical interpretation. Faulkner's omniscient narration of the episode is almost twice as long as Ratliff's simple monologue, and rises to an altogether different plane of conception and diction. The contrast is almost like that between a ballad and a tone poem.

This difference, which certainly must indicate Faulkner's free and considered choice and his fundamental aesthetic inclination, can be defined by a comparison of parallel passages from the horse-auction scene, when the Texan tries to hold one of the animals and continue his salestalk. The Scribner short story, with Ratliff as first-person narrator, reads as follows:

"Look it over," he says, with his heels dug too and that white pistol sticking outen his pocket and his neck swole up like a spreading adder's until you could just tell what he was saying, cussing the horse and talking to us all at once: "Look him over, the fiddle-headed son of fourteen fathers. Try him, buy him, you will get the best—" Then it was all dust again, and we couldn't see nothing but spotted hide and mane, and that ere Texas man's boot-heels like a couple of walnuts on two strings, and after a while that two-gallon hat come sailing out like a fat old hen crossing a fence. When the dust settled again, he was just getting outen the far fence corner, brushing himself off. He come and got his hat and brushed it off and come and clumb onto the gate post again.

In the novel the parallel passage has been recast in the third person thus:

"Look him over, boys," the Texan panted, turning his own suffused face and the protuberant glare of his eyes toward the fence. "Look him over quick. Them shoulders and—" He had relaxed for an instant apparently. The animal exploded again; again for an instant the Texan was free of the earth, though he was still talking: "—and legs you whoa I'll tear your face right look him over quick boys worth fifteen dollars of let me get a holt of who'll make me a bid whoa you blare-eyed jack rabbit, whoa!" They were moving now—a kaleidoscope of inextricable and incredible violence on the periphery of which the metal clasps of the Texan's suspenders sun-glinted in ceaseless orbit, with terrific slowness across the lot. Then the broad clay-colored hat soared deliberately outward; an instant later the Texan followed it, though still on his feet, and the pony shot free in mad, stag-like bounds. The Texan picked up the hat and struck the dust from it against his leg, and returned to the fence and mounted the post again.

Obviously the difference is not only quantitative but qualitative. Instead of Ratliff's "that old two-gallon hat come sailing out like a fat old hen crossing a fence" there is Faulkner's "the broad clay-colored hat soared deliberately outward"; Ratliff sees "that ere Texas man's bootheels like a couple of walnuts on two strings," but Faulkner shows a "kaleidoscope of inextricable and incredible violence on the periphery of which the metal clasps of the Texan's suspenders sun-glinted in ceaseless orbit with terrific slowness across the lot." This latter represents the style Faulkner has chosen to develop; he can do the simpler and more objective narration, but when given such an opportunity as in the amalgamating of these magazine stories into a novel, he insists on transmuting the factual-objective into the descriptive-definitive colored by his imagination and elaborated by his resourcefulness in language.

In its typical exercise this style gives image only incidentally and exists primarily to enhance and sustain mood. Thus Wilbourne's first approach to the house where his meeting with Charlotte is to begin their passionate and disastrous love story is set in this key:

...they entered: a court paved with the same soft, quietly rotting brick. There was a stagnant pool with a terra-cotta figure, a mass of lantana, the single palm, the thick rich leaves and the heavy white stars of the jasmine bush where light fell upon it through open French doors, the court balcony—overhung too on three sides, the walls of that same annealing brick lifting a rampart broken and nowhere level against the glare of the city on the low eternally overcast sky, and over all, brittle, dissonant and ephemeral, the spurious sophistication of the piano like symbols scrawled by adolescent boys upon an ancient decayed rodent-scavengered tomb.

The reporter's mood of anxious inquiry and the frustration which is thematic in *Pylon* are both represented as he telephones:

Now he too heard only dead wirehum, as if the other end of it extended beyond atmosphere, into cold space; as though he listened now to the profound sound of infinity, of void itself filled with the cold unceasing murmur of aeonweary and unflagging stars.

This organic quality of Faulkner's style, sustaining through essentially poetic devices an orchestration of meaning, makes it impossible to judge him adequately by brief quotation. In the description of Temple's first hours in Madam Reba's brothel, for instance, the thematic recurrence from page to page to subjectively interpreted imagery builds up in a time continuum the mood of the girl's trance-like state of shock and also the larger fact of her isolation in the sordid. First,

The drawn shades, cracked into a myriad pattern like old skin, blew faintly on the bright air, breathing into the room on waning surges the sound of Sabbath traffic, festive, steady, evanescent . . .

and then, three pages further,

The shades blew steadily in the windows, with faint rasping sounds. Temple began to hear a clock. It sat on the mantel above a grate filled with fluted green paper. The clock was of flowered china, supported by four china nymphs. It had only one hand, scrolled and gilded, halfway between ten and eleven, lending to the otherwise blank face a quality of unequivocal assertion, as though it had nothing whatever to do with time.

and then, two pages further,

In the window the cracked shade, yawning now and then with a faint rasp against the frame, let twilight into the room in fainting surges. From beneath the shade the smoke-colored twilight emerged in slow puffs like signal smoke from a blanket, thickening in the room. The china figures which supported the clock gleamed in hushed smooth flexions: knee, elbow, flank, arm and breast in attitudes of voluptuous lassitude. The glass face, become mirror-like, appeared to hold all reluctant light, holding in its tranquil depths a quiet gesture of mori-

bund time, one-armed like a veteran from the wars. Half past ten
o'clock. Temple lay in the bed, looking at the clock, thinking about
half-past-ten-oclock.

Yet side by side with this richly interpretative style there
exists in almost all of Faulkner's work a realistic colloquialism,
expressing lively dialogue that any playwright might envy, and
even carrying over into sustained first-person narrative the flavor
of regionalism and the idiosyncrasies of character. In the colloquial vein Faulkner's brilliance is unsurpassed in contemporary
American fiction. He has fully mastered the central difficulty, to
retain verisimilitude while subjecting the prolix and monotonous
raw material of most natural speech to an artistic pruning and
pointing up. *Sanctuary*, for an example, is full of excellent
dialogue, sharply individualized. And Faulkner's latest book[1] not
only contains some of his most poetic writing but has one of his
best talkers, Ratliff, both in extended anecdote in monologue and
in dramatic conversations. Ratliff's reflective, humorous, humane,
but skeptical nature, a triumph in characterization, is silhouetted
largely out of his talk about the hamlet's affairs.

Faulkner also can weave colloquial bits into the matrix of a
more literary passage, with the enlarging effect of a controlled
dissonance. Thus Quentin imagines Henry Sutpen and Charles
Bon, at the end of the war, Charles determined to marry Judith,
Henry forbidding; and then into Quentin's elaboration of the
scene breaks the voice of his father, continuing the story, giving
its denouement in the words vulgarly uttered by Wash Jones:

(It seemed to Quentin that he could actually see them. . . . They faced
one another on the two gaunt horses, two men, young, not yet in the
world, not yet breathed over long enough, to be old but with old eyes,
with unkempt hair and faces gaunt and weathered as if cast by some
spartan and even niggard hand from bronze, in worn and patched gray
weathered now to the color of dead leaves, the one with the tarnished
braid of an officer, the other plain of cuff, the pistol lying yet across
the saddle bow unaimed, the two faces calm, the voices not even

1. *The Hamlet* (New York, 1940) [editor's note].

raised: *Dont you pass the shadow of this post, this branch, Charles*;
and *I am going to pass it, Henry*)—and then Wash Jones sitting that
saddleless mule before Miss Rosa's gate, shouting her name into the
sunny and peaceful quiet of the street, saying, "Air you Rosie Coldfield? Then you better come on out yon. Henry has done shot that
durn French feller. Kilt him dead as a beef."

Master of colloquialism in dramatic scene though he is,
Faulkner sometimes lays aside this power in order to put into
a character's mouth the fullest expression of the narrative's meaning. The mature Bayard Sartoris, looking back to Civil War times,
telling the story of his boyhood and youth in *The Unvanquished*,
opens what is Faulkner's most straightforward narrative, and his
only novel related throughout by one character in first person,
in this strain:

Behind the smokehouse that summer, Ringo and I had a living map.
Although Vicksburg was just a handful of chips from the woodpile
and the River a trench scraped into the packed earth with the point of
a hoe, it (river, city, and terrain) lived, possessing even in miniature
that ponderable though passive recalcitrance of topography which
outweighs artillery, against which the most brilliant of victories and
the most tragic of defeats are but the loud noises of a moment.

At times it seems as though the author, after having created an
unsophisticated character, is elbowing him off the stage, as when
the rustic Darl Bundren sees "the square squat shape of the coffin
on the sawhorses like a cubistic bug," or as when in the short
story, "All The Dead Pilots," the World War flier John Sartoris is
characterized as having a vocabulary of "perhaps two hundred
words" and then is made to say,

...I knew that if I busted in and dragged him out and bashed his head
off, I'd not only be cashiered, I'd be clinked for life for having infringed
the articles of alliance by invading foreign property without warrant
or something.

For the most part, however, the transcending of colloquial verisimilitude in the novels is a fairly controlled and consistent technique, the characters Faulkner most often endows with pene-

tration and eloquence being his philosophical spectators. Undoubtedly his chief concern, though, is with a lyric encompassment of his narrative's whole meaning rather than with the reticences of objective dramatic representation.

Thus many of his characters speak with the tongues of themselves and of William Faulkner. As Quentin and his Harvard roommate Shreve evolve the reconstruction of Thomas Sutpen's story which constitutes the second half of *Absalom, Absalom!*, Quentin thinks when Shreve talks, "He sounds just like father," and later, when Quentin has the floor, Shreve interrupts with "Don't say it's just me that sounds like your old man," which certainly shows that Faulkner realizes what he is doing. Actually he does make some differences among these voices: Miss Rosa rambles and ejaculates with erratic spinsterish emotion, Mr. Compson is elaborately and sometimes parenthetically ironic, Quentin is most sensitively imaginative and melancholy, Shreve most detached and humorous. What they have in common is the scope and pitch of an almost lyrical style which Faulkner has arbitrarily fixed upon for an artistic instrument. The justification of all such practices is empirical; imaginative writing must not be judged by its minute correspondence to fact but by its total effect; and to object against Faulkner's style that men and women don't really talk in such long sentences, with so full a vocabulary so fancifully employed, is as narrowly dogmatic as was Sinclair Lewis, in *Main Street*, insisting that Sir Launcelot didn't actually speak in "honeyed pentameters."

Typical instances of Faulkner's endowing his characters with precise diction and fluency may show that on the whole it is not an unacceptable convention. Thus Wilbourne's full and finished sentence,

We lived in an apartment that wasn't bohemian, it wasn't even a tabloid love-nest, it wasn't even in that part of town but in a neighborhood dedicated by both city ordinance and architecture to the second year of wedlock among the five-thousand-a-year bracket.

though it is not stylistically rooted in his manner as characterized up to this point, is not inconsistent with his personality and sensibilities, and it does get on with the story. Equally acceptable is Ratliff's remark about the platitudinous family-fleeing I. O. Snopes,

What's his name? that quick-fatherer, the Moses with his mouth full of mottoes and his coat-tail full of them already half-grown retroactive sons?

Its keen diction and nice rhythm are not essentially false to Ratliff, but only an idealization in language of the percipient humorous sewing-machine salesman the reader already knows. The same is true of those tumbling floods of phrases, too prolonged for human breath to utter, with which the reporter in *Pylon* assaults the sympathies of editor Hagood; they are not so much a part of dialogue as an intense symbol of the pace of racing aviation and the reporter's frantic concern for his protégés among the fliers.

It is interesting to note that Faulkner's full style somewhat resembles older literary uses, such as the dramatic chorus, the prologue and epilogue, and the *dramatis personae* themselves in soliloquy and extended speech. The aim of any such device is not objective realism but revelation of theme, a revelation raised by the unstinted resourcefulness and power of its language to the highest ranges of imaginative outlook. No wonder that with such a purpose Faulkner often comes closer than is common in these times to Shakespeare's imperial and opulent use of words. If unfortunately his ambition has sometimes led Faulkner to perpetrate some rather clotted prose, perhaps these lapses may be judged charitably in the light of the great endeavor they but infrequently flaw.

More particularly Faulkner's full sentence structure springs from the elaborateness of his fancies ramifying in descriptive imagery. Thus editor Hagood, perpetually beset by small annoyances and chronically irritated by them, drops himself wearily into his roadster's low seat,

... whereupon without sound or warning the golfbag struck him across the head and shoulder with an apparently calculated and lurking viciousness, emitting a series of dry clicks as though produced by the jaws of a beast domesticated though not tamed, half in fun and half in deadly seriousness, like a pet shark.

Another typical source of fullness in Faulkner's sentences is a tendency to musing speculation, sometimes proceeding to the statement of alternative suggestions. Thus Miss Rosa speaks of wearing garments left behind by the eloping aunt in "kindness or haste or oversight," that doing its bit in a sentence well over three hundred words long. Such characteristic theorizing may run to the length of this postscript to a description of Flem Snopes:

...a thick squat soft man of no establishable age between twenty and thirty, with a broad still face containing a tight seam of mouth stained slightly at the corners with tobacco, and eyes the color of stagnant water, and projecting from among the other features in startling and sudden paradox, a tiny predatory nose like the beak of a small hawk. It was as though the original nose had been left off by the original designer or craftsman and the unfinished job taken over by someone of a radically different school or perhaps by some viciously maniacal humorist or perhaps by one who had only time to clap into the center of the face a frantic and desperate warning.

Even the most elaborate and esoteric of these speculations are not limited to third-person narrative; Faulkner's pervasive subjectivity injects such abstractions too, as well as extended imagery, into the reflections and speech of many of his characters, again most typically those who contemplate and interpret the action of the stories, who act as chorus or soliloquize. Here too the device proves itself in practice. When such characters brood over the events, painstakingly rehearsing details, piling one hypothesis upon another, their very tentativeness creates for the reader the clouded enigmatic perspective of reality itself. Thus Miss Rosa's account, with reinterpretation imposed upon memory, of Sutpen's driving in to church with his family:

It was as though the sister whom I had never laid eyes on, who before I was born had vanished into the stronghold of an ogre or a djinn, was now to return through a dispensation of one day only, to the world which she had quitted, and I a child of three, waked early for the occasion, dressed and curled as if for Christmas, for an occasion more serious than Christmas even, since now and at last this ogre or djinn had agreed for the sake of the wife and the children to come to church, to permit them at least to approach the vicinity of salvation, to at least give Ellen one chance to struggle with him for those children's souls on a battleground where she could be supported not only by Heaven but by her own family and people of her own kind; yes, even for the moment submitting himself to redemption, or lacking that, at least chivalrous for the instant even though still unregenerate.

The foregoing examples, however, do not illustrate Faulkner's style at its most involved, as in this passage from Quentin's consciousness, while he listens to Miss Rosa's reconstruction of the Sutpen family history:

It should have been later than it was; it should have been late, yet the yellow slashes of mote-palpitant sunlight were latticed no higher up the impalpable wall of gloom which separated them; the sun seemed hardly to have moved. It (the talking, the telling) seemed (to him, to Quentin) to partake of that logic- and reason-flouting quality of a dream which the sleeper knows must have occurred, stillborn and complete, in a second, yet the very quality upon which it must depend to move the dreamer (verisimilitude) to credulity—horror or pleasure or amazement—depends as completely upon a formal recognition of and acceptance of elapsed and yet-elapsing time as music or a printed tale.

By its parentheses and involution and fullness this last sentence illustrates that occasionally extreme eccentricity most often and most rightfully objected to in its author's style. At the same time this sentence may give a key to Faulkner's entire method and typify its artistic purposefulness—to create "that logic- and reason-flouting quality of a dream," yet to depend upon the recognized verisimilitude of "elapsed and yet-elapsing time." Such a product is not necessarily mere nightmare; it is often a real quality of experience at its greatest intensity and acuteness. In his most characteristic writing Faulkner is trying to render the transcendent life of the mind, the crowded composite of associative and analytical consciousness which expands the vibrant moment into the reaches of all time, simultaneously observing, remembering, interpreting, and modifying the object of its awareness. To this end the sentence as a rhetorical unit (however strained) is made to hold diverse yet related elements in a sort of saturated solution, which is perhaps the nearest that language as the instrument of fiction can come to the instantaneous complexities of consciousness itself. Faulkner really seems to be trying to give narrative prose another dimension.

To speak of Faulkner's fiction as dream-like (using Quentin's notion as a key) does not imply that his style is phantasmagoric, deranged, or incoherent. Dreams are not always delirium; and association, sometimes the supplanter of pattern, can also be its agent. The dreaming mind, while envisaging experience strangely, may find in that strangeness a fresh revelation, all the more profound in that the conventional and adventitious are pierced through. Similarly inhibitions and apathies must be transcended in any really imaginative inquiry, and thus do Faulkner's speculative characters ponder over the whole story, and project into cumulative drama its underlying significations. Behind all of them, of course, is their master-dreamer; Faulkner's own dominating temperament, constantly interpreting, is in the air of all these narratives, reverberant. Hence no matter how psychological the story's material, Faulkner never falls into the mere enumeration which in much stream-of-consciousness writing dissolves all drama and reduces the narrative to a case history without the shaping framework of analysis, or even to an unmapped anachronistic chaos of raw consciousness. Faulkner is always a dynamic story-teller, never just a reporter of unorganized phenomena. His most drastic, most dream-like use of stream-of-consciousness, for instance, in *The Sound and the Fury*, is not only limited to the first two sections of the book, but it sketches a plot which in the lucid sections that follow gradually emerges clear-cut.

As clear-cut, at least, as Faulkner's stories can be. Here

again is illustrated the close relation of his style to his whole point of view. If Faulkner's sentences sometimes soar and circle involved and prolonged, if his scenes become halls of mirrors repeating tableaux in a progressive magnification, if echoes multiply into the dissonance of infinite overtones, it is because the meanings his stories unfold are complex, mysterious, obscure, and incomplete. There is no absolute, no eternal pure white radiance in such presentations, but rather the stain of many colors, refracted and shifting in kaleidoscopic suspension, about the center of man's enigmatic behavior and fate, within the drastic orbit of mortality. Such being Faulkner's view of life, such is his style.

To this view the very rhythm of Faulkner's prose is nicely adjusted. It is not emphatic; rather it is a slow prolonged movement, nothing dashing, even at its fullest flood, but surging with an irresistible momentum. His effects insofar as they depend on prose rhythms are never staccato, they are cumulative rather than abrupt. Such a prose rhythm supplements the contributions of full vocabulary and lengthy sentence toward suspension rather than impact, and consequently toward deep realization rather than quick surprise. And the prolonged even murmur of Faulkner's voice throughout his pages is an almost hypnotic induction into those detailed and darkly colored visions of life which drift across the horizons of his imagination like clouds—great yet vaporous, changing yet enduring, unearthly yet of common substance. It might be supposed that his occasionally crowded and circumlocutory style would destroy narrative pace and consequence. Actually this hovering of active imagination, while employing the sustained lyricism and solid abstraction which differentiate Faulkner from the objective realist, furnishes the epitome of drama. The whole aim is at perspective, through the multiple dimensions of experience, upon a subject in that suspension which allows reflection. The accomplishment is the gradual, sustained, and enriched revelation of meaning; in Faulkner's novels drama is of that highest form which awaits the unfolding of composite action, characterization, mood, and idea, through the medium of style.

Faulkner himself probably would admit the relative inadequacy of instrument to purpose, would agree with Mr. Compson in calling language "that meager and fragile thread by which the little surface corners and edges of men's secret and solitary lives may be joined for an instant." Faulkner perhaps has no greater faith in the word than have his contemporaries who have partially repudiated it, but instead of joining that somewhat paradoxical literary trend, he seems determined to exploit an imperfect device to the uttermost within the limits of artistic illusion. Thus although in certain passages he has demonstrated his command of a simplified objective method, he has not made it his invariable device, nor does he allow its contemporary vogue to prevent his using words in the old-fashioned way for whatever they are worth descriptively and definitively.

Faulkner's whole narrative method, as described, may seem to be a retrogression in technique. Two main tendencies in modern fiction have been toward a more and more material dramatic presentation, depending simply upon the naming of objects and acts and the reporting of speech, and on the other hand, toward an ostensibly complete and unbroken reproduction of the free flow of consciousness. These methods have produced books as radically different as *The Sun Also Rises* and *Ulysses*, yet they have elements in common. In both types the author attempts to conceal himself completely behind his materials, to give them the quality of integral phenomena, and in line with this purpose the style aims at pure reproduction, never allowing definition and interpretation from any detached point of view. These have been honest attempts, a great deal of fine craftsmanship has gone into them, and some of the products have been excellent in their kind. Yet at their most extreme these have been movements in the one direction toward bareness, impoverishment, and in the other toward incoherence. Confronted by the imperfections and confusions of the present scene, and made hyperskeptical by deference to scientific method, the writers who have attempted absolute objectivity (whether dramatic or psychological, whether in overt event or stream of association) have sometimes produced what looks like an anti-intellectual aesthetic of futility and inconsequence. So in another sense Faulkner's narrative technique, particularly as implemented by his full style, instead of being a retrogression may represent one kind of progression through the danger of impasse created by too great submission to vogues of photographic or psychographic reproduction.

Yet Faulkner's is not altogether a return to an older expressiveness, not a complete departure from the modern schools of Hemingway and Joyce. In his colloquial passages he is quite as objectively dramatic as the one, in his rehearsal of the fantasies of acute consciousness he follows the other—and it should be remembered that he is superlatively skillful at both, so that it cannot be said that he puts these objective methods aside because he cannot use them. Furthermore, Faulkner is fond of employing in extended passages one of the favorite modern means of objectivity in fiction, the first-person narrator, using the device toward its most honored modern purpose, the attainment of detached perspective and the creation of realistic illusion concerning large vistas of the story. In short, there is no method in modern fiction which Faulkner does not comprehend and use on occasion. Fundamentally Faulkner's only heterodoxy by present standards of style is his fullness, especially as it takes the form of descriptive eloquence or abstraction and definitiveness. What is stylistically most remarkable in his work is the synthesis he has effected between the subtleties of modern narrative techniques and the resources of language employed in the traditionally poetic or interpretative vein. That such a synthesis is feasible is demonstrated in the dynamic forms of his novels, and it may be prelude to significant new developments in the methods of fiction.

IV. The Work:

Studies of Individual Novels and Stories

THE TECHNIQUE OF *THE SOUND AND THE FURY*

LAWRENCE EDWARD BOWLING

ALTHOUGH Faulkner's critics are frequently at variance on many issues, they all concur on one point—that his narrative technique is extremely intricate and perplexing. Having agreed upon this, however, they divide into two groups: those who feel that this complexity is justified and those who hold that it is an unnecessary obstacle. Taking the latter point of view, Granville Hicks says, "One can almost imagine Mr. Faulkner inventing his stories in the regular chronological order and then recasting them in some distorted form."[1]

Of all Faulkner's prose writings *The Sound and the Fury* is the most complex; it is also one of his best works. It is not one of his most popular works, for its unusual technique is confusing to most readers and prejudices many of them against the book to the point of laying it aside without a complete and fair hearing. Therefore, if Faulkner is to go on trial for his involved technique, this novel makes an appropriate test case.

There is certainly nothing about the first two pages of this novel to entangle or frighten away the average reader. The most unusual characteristic of the writing is its flat simplicity. It is

Reprinted with permission from *The Kenyon Review*, Autumn, 1948, pp. 552–566.
1. "The Past and Future of William Faulkner," *The Bookman*, September, 1931, p. 22.

composed of simple words and much repetition; the basic structural unit is the simple sentence; the question mark and the exclamation point are reduced to the period. The narrator formulates no abstract ideas or explanations but records only what he perceives through the physical senses. All this implies on the part of the narrator an undiscriminating mind—a mind which does not distinguish among a statement of fact, an exclamation, a question and a command, and does not recognize any relation between one external fact and another. As the reader soon discovers, Benjy is an idiot, to whom life is a tale full of sound and fury signifying very little.

On the basis of the author's use of the first person and the past tense, the reader assumes that the story is going to be an ordinary first-person, objective rendering of a past experience, similar in technique to Hemingway's *A Farewell to Arms*. In the first two pages of the book, there is nothing to contradict and everything to support this assumption, until the reader encounters the italicized paragraphs on page three. This passage introduces the first main hurdle in the book and requires detailed consideration, for without a clear understanding of what is taking place here, the reader can never hope to get even to first base with *The Sound and the Fury*:

We went along the fence and came to the garden fence, where our shadows were. My shadow was higher than Luster's on the fence. We came to the broken place and went through it.

"Wait a minute." Luster said. "You snagged on that nail again. Cant you never crawl through here without snagging on that nail."

Caddy uncaught me and we crawled through. Uncle Maury said to not let anybody see us, so we better stoop over, Caddy said. Stoop over, Benjy. Like this, see. We stooped over and crossed the garden, where the flowers rasped and rattled against us. The ground was hard. We climbed the fence, where the pigs were grunting and snuffing. I expect they're sorry because one of them got killed today, Caddy said. The ground was hard, churned and knotted.

Keep your hands in your pockets, Caddy said. Or they'll get froze. You don't want your hands froze on Christmas, do you.

"It's too cold out there." Versh said. "You dont want to go out doors."

"What is it now." Mother said.

"He want to go out doors." Versh said.

"Let him go." Uncle Maury said.

If the reader can grasp the key to this passage, he is well on the way to understanding the technique employed in the first section of the book. The problem is to discover by what means the story is suddenly shifted from Benjy and Luster on April 7, 1928, to Benjy and Caddy in the Christmas season of some other year, and just as suddenly shifted again to Benjy, Versh, and Mother. In solving this problem, the reader finally realizes that the first two pages of the novel (up to the italicized passage) are not a regular first-person, external rendering of a *past* experience but are, despite the use of the past tense, a stream of consciousness rendering of a *present* action.

In the first paragraph of this passage, the thirty-three-year-old idiot Benjy and his fourteen-year-old colored bodyguard Luster are coming back from the golf course. They arrive at a broken place in the fence and start to crawl through. Benjy snags on a nail. This snagging experience recalls to his mind a similar childhood experience of crawling through a fence with his sister Caddy and snagging on a nail about twenty-five years ago. This association of ideas causes his mind to break off from the present experience and continue in the earlier experience.

However, at the end of the italicized passage Benjy's mind does not return to the present but shifts again (because of certain associations) to another past experience with Mother, Versh, and Uncle Maury. His mind continues in this second past experience until Caddy comes in from school (in the past experience) and takes him out for a walk; while she is talking to him, he begins crying (in the present experience) and this causes Luster to interrupt the recall of the past experience by scolding Benjy.

As is characteristic of Benjy, his backward-looking mind returns to the present only long enough to be reminded of another fragment from his past. In this case, the sight of a carriage becomes a new associative stimulus (as the nail had been before) and causes the needle of Benjy's attention to drop into the recording at the point of his going to the cemetery with his mother ten or twelve years ago. In this manner, Benjy's mind continues throughout the first section of the book, jumping capriciously back and forth between the present and thirty years of transcribed past experience. What first appeared to be a straightforward, first-person narrative turns out to be a unique stream of consciousness rendering of Benjy's mind during part of one day in this idiot's life.

Although this discovery is a major move in the right direction, there are numerous other problems which arise out of the nature of this narrative method, for the stream of consciousness technique tends to break down three stabilizing elements traditionally considered fundamental in narrative fiction: exposition, plot, and chronological order. The average reader is accustomed to the type of novel which begins with a certain amount of exposition, moves into the main plot, and follows this action in chronological order to the resolution of the conflict. He has become accustomed to reading stories with a beginning, a middle, and an end—for this has been the conventional method of storytelling employed all the way back to the *Iliad* and the Book of Genesis, which begins with "the beginning."

But this is not Faulkner's method in *The Sound and the Fury*. He begins at the end and works backward. The fragments from Benjy's past are presented not in the chronological order in which they occurred but in the order in which chance associations cause him to recall them. The last pages of this section deal with the earliest of Benjy's recalled experiences, his going to bed with his brothers Quentin and Jason and his sister Caddy when he was three years old. Thus, Benjy's section ends on a note thirty years before it began.

Serious violation of chronology is not in itself an insuperable obstacle, provided that the separate units are fairly large and are focused around a central plot, as is the case in Conrad's stories. But in the first section of *The Sound and the Fury* many of the recalled passages are only a few lines in length and appear to have almost no relation to each other or to a central plot. Furthermore, the author offers absolutely no assistance by way of exposition. The only editorial liberty which he takes with Benjy's mental processes is the use of italics to indicate the point at which his mind shifts from one fragment to another. It is as if the author said: "Here's an idiot; it's you and him for it"—except that Faulkner never goes so far as to say that Benjy is an idiot.

We find ourselves alone with the idiot Benjy, trying to get the necessary information from him. In this we are handicapped on two counts: first: since Benjy is not aware that we are eavesdropping his thoughts, it does not occur to him to explain things for our benefit; second, he could not explain anything if he tried, for he is incapable of the simplest abstraction. His best efforts in this direction are the turning of a few simple direct quotations into indirect quotations. Even this much cerebration seems almost out of character for Benjy. Throughout the whole book, he does not manage to speak one word and gives little indication that he understands human speech, except what he can gather from the tone of the voice. To expect Benjy to explain the phenomena which his mind perceives is like expecting a phonograph to comment upon a recording. All his mind does is reproduce what it takes in through the physical senses. His section of the book is probably the most thoroughgoing sustained effort in impressionistic writing in all literature. Any passage from his section will illustrate this point, but the best example is the description of his burning his hand:

> I put my hand out to where the fire had been.
> "Catch him." Dilsey said. "Catch him back."
> My hand jerked back and I put it in my mouth and Dilsey caught me. I could still hear the clock between my voice. Dilsey reached back and hit Luster on the head. My voice was going loud every time.
> "Get that soda." Dilsey said. She took my hand out of my mouth.

My voice went louder then and my hand tried to go back to my mouth, but Dilsey held it. My voice went loud. She sprinkled soda on my hand.

This report is as objective and impressionistic as if it were rendered by an observer; it is even more impressionistic than an observer's report would be, for an observer would probably say that Benjy burned his hand. But Benjy does not once use the word *burned.* He tells us only what we would hear and see if we were there. Any conclusion on our part that he burned his hand or that pain resulted would be a pure abstraction and not a sensation perceived by the physical senses—for as Joseph Conrad and Ford Madox Ford were discovering half a century ago, "Life does not narrate but makes impressions on our brains. We in turn, if we wished to produce on you an effect of life, must not narrate but render impressions."[2]

Most of what has been said about the first section of the book will apply also to the second section, "June 2, 1910." This section is rendered exclusively by means of the stream of consciousness technique and from the mind of Benjy's oldest brother, Quentin, during one day at Harvard, where he commits suicide by drowning. Like Benjy's section, Quentin's section may be divided into two parts: that which takes place on June 2, 1910, and that which is recalled from various past experiences. It is further like Benjy's section in that it employs the past tense for present events and at first gives the impression of being a first-person narrative. In the first paragraphs, the sentence structure and the word order are as regular and logical as any first-person narrative is expected to be. A recalled speech by the father is led up to gradually and is exactly the sort of thing which a first-person narrator might put into his story in just this way. It certainly cannot be said of the first two pages that they give the reader the impression of looking directly into Quentin's mind and there observing his most intimate and fragmentary thoughts just as they

2. Ford Madox Ford: *Joseph Conrad: A Personal Remembrance,* pp. 180 ff.

are born. Rather these pages give the reader the impression that he is hearing or reading a summary narration of past events. This is true of almost all the passages dealing with the events of June 2, 1910. The writing has the tone of communication rather than the tone of self-expression. It is in the presentation of fragments from the past that this section is most convincing as stream of consciousness writing.

The technique in this section is not quite the same as that employed in the first section. The difference is due to the fact that Quentin's mind is much more complex than Benjy's. Since Benjy is incapable of the simplest abstraction, there is in his section nothing that can truly be called soliloquy. Quentin, however, is capable of thought, and we find throughout his section numerous soliloquies. Since Quentin's intellect is more highly developed than Benjy's, it is more nimble in shifting from one experience or idea to another. Although such capriciousness often makes Quentin's mental processes difficult to follow, this is no mere personal whim on the part of the author to make the section unduly perplexing. Even in the most complex and realistic passages, Faulkner has greatly simplified Quentin's mental processes in order that the reader may be able to understand them. The following representative excerpt will illustrate this point. Quentin is on a street car in Cambridge, but his mind is preoccupied with recalling a drive with his mother, his sister Candace, and her husband Herbert, shortly after their marriage on April 25, 1910. The mother is doing most of the talking:

Herbert has spoiled us all to death Quentin did I write you that he is going to take Jason into his bank when Jason finishes high school Jason will make a splendid banker he is the only one of my children with any practical sense you can thank me for that he takes after my people the others are all Compson *Jason furnished the flour. They made kites on the back porch and sold them for a nickel a piece, he and the Patterson boy. Jason was treasurer.*

There was no nigger in this street car, and the hats unbleached as yet flowing past under the window. Going to Harvard. We have sold Benjy's *He lay on the ground under the window, bellowing. We*

have sold Benjy's pasture so that Quentin may go to Harvard a brother
to you. Your little brother.

You should have a car it's done you no end of good dont you
think so Quentin I call him Quentin at once you see I have heard so
much about him from Candace.

Why shouldn't you and I want my boys to be more than friends
yes Candace and Quentin more than friends *Father I have committed*
what a pity you had no brother or sister *No sister no sister had no
sister* Dont ask Quentin he and Mr. Compson both feel a little insulted
when I am strong enough to come down to the table I am going on
nerve now I'll pay for it after it's all over and you have taken my little
daughter away from me *My little sister had no. If I could say Mother.
Mother.*

The mother's mention of Jason's practical sense and his future
job in Herbert's bank reminds Quentin of the time that Jason
demonstrated his practical wisdom at an early age. As Quentin
looks around him in the street car, his mind is temporarily recalled
to the present and to the people on the street who are "going to
Harvard." This phrase reminds him of a speech (probably by his
mother) about his own going to Harvard, but when he gets to
Benjy's name in the recalled speech, he is reminded of Benjy's
bellowing under the window at Caddy's wedding. In the next
paragraph, Herbert is obviously the speaker, and the mother is
talking again in the last paragraph. Her phrase "more than
friends" recalls to Quentin's mind the conversation in which he
tried to convince his father that he and Candace had committed
incest. The mother's remark about Herbert's not having a sister is
echoed in Quentin's mind with added emphasis until he again
begins attending what his mother is saying and follows her to
"my little daughter." He snatches up this phrase and fuses it with
had no sister to form the ambiguous fragment *My little sister had
no*—for which there are three possible interpretations, depending upon the omitted object. First, Quentin is thinking that his
sister Caddy had no *mother*, for Mrs. Compson, instead of being
the mother that she should have been to her children, has always
taken refuge in a halo of camphor and self-pity, just as she is now

doing throughout this passage; if she had been a real mother, Caddy probably would not have lost her personal honor and her family pride by allowing herself to be seduced and by finally marrying a northern banker. Second, Quentin is thinking that his little sister had no *sister*, and therefore can never understand what a sister's loss of honor means to a brother. Third, the uncompleted fragment *My little sister had no* suggests The Song of Solomon 8:8–10.[3] What is worrying Quentin is not that his sister had no *breasts* when she was little, but that she proved to be a *door* instead of a *wall* when she grew to maturity. Then was she in his eyes (and later in the eyes of her husband and the rest of her family) as one that found *dis*favor.

Since this short passage contains fragments dealing with six different time-scenes, the reader may conclude that the author has unnecessarily exaggerated the complexity of Quentin's mind. However, if he will try to imagine what a representative excerpt from his own mind would look like if transcribed onto the printed page, the reader will realize that Faulkner has actually simplified Quentin's mental activity in this passage (and throughout his section). He has eliminated all extraneous details which would not contribute to the main theme, and he has presented Quentin's mind as operating much more logically than it would in reality.

In one instance, Faulkner carries this simplification to the extreme of having Quentin's mind continue in chronological order in the same recalled experience for eighteen pages (185–203). He wants to present in an uninterrupted, dramatic unit the central memory which is the basis of Quentin's internal struggle. Since it would be unusual and out of character for Quentin's mind to recall this much of one past experience at one time without interruption, the author makes this particular in-

3. We have a little sister and she hath no breasts: what shall we do for our sister in the day when she shall be spoken for?
If she be a wall, we will build upon her a palace of silver: and if she be a door, we shall inclose her with boards of cedar.
I am a wall, and my breasts like towers: then was I in his eyes as one that found favor.

stance plausible by having the recalled unit pass through Quentin's mind while he is temporarily unconscious. The unit is not difficult to understand, but it does raise certain interesting questions. A short excerpt from near the first of the unit will illustrate the technique. Caddy has just come home after being out with Dalton Ames, and Benjy has sensed her shame and started screaming. She runs out to a nearby stream and plunges in. Quentin follows her:

> the water sucked and gurgled across the sand spit and on in the dark among the willows across the shallow the water rippled like a piece of cloth holding still a little light as water does
>
> he's crossed all the oceans all around the world
>
> then she talked about him clasping her wet knees her face tilted back in the grey light the smell of honeysuckle there was a light in mothers room and in Benjys where T. P. was putting him to bed
>
> do you love him
>
> her hand came out I didnt move it fumbled down my arm and she held my hand flat against her chest her heart thudding.
>
> no no
>
> did he make you then he made you do it let him he was stronger than you and he tomorrow Ill kill him I swear I will father neednt know until afterward

In this passage and throughout the unit, the author steers a middle course between making the material comprehensible and at the same time keeping it convincing as a stream of consciousness rendering of a past experience. The speeches and the descriptive fragments are paragraphed separately to avoid confusion. The general absence of orthodox punctuation and capitalization causes no real difficulty but does succeed in distinguishing the unit from ordinary narration and giving it the desired appearance.

One may ask: why did the author not render all of Quentin's recalled experiences in some such simplified, chronological manner as this? It would certainly have made it far less difficult for the reader to follow the main threads of the plot. This is just the question raised by Mr. Hick's remark that Faulkner seems first to have invented his stories in the regular chronological order and then recast them in a distorted form. The answer is that in the first three sections of _The Sound and the Fury_ the author is not primarily concerned with presenting the facts of a story, but with presenting the _reactions_ of certain characters to these facts and thereby revealing individual states of mind. Every simplification of the technique necessitates a corresponding simplification of the character's mental reaction and alters his state of mind to a slightly different state of mind. In the particular unit under discussion, for example, Quentin's state of mind is much less complex than it is in other parts of his section. The author had to sacrifice complexity in order to gain something else which he considered worth the temporary sacrifice. However, if the whole of Quentin's recalled experiences were rendered in this manner, the distinguishing characteristics of Quentin's state of mind would certainly be lost. That this would be the case can be seen by comparing the first three sections of the book. In each section a different variation of the stream of consciousness technique is used, and in each case the resulting state of mind of the character is different and the effect upon the reader is different.

While dealing with the interrelations of technique, content, and the desired effect upon the reader, one may ask another question: if the absence of standard punctuation and capitalization in the above passage is effective in setting it apart and giving it the illusion of a recalled experience, why did the author not use some such method as this in the first section for presenting Benjy's recalled experiences? The answer is that, by using the same punctuation and capitalization for the past experiences as for the present, the author is trying to suggest that to Benjy's undiscriminating mind the past is no less real and immediate than the present. To have made even a formal distinction between the two would have implied that Benjy was himself aware of a difference.

The third section of _The Sound and the Fury_ is almost wholly orthodox both in content and in technique and requires no detailed analysis. Although one can detect on examination that Jason's section, "April 6, 1928," is presented through a simplified version of the stream of consciousness technique, it is not necessary that the reader give any particular attention to this fact in order to understand the section. Except for a few recalled fragments, Jason's section is a straightforward first-person narrative of events taking place on April 6.

The last section, "April 8, 1928," is the most orthodox of all the sections, for it is a regular omniscient rendering of this day's events. The only characteristic which it has in common with the other three sections is the strictly objective attitude which the author maintains toward his material. Although there are a few interpretative statements in this section, these are kept at a minimum and incorporated into the main body of the material in such a way as not to attract attention to themselves or alter the prevailing tone of the section.

Most readers and critics have been baffled by the unusual arrangement of the four sections in the following unchronological order: "April 7, 1928," "June 2, 1910," "April 6, 1928," "April 8, 1928." Commenting upon this aspect of the novel, Granville Hicks says, "It is not certain that Benjy was the inevitable narrator of the history of the Compson family, or that the story could only have been told in four episodes, or that in the arrangement of these episodes chronological order had to be violated." This statement, as well as the other one quoted earlier, assumes that *The Sound and the Fury* is fundamentally a conventional type of "story" which the author is unnecessarily distorting into a difficult form. But this is hardly the case. According to this method of reckoning, Benjy's section is almost eighteen years out of its chronological order. This conclusion would be correct if each section were devoted entirely to events of the designated date. But this is true for only one section of the book, "April 8, 1928." Each of the other sections deals with two sets of events: those which take place on the designated date and those which are recalled from the past; and these recalled events are no less important than the present. In the first two sections, recalled experiences are far more important than the present enveloping action. If one is to determine the fundamental chronology of the four sections, he must consider the dates of the recalled experiences.

In his introduction to *The Portable Faulkner*, Malcolm Cowley raises another stimulating question for discussion. "In *The Sound and the Fury*, which is superb as a whole," he says, "we can't be sure that the four sections of the novel are presented in the most effective order." What disturbs Mr. Cowley is not the violation of surface chronology but the fact that "we can't fully understand and perhaps can't even read the first section until we have read the other three." By "most effective order" he seems to mean the order in which a section would be most easily understood and most effective individually. One may very well agree with Mr. Cowley that some other order of arrangement might have made Benjy's section more comprehensible on the first reading; however, the shifting of this section would merely mean that some other section would then come into first position, and the same trouble would start all over again, for each of the four sections is interdependent upon the other three. This is true even of the fourth and simplest section—as Cowley discovered when he considered printing this unit in *The Portable Faulkner*. "I thought that the last part of the book would be most effective as a separate episode, but still it depended too much on what had gone before."

Let us consider some of the ways in which the present position of Benjy's section does contribute to the desired effect of the novel as a whole. If the childhood experiences are to be included at all, it does seem definitely preferable that they be presented early, before the reader advances too far into the problems of adult life dealt with in the following three sections. But Benjy's section is far more than a mere background summary of ordinary childhood experiences. From one point of view, it is the whole novel in miniature. It presents all the main characters in situations which foreshadow the main action. This is particularly true of the recalled water-splashing episode which took place when Caddy was seven, Quentin nine, Jason about five, and

Benjy about three. These children and a little colored boy, Versh, are playing in the branch one evening. Caddy gets her dress wet and, in order to avoid punishment, pulls off the dress to let it dry. Quentin is perturbed because she gets her dress wet and also because she pulls it off before Versh and the other children. He slaps her and she falls down in the water, getting her bodice and drawers wet. He then feels partly responsible for Caddy's guilt and says that they will both get whipped. She says it was all his fault. However he and she and Versh agree not to tell; but Jason decides to tell if Caddy and Quentin do not give him a bribe. When the children go to bed, Dilsey the Negro cook discovers the stain on Caddy's buttocks, but she is unable to remove the spot.

The parallels between this and the main plot are obvious. When Caddy becomes a young woman, she soils her honor with a serious stain which will not come off; Quentin assumes responsibility for her shame and finally commits suicide in an attempt to expiate her sin; Jason, true to form, makes the most of Caddy's shame by blackmailing her for all he can get. In the childhood experience, Jason walks with his hands in his pockets (as if "holding his money") and once falls down because he does not have his arms free to balance himself; in the main action later, his "holding his money" (by keeping it at home in a box instead of banking it) results in his being robbed by his niece. Since this childhood experience is obviously intended to foreshadow the adult action, it can accomplish this purpose only if it comes before the other three sections.

The Sound and the Fury is a novel about disorder, disintegration, and the absence of perspective. As an introduction to this theme, what could be more appropriate than the flat, perspectiveless language of Benjy's section? The novel is essentially about the internal chaos of the characters—their intellectual, moral, and spiritual confusion. It is therefore appropriate that the first section be presented from the point of view of an idiot who symbolizes this general disorder and exemplifies the simplest variation of it—intellectual confusion; Benjy is incapable of intellectual discrimination, constantly mistaking the past for the present.

Two of the four sections are restricted in two respects and two are restricted in only one respect. Quentin's and Jason's sections are restricted to the internal point of view and to a limited phase of Caddy's transgression. Quentin is preoccupied almost exclusively with Caddy's loss of honor; Jason's attention is concentrated upon Caddy's illegitimate daughter. Benjy's section, although it is restricted in point of view to the mind of Benjy, is not restricted to Caddy or to any one phase of her problem to the exclusion of other matters and other characters. The last section of the novel is similar to Benjy's section in that it too deals with the Compson situation in a general manner, but it accomplishes the effect of comprehensiveness by another means. Whereas Benjy's section is restricted in point of view and not narrowly restricted in time-span, the last section is restricted in time-span to the events of one day but still acquires breadth of outlook by being written from the omniscient-omnipresent point of view, which gives the reader the impression of being outside the characters and at a sufficient remove to view the whole general panorama. The comprehensive quality of the first and the last sections, as contrasted with the two middle sections, gives a good architectural balance to the structure of the novel as a whole. It also allows the reader to begin with the general situation, move into two particular phases of this situation, and emerge again on the other side with a broad, general view. By beginning and ending the novel in this way, the author gives extension to the theme by making clear that the novel is not merely about Caddy's transgression and the reaction of her family, but about a much more comprehensive theme. The disorder, disintegration, and absence of perspective in the lives of the Compsons is intended to be symbolic and representative of a whole social order, or perhaps it would be better to say a whole social disorder.

TIME IN FAULKNER: *THE SOUND AND THE FURY*

JEAN-PAUL SARTRE

THE READER OF *The Sound and the Fury* is at first struck by the oddities of its technique. Why has Faulkner broken up the time of his story and disarranged the fragments? Why does the mind of an idiot provide the first window opened on Faulkner's imaginary world? The reader is tempted to look for points of reference and to re-establish the chronology for himself: "Jason and Caroline Compson had three sons and a daughter. The daughter, Caddy, was seduced by Dalton Ames and driven to find a husband. . . ." But he stops here, because he notices that he is telling another story. Faulkner did not first think in terms of an orderly narrative and then shuffle the parts like a pack of cards; he could not have told the story in any other way. In the classical novel, the action has a focus: for example, the murder of the Karamazov father, or the meeting between Edouard and Bernard in *The Counterfeiters*. It would be futile to look for this kind of focus in *The Sound and the Fury*: is it Benjy's castration? Caddy's unfortunate love affair? Quentin's suicide? Jason's hatred for his niece? Each episode, once it has been grasped, invokes others—in fact, all the other episodes connected with it. Nothing happens, the story does not progress; rather, we discover it behind each word as an oppressive and hateful presence, varying in intensity with each situation. It is a mistake to think of these anomalies as mere exercises in virtuosity; the novelist's aesthetic always sends us back to his metaphysic. The critic's task is to bring out the author's meta-

Reprinted by permission of Librairie Gallimard, Paris, from *Situations* I, "Le Bruit et la Fureur" (Paris: Gallimard, 1947), pp. 70-81. Originally published in *La Nouvelle Revue française*, June and July, 1939. Translated by Martine Darmon, with the assistance of the editors.

physic before evaluating his technique. And it is obvious that Faulkner's is a metaphysic of time.

It is man's misfortune to be confined in time. ". . . a man is the sum of his misfortunes. One day you'd think misfortune would get tired, but then time is your misfortune. . . ."[1] This is the true subject of the novel. And if the technique adopted by Faulkner seems at first to be a negation of time, that is because we confuse time with chronology. Dates and clocks were invented by man: ". . . constant speculation regarding the position of mechanical hands on an arbitrary dial which is a symptom of mind-function. Excrement Father said like sweating."[2] To reach real time, we must abandon these devices, which measure nothing: ". . . time is dead as long as it is being clicked off by little wheels; only when the clock stops does time come to life."[3] Quentin's breaking his watch has, therefore, a symbolic value; it forces us to see time without the aid of clocks. The time of the idiot, Benjy, is also unmeasured by clocks, for he does not understand them.

As for Faulkner's concept of the present, it is not a circumscribed or sharply defined point between past and future. His present is irrational in its essence; it is an event, monstrous and incomprehensible, which comes upon us like a thief—comes upon us and disappears. Beyond this present, there is nothing, since the future does not exist. One present, emerging from the unknown, drives out another present. It is like a sum that we compute again and again: "And . . . and . . . and then." Like Dos Passos, but with greater subtlety, Faulkner makes his story a matter of addition. Even when the characters are aware of them, the actions, when they emerge in the present, burst into scattered fragments: "I went to the dresser and took up the watch, with the face still down. I tapped the crystal on the corner of the dresser and caught the fragments of glass in my hand and put them into the ashtray and twisted the hands off and

1. *The Sound and the Fury* (New York: Modern Library, 1946), p. 123.
2. *Ibid.*, p. 96.
3. *Ibid.*, p. 104.

put them in the tray. The watch ticked on."[4] The other characteristic of Faulkner's present is *suspension*.* I use this word,
for lack of a better one, to indicate a kind of arrested motion
in time. In Faulkner, there is never any progression, nothing
which can come from the future. The present does not contain
in itself the future events we expect—as it seems to when I say
that the friend I have been waiting for finally appears. On the
contrary, to be present is to appear without reason and to be
suspended. Faulkner does not see this suspension in abstract
terms; he perceives it in things themselves and tries to make it
felt. "The train swung around the curve, the engine puffing with
short, heavy blasts, and they passed smoothly from sight that
way, with that quality about them of shabby and timeless
patience, of static serenity. . . ."[5] And again: "Beneath the sag
of the buggy the hooves neatly rapid like the motions of a lady
doing embroidery, *diminishing without progress* like a figure on
a treadmill being drawn rapidly offstage."[6] Faulkner appears to
arrest the motion at the very heart of things; moments erupt and
freeze, then fade, recede and diminish, still motionless.

However, this fugitive and incomprehensible state can be
grasped and made verbal. Quentin can say: I broke my watch.
But when he says it, his gesture will be *past*. The past can be
named and described. Up to a certain point it can be fixed by
concepts or intuitively grasped. We have already noted, in connection with *Sartoris,* that Faulkner always shows us events when
they are already completed. In *The Sound and the Fury*, everything occurs in the wings; nothing happens, everything has happened. This is what enables us to understand that strange formula
of one of the heroes: "I am not is, I was." In this sense also,
Faulkner can make of man a being without future, "sum of his
climactic experiences," "sum of his misfortunes," "sum of

4. *Ibid.,* p. 99.
* The French word is *l'enfoncement,* for which the word *suspension*
seemed the most suitable translation, in view of the context. [translator's
note]
5. *Ibid.,* p. 106.
6. *Ibid.,* p. 143. Italics mine.

what have you." At every instant we draw a line, since the present
is nothing but disordered rumor, a future already past. Faulkner's vision of the world can be compared to that of a man
sitting in a convertible looking back. At every moment shadows
emerge on his right, and on his left flickering and quavering
points of light, which become trees, men, and cars only when
they are seen in perspective. The past here gains a surrealistic
quality; its outline is hard, clear and immutable. The indefinable
and elusive present is helpless before it; it is full of holes
through which past things, fixed, motionless and silent, invade it.
Faulkner's soliloquies make us think of plane flights made
rough by air pockets; at every point the consciousness of the
hero "falls into the past" and rises once more, to fall again. The
present does not exist, it becomes; everything *was*. In *Sartoris,*
the past was seen in terms of "stories" because it consisted of a
store of familiar memories and because Faulkner had not yet
found his technique. In *The Sound and the Fury* he is more experimental and therefore less certain. But his preoccupation with
the past is so strong that he sometimes disguises the present—
and the present makes its way in the shadows, like an under-
ground river, to reappear only when it has become past. Thus,
Quentin is not even conscious of having insulted Bland, for he
is reliving his quarrel with Dalton Ames.[7] And when Bland
hits him, the fight is identified with the past fight between
Quentin and Ames. Later, Shreve will *relate* how Bland struck
Quentin; he will describe the scene because it has become history
—but when it was taking place in the present it was nothing
more than a shadowy and obscure event. I have been told of an
old school principal whose memory had stopped like a broken
watch; it remained forever fixed at his fortieth year. Though
he was sixty, he was not aware of his age; his last memory
was of the schoolyard and his daily rounds in the playground.
Thus he interpreted his present by means of this fixed past and

7. *Ibid.,* pp. 178-184. Cf. p. 179, the dialogue with Bland inserted in the
middle of the dialogue with Ames: "did you ever have a sister did you,"
and the inextricable confusion of the two battles.

he walked around his table, convinced that he was watching students at their play. Faulkner's characters behave in a similar fashion. Worse than that, their past is not ordered according to chronology but follows certain impulses and emotions. Around some central themes (Caddy's pregnancy, Benjy's castration, Quentin's suicide) innumerable fragments of thought and act revolve. Hence the absurdity of chronology, of "the round and stupid assertion of the clock." The order of the past is the order of the heart. We must not believe that the present event, after it has gone, becomes the most immediate of our memories. The shift of time can submerge it at the bottom of memory or leave it on the surface. Only its own intrinsic value and its relevance to our lives can determine its level.

This, then, is the nature of Faulkner's time. How valid is it? This indefinable present; these sudden invasions of the past; this affective order, opposed to the rational order which, though chronological, lacks reality; these memories, monstrous and recurring; these fluctuations of the heart—don't we recognize in them Marcel Proust's lost and recaptured time? I am aware of the differences; I know, for instance, that in Proust, salvation lies in time itself, in the total recovery of the past. For Faulkner, on the contrary, the past is unfortunately never lost; it is always there, almost as an obsession. Mystical ecstasies are our only means of escaping from the temporal world; and a mystic is always a man who wants to forget something: his Self, or more generally, language or formal representation. Faulkner wants to forget time: ". . . Quentin, I give you the mausoleum of all hope and desire; it's rather excruciating-ly apt that you will use it to gain the reducto absurdum of all human experience which can fit your individual needs no better than it fitted his or his father's. I give it to you not that you may remember time, *but that you might forget it now and then for a moment* and not spend all your breath trying to conquer it. Because no battle is ever won, he said. They are not even fought. The field only reveals to man his own folly and despair, and victory is an illusion of philosophers and fools."[8] Because he has forgotten time, the hunted Negro in *Light in August* suddenly achieves a strange and unnatural happiness: "It's not when you realize that nothing can help—religion, pride, anything—it's when you realize that you dont need any aid."[9] But for Faulkner, as for Proust, time is above all that which isolates. We remember the lovers in *Les Plaisirs et les Jours,* holding on to their passions which they are afraid will pass, which they know will pass. The same anguish is found in Faulkner: ". . . people cannot do anything that dreadful they cannot do anything very dreadful at all they cannot even remember tomorrow what seemed dreadful today . . ."[10] and ". . . a love or a sorrow is a bond purchased without design and which matures willynilly and is recalled without warning to be replaced by whatever issue the gods happen to be floating at the time. . . ."[11] Proust really *should have* employed a technique like Faulkner's; that was the logical outcome of his metaphysic. Faulkner, however, is a lost man, and because he knows that he is lost he risks pushing his thought to its conclusion. Proust is a classicist and a Frenchman; and the French lose themselves with caution and always end by finding themselves. Eloquence, a love of clarity and a rational mind led Proust to preserve at least the appearance of chronology.

We can find the real reason for their similarities in a widely shared literary preoccupation. Most of the great contemporary writers—Proust, Joyce, Dos Passos, Faulkner, Gide, and Virginia Woolf—have tried, each in his own way, to mutilate time. Some have deprived it of past and future and reduced it to the pure intuition of the moment; others, like Dos Passos, make it a limited and mechanical memory. Proust and Faulkner have simply decapitated it; they have taken away its future—that is to say, the dimension of free choice and act. Proust's heroes never undertake anything: they foresee, yes, but their previsions, like day-

8. *Ibid.,* p. 95. Italics mine.
9. *Light in August* (New York: Modern Library, 1950), p. 99.
10. *The Sound and the Fury,* p. 99.
11. *Ibid.,* p. 196.

dreams that put reality to flight, cling to them and therefore they cannot go beyond the present. The Albertine who appears is not the one we expected, and the interlude proves to be only a small, inconsequential agitation, limited to an instant. As for Faulkner's heroes, they never foresee: the car takes them away, as they look back. The approaching suicide which throws its dark shadow over Quentin's last day is not in the realm of human choice. Quentin cannot, for one second, conceive of the possibility of *not* killing himself. The suicide is an issue already determined, something which he approaches blindly without either desiring or conceiving it: ". . . you seem to regard it merely as an experience that will whiten your hair overnight so to speak without altering your appearance at all. . . ." Suicide is not consciously chosen, for it is inevitable. In losing its character of the possible, it ceases to exist in the future; it has become part of the present, and all Faulkner's art aims to suggest to us that Quentin's soliloquy and his last walk *are already* his suicide. I believe we can explain in this fashion a curious paradox: Quentin thinks of his last day as being in the past, like someone who remembers. But who is it that remembers, since the last thoughts of the hero almost coincide with the sudden eruption and destruction of his memory? The answer lies in the novelist's skill in choosing the particular moment of the present from which he describes the past. Like Salacrou in *L'Inconnue d'Arras*, Faulkner has chosen for his present the infinitesimal instant of death. Thus, when Quentin's memory begins to enumerate his impressions ("Through the wall I heard Shreve's bed-springs and then his slippers on the floor hishing. I got up. . . ."), *he is already dead*. So much art and, in fact, so much dishonesty only aim to compensate for the author's lack of any intuitive knowledge of the future. Everything, and in particular the irrationality of time, in Faulkner now becomes clear. Since the present is the unexpected, the unshaped future can be determined only by an excess of memories. We realize that duration is "man's own misfortune." If the future has reality, time moves from the past and draws near the future; but if the future is suppressed, time is no longer that which separates, which cuts the present off from itself: ". . . you cannot bear to think that someday it will no longer hurt you like this. . . ." Man spends his life struggling against time; and, acid-like, time corrodes man, tears him from himself and keeps him from realizing his humanity. Everything becomes absurd: "[Life] is a tale told by an idiot, full of sound and fury, signifying nothing."[12]

But is the time of man without a future? I can see that the nail, the clod of earth, the atom live in a perpetual present. But is man only a thinking nail? If we begin by plunging him into universal time, the time of nebulae and of planets, of tertiary formations and of animal species, as in a bath of sulfuric acid, the answer is obvious. It is nevertheless true, if we believe that time can be imposed from the outside, that a consciousness thus tossed from instant to instant would be a consciousness *first* and temporal *afterwards*. Consciousness can be "in time" only if it becomes time by that movement itself which makes it consciousness; to use Heidegger's phrase, it must "become time." In that case, it is no longer possible to stop man at each successive moment and to define him as the "sum of what have you." On the contrary, the nature of consciousness implies that it is projected into the future; we can understand what it is only by what it will become; it is determined in its present being by its own potentialities. This is what Heidegger calls "the silent strength of the possible." You won't recognize in yourself the Faulknerian man, a creature deprived of potentiality and explained only by what he was. If you try to fix your consciousness and examine it, you will see that it is hollow; you will find only futurity. I am not even talking about your plans or expectations; but the very gesture that you notice in its passing has meaning for you only if you project its completion outside itself, outside yourself, into the not-yet. This cup with its bottom which you do not see but which you could see, at the end of a movement not yet made— this white sheet of paper with its hidden verso which you could see if you turned the sheet—these, and all the stable and massive objects which surround us, extend their most immediate and solid

12. *Macbeth,* Act V, scene v.

qualities into the future. Man is not the sum of what he has, but the totality of what he does not yet have, of what he could have. And if we are thus immersed in the future, is not the irrational brutality of the present diminished? The event does not pounce upon us like a thief, since it is by its very nature a future-that-has-been. And is it not the task of the historian who explains the past to inquire first into its future? I am afraid that the absurdity Faulkner finds in human life was originally placed there by him. Not that life is not absurd, but that it has an absurdity different from what Faulkner ascribes to it.

Why have Faulkner and so many other writers chosen this particular absurdity, which is so far from the creative imagination and from truth? We must look for the reason in the social conditions of our present life. Faulkner's despair seems to me to be anterior to his metaphysic; for him, as for all of us, the future is barred. All that we see, all that we live through, incites us to say: "It can't last much longer"; we cannot, however, conceive of any change but a violent one. We live in a time of incredible revolutions, and Faulkner uses his extraordinary art to describe a world dying of old age, with us gasping and choking in it. I like his art, but I don't believe in his metaphysic. A barred future is still a future. "Even if human reality has nothing more 'ahead,' even if it has 'closed its accounts,' its being is still determined by this 'anticipation of itself.' " The loss of all hope, for example, does not deprive human reality of all possibilities; it is simply "a way of *being* in terms of those possibilities."[13]

13. Heidegger, *Sein und Zeit.*

AS I LAY DYING

OLGA VICKERY

WILLIAM FAULKNER has referred to the novel *As I Lay Dying*[1] as his best work. It was written while he was on the night shift of a power plant; completed in six weeks; published without a single line of revision. Critical appraisal, on the basis of objective analysis, must test the validity of Faulkner's own judgment. *As I Lay Dying* seems to be the one novel in which the author is in full control of his material. As a result it is an organic unit. The form is the content; hence the precision and economy is the cause of the suggestiveness and the richness. The novel exists as an illustration and justification of Mark Schorer's statement in his essay "Technique as Discovery."

Technique is the means by which the writer's experience, which is his subject matter, compels him to attend to it; technique is the only means he has of discovering, exploring, developing his subject, of conveying its meaning and finally of evaluating it.

It is interesting to note that Cowley includes no portion of this novel in the Faulkner *Portable*. Yet the Bundrens live only forty miles from Jefferson. They are neighbors to the Tulls. They know the MacCollums and the Snopeses. Dr. Peabody doctors them all as well as the Sartorises. The same South has shaped them all. Yet the Bundrens do not fit easily into the Faulkner myth as shaped by Cowley in the *Portable*. The reason for the exclusion appears to be twofold. *As I Lay Dying* is an extremely closely woven novel even though a technique of separate, distinct scenes is used. Each of the scenes depends for its effectiveness on those that precede it and for its significance on those that

Reprinted with permission from *Perspective*, Autumn, 1950, pp. 179–191.

1. All quotations in this paper from *As I Lay Dying* are from the Modern Library Edition, New York, 1946.

follow it. The novel does not permit its unity to be arbitrarily broken.

Cowley sees the Southern myth as dependent on, and rising from, the destructive interaction of the Sartorises and the Snopeses, of the self-destroying and destructive whites and the suffering yet provoking Negro. The position of the Bundrens within this central situation is not expressed within the novel itself nor can it be deduced from the body of his works. Their actions have no bearing on the life of the Sartorises, nor can these actions be interpreted in terms of the "Doom of the South." They are, of course, a specific social and economic level in the Yoknapatawpha County, but Faulkner has not yet made clear the significance of this level in his saga. If the connection with the Southern myth is there, it is one of analogy, of parallel development which takes place in the backyard of the manor unseen and sensed only as an odor.

As I Lay Dying was written immediately after *The Sound and the Fury*. The two show certain structural similarities but the later book has an increased degree of complexity. *The Sound and the Fury* seems to employ the technique diagrammed by Henry James in "the neat figure of a circle consisting of a number of small rounds disposed at equal distances about a central object." The central object was the situation, the subject in itself. The small rounds were lamps which threw light on the object until it had reached maximum illumination, after which it, in turn, would throw light back to the lamps. Benjy, Quentin, and Jason act as such lamps illuminating and in turn being illuminated by the central situation. It is important that these three reflectors remain static. The style is consistently appropriate to each of them, but it also remains static on the level of the characters it expresses. It is only our understanding of the characters and of the situation that grows.

This method is used also in *As I Lay Dying*, but it is further complicated. Each of the lamps can be regulated, can vary in degree of illumination cast on the central problem. They can operate on the four different levels: action, words, conscious thought, and the unconscious. Moreover each of these levels has its own particular blending of observation, association, reflection, and emotion. Certain of the characters are limited to only one of these levels. Darl, the most complex of the characters, owes his complexity and his madness to the fact that he partakes of them all. The different levels of consciousness are rendered by Faulkner through variations of style rising from the dialect of actual speech to the intricate imagery and poetic rhythms of the unconscious.

As a further complication, the disinterested spectator of James, who had been Dilsey or the Negro consciousness in *The Sound and the Fury*, is now broken up into eight different characters. They are used to comment and to provide a larger frame of reference. They are not implicated in the central problem but in the actions which are the result of it. Accordingly, their observations can be made only with reference to the lamps, not to the object of illumination. However, they have the necessary alertness of the physical eye which projects the action into the outside world.

In speaking of Henry James' novels, Joseph Warren Beach quoted James himself: "the thing is all beautifully a matter of interpretation and of the particular conditions without a view of which latter some of the most prodigious adventures . . . may vulgarly show for nothing." Beach was concerned with explaining the seeming inactivity of James' characters, but his statement is even more necessary for our comprehension of *As I Lay Dying*. Without the interpretation, without the view of particular conditions, the journey to Jefferson becomes nothing—a meaningless chaos of idiocy and violence. However, we cannot borrow facile explanation from the non-Bundren world in order to provide the novel with meaningfulness. The meaning and our interpretation of it must grow out of the novel, not be imposed on it. To make the promise a matter of Christian ethics and the journey "an act of traditional morality" is to distort both characters and actions.

The central problem is not the fulfillment of a promise made complicated and hazardous by accidents of nature. Rather it is

Addie, not as mother, corpse, or promise but as an element in
the blood of her children which they must integrate whether she
lives or dies. Within her we must seek their motivation, their
knowing and doing. She is the source of the tension and the
latent violence. Her death forces them to face the problem and
to attempt to solve it in their own terms. The flood and the fire
are external manifestations of the internal violence. In Dr. Peabody's words:

> I can remember how when I was young I believed death to be
> a phenomenon of the body; now I know it to be merely a function of
> the mind—and that of the minds of the ones who suffer the bereave-
> ment [p. 368].

This statement comes after the tensions centering upon Addie
have been established but before any action has occurred. The
rest of the novel is concerned with the expression of the bereavement of the survivors and with the resolution of the tension
whose source was Addie.

Addie is the only one of the Bundrens whose past goes
beyond the family. Although all her relatives are buried in
Jefferson, their presence is voiced in her father's phrase "the
reason for living was to get ready to stay dead a long time"
[p. 461]. Only through the violence of life can we achieve the
peace of death. Birth is, in a sense, the first and only violation,
and life becomes an effort to learn how to live with the results
of it until the final violation and expiation of life comes. This
cycle of human life arises out of the land, "opaque, slow, violent;
shaping and creating the life of man in its implacable and brooding image" [p. 369].

Since the source of life is violation, only through the violence of action can a meaningful communication between people
be established. Words are without meaning, ineffectual:

> I would think how words go straight up in a thin line, quick and
> harmless, and how terribly doing goes along the earth, clinging to it,
> so that after a while the two lines are too far apart for the same person
> to straddle from one to the other...[p. 465].

Yet Addie, who is part of "the wild blood boiling along the earth," accepts Anse. The realization of betrayal is swift upon the coming of Cash. She accepts her first child as the price of her realization of the complete separation of the word and the act. After this, the two lines begin to diverge until all communication between her and Anse is lost. It is impossible for either of them to reach across to the other. Darl, then, comes as the ultimate outrage because she and Anse have diverged too far for that birth to have been possible. She rejects almost immediately the thought of Anse as agent of her betrayal. He also has been tricked. Violence has been committed upon her by life itself. When this fact becomes clear to her in her mind, Anse, already ineffectual as word, becomes nullified as action also.

Her meeting with Whitfield is sudden and swift. It is part of the unconscious violence of the land and also something beyond the land, beyond even consciousness. Although he can withdraw again into words, into "sin" and "repentance" and "duty," for her "it was not over . . . over in the sense of beginning and ending, because . . . there was no beginning nor ending to anything then" [p. 467]. Addie sees Whitfield as the symbol of the act stripped of all words because he must discard all the words of which he is the guardian to come to her. Using Whitfield as the instrument she enacts her own violence. Out of this act comes Jewel, mothered by violence and fathered by no one. The relationship between Jewel and his mother is maintained on the level of unexpressed but understood fury and love. And it is on this basis that she can prophesy:

He is my cross and he will be my salvation. He will save me from the water and from the fire. Even though I have laid down my life, he will save me [p. 460].

After this acceptance of and participation in the life which is part of the land, Addie is ready to set her house in order for death. She consciously gives Anse Dewey Dell to "negative" Jewel and Vardaman to replace him. Both of these births are acts on the levels of consciousness. Anse takes no part in their conception. Addie has the final moment of exhilarated realization:

> My children were of me alone, of the wild blood boiling along the earth, of me and of all that lived; of none and of all [p. 467].

The circumstances of the birth of each of the children establish the level of their awareness of her and the mode of their participation in her burial. This accounts for the structural form of the novel. The progression is centrifugal as well as linear. Centrifugally each scene establishes the relationship between Addie and the character concerned. Accordingly each action must be restated by each of the characters as it affects him. Linearly we have the sequence of action and the establishment of communication through violence among the characters.

Anse, as characterized by Addie, lives only on the level of the spoken word, which is ineffectual. This combination of words and of ineffectuality in his nature is sustained throughout his three scenes as well as in the comments of others upon him. Realization of this justifies the statement: "It is as though upon a face carved by a savage caricaturist a monstrous burlesque of all bereavement flowed" [p. 394]. The bereavement is a word for him and he acts up to it not out of it: "God's will be done. . . . Now I can get them teeth" [p. 375].

Because he exists only on the level of words, Addie has no influence on him except for the projection of enough of her vital energy to make him feel the necessity for action. That is her revenge: to exact a promise which is a word but which will force Anse into an act. As she foresees, Anse insists on the letter of the promise even though he does not know what it signifies. But he is incapable of performing or even of directing the action implied in the promise. At every crisis he is the bystander. It is significant that all the violence of the journey penetrates to his consciousness only in the form of words with no action resultant. For him the whole episode of the flood is summed up in the phrase: "It's a trial. . . . But I don't begrudge her it. No man can say I begrudge her it" [p. 458]. Nor can any of the children establish a meaningful contact with him. Each action seen with the physical eye is strained through his self-centered mind and rendered futile by his platitudes. Hence his language, on the level of dialect, revolves around himself.

Considering the level on which Anse lives, his second marriage is no shock, nor does it catapult the novel into farce. It is profoundly in keeping with his character. In his life the second Mrs. Bundren is as meaningless in terms of vital action as the first one was. No ethical judgment can be leveled at the words which are Anse, simply because they are words. For him the burial of Addie is identified with the verbal promise which is carried out by others for him. Then, once more treating marriage as a word to which no responsibility of action is attached, he introduces the "duck-shaped woman with the hard looking pop eyes" as his wife.

In contrast to his father, Cash exists on the level of action. He seems peculiarly removed from the tension and the violence, as if there were a screen between his building of the coffin and the fury of the others. At his birth Addie had realized the separation of word and act and had retreated into that realization. Violence and violation had been recognized but not embraced. This situation is recreated in Cash. It is he who actually builds the coffin, directs the journey and manages the burial, without ever partaking of the loquacity of Anse. He speaks directly only after something concrete has been accomplished, after the coffin has been finished. His occupation befits his character and his level of consciousness. As a carpenter he is concerned with working with his hands and building well. As Addie's son he uses those hands and that skill to express her meaning for him. "And Cash likes sawing the long hot sad yellow days up into planks and nailing them to something" [p. 355].

There is very little contact between Cash and the rest of the family because he does not intrude into the realm of their fury and their tension. In the scene of the flood the circumstances of his birth are recreated. Violence is thrust upon him; he is made to recognize its existence. His twice-broken leg, the inflicted, un-

sought violence, paves the way for his development, for his increased awareness. This makes plausible the difference between
his first scene in which he enumerates the stages in making a coffin
and the last one in which he alone seems to have an understanding of the family that is valid in terms of the outside world.

His greater degree of comprehension of and sympathy with
Darl is established during the fire, the second stage of the violence. Setting fire to the barn is an act which is foreign to Darl,
which should have been his own, since once having suffered the
violence he should have embraced it through act as Addie had
done. He realizes this: "It's because me and him was born close
together. . . . And me being the oldest, and thinking already the
very thing that he done: I don't know" [p. 511]. By allowing
Darl to commit his act, Cash has assumed responsibility for him.
Darl senses this when he makes his departure to Jackson dependent on Cash's word. This reversal of natural roles is also a means
of developing his awareness. This combined with his own firm
foundation in action makes him the only effective character in
the novel. It is his judgments which seem to possess the greatest
degree of value.

> Sometimes I ain't so sho who's got ere a right to say when a man
> is crazy and when he ain't. Sometimes I think it ain't none of us pure
> crazy and ain't none of us pure sane until the balance of us talks him
> that-a-way. It's like it ain't so much what a fellow does, but it's the
> way the majority of folks is looking at him when he does it [p. 510].

In this passage there are elements of both Darl and Cash. It is
the thought of Darl forced into validity by the dialect of Cash.
And both elements re-echo and once again reaffirm the separation
of words and acts.

Darl, the second son, is the most complicated and complicat-
ing of the characters. Each of the others collides with him in some
way or other, thus setting up new tensions. For him, moreover,
the problem of Addie is insoluble because his awareness of it is
on too many levels for him to be able to meet it on any one

effective plane: "That's why I am not *is*. *Are* is too many for one woman to foal" [p. 409].

The stages of awareness in Darl are expressed by Faulkner through corresponding levels of language. While he is involved in action or observing it with his physical eye, his words are in dialect. His conscious thought is rendered in terms of formal language coherently and logically ordered. When he passes into the unconscious, Faulkner makes no attempt to modulate the stream of consciousness in terms of the character. Since the thoughts no longer pass through the conscious mind all peculiarities of the character's expression are abandoned. The style used is ornate, heightened, poetic prose. The images are not derived from Darl's experience but rather snatched from some region beyond his knowledge and comprehension.

How do our lives ravel out into the no-wind, no-sound, the weary gestures wearily recapitulant: echoes of old compulsions with no-hand on no-strings...[p. 491].

This passage not only typifies the texture of Darl's stream of consciousness on this level; it also conveys poetically the process of reaching it.

Because of the range of his awareness Darl is able to meet any of the other characters in his own sphere. Thus at every instance he is able to identify himself with another character, to know instinctively his motivation and yet remain detached: "It's like he had got into the inside of you, someway. Like somehow you was looking at yourself and your doings outen his eyes" [p. 426]. In this way he had performed the action which was Cash's. But at the same time he is incapable of performing any act that is truly his own because he is incapable of integrating all the levels of awareness in terms of an action. As the novel progresses, he moves further and further away from doing. Tull expresses this on a very elementary level.

For the Lord aimed for him to do and not to spend too much time thinking, because his brain it's like a piece of machinery: it won't stand a whole lot of racking. It's best when it all runs along the same,

doing the day's work and not no one part used no more than needful.
... that's ever living thing the matter with Darl: he just thinks by himself too much [p. 389].

It is implied that there was a time when Darl was of the land,
partaking of its strength and its validity, capable of action:

Darl ... that sits at the supper table with his eyes gone further
than the food and the lamp, full of the land dug out of his skull and
the holes filled with distance beyond the land [p. 355].

Addie had talked of her identification with the land at the time
of his birth. But at the same time she had considered him an outrage and a violation because the lines of thinking and doing had
diverged too far for him to be possible. The same distance between thought and act is felt in his lighting the fire. It is as if he
were attempting to dispose of her in the same terms in which
she had conceived him. His increasing separation from the land
means finally a separation from himself: "*Are* is too many for one
woman to foal."

It's like there was a fellow in every man that's done a-past the
sanity or the insanity, that watches the sane and the insane doings of
that man with the same horror and the same astonishment [p. 515].

In the stage of complete madness Darl expresses this watching
of himself by referring to his actions as those of Darl.
There is no conflict between Darl and Cash, since he has
passed beyond the circle of action on which Cash exists. The
reversal of roles at the time of the fire produces understanding
between them. On the other hand, any meeting of Darl and Jewel
increases the tension. The reason is that Darl knows the circumstances of Jewel's birth and his relationship with Addie:

She cried hard, maybe because she had to cry so quiet; maybe
because she felt the same way about tears she did about deceit, hating
herself for doing it, hating him because she had to. And then I knew
that I knew. I knew that as plain on that day as I knew about Dewey
Dell on that day [p. 435].

Darl's claim that he is motherless is justifiable when we consider his birth. However, it is her he is facing when he taunts and provokes Jewel. This explains the peculiar degree of intensity in the moments of contact between them. Because he refuses to assume responsibility for his knowledge, because he refuses to act from it and out of it, he forces Jewel into its enactment through violence which reaches its resolution only when Jewel beats him up at Jefferson.

Darl's relationship with Dewey Dell is similar to that with Jewel. The fact of her pregnancy by Lafe corresponds to Addie's affair with Whitfield. And as Darl has known of the latter, so he grasps the implications of the former. Again, in admitting his knowledge to himself and to her, he takes responsibility for it. The knowing must result in doing. This is why Dewey Dell's first words to him are: "Are you going to tell pa are you going to kill him?" [p. 356]. Darl refuses both acts, thus setting up the bridge and the enmity between them. As with Jewel, by knowing and not doing, he forces Dewey Dell into physical violence directed at himself.

As Darl progresses further and further away from the sanity of the act, his resemblance to Vardaman becomes more pronounced. When the wagon reaches the Gillespies, the monologues of Darl and Vardaman are juxtaposed five times. The two of them have reached an understanding beyond logic or rational coherence. Just before the fire their attitudes towards Addie become identical. As Vardaman states in one scene and Darl repeats in the next, both hear Addie stirring in the coffin and speaking to them: "She's talking to God. . . . She is calling on Him to help her. . . . She wants Him to hide her away from the sight of man. . . . So she can lay down her life" [p. 495]. It is on this level of unconsciousness which is beyond reason and so considered as madness that Darl grasps Addie's very thought, her very phrase. The "echo of a dead compulsion" is transmitted into the sphere of action with no intervening stage. In that respect it is analogous to Vardaman's act of drilling holes into the coffin. Because the act and the compulsion are too far diverged, bridging the gap destroys him. "But it is better so for him. This world is not his world; this life his life" [p. 532].

Although Jewel is most closely connected with Addie and the problem she presents, he speaks only once throughout the novel. The reason is that he transforms emotion into action without an intervening stage of conscious thought. And so it is Darl who expresses his motivation. Jewel's roots are grounded in Addie's violence and love and his burial of her is carried out in the same terms. Only he of all the characters sees her emotionally and the emotion is shot through with violence. Blows and caresses, curses and endearments—the echo of Addie "hating herself for doing it, hating him because she had to."

As Darl keeps reiterating, Jewel has no father. He has been born completely of the emotional violence of his mother. The intensity of their relationship borders on emotional incest. Jewel has to break the connection through some act. He does it by the purchase of a wild horse on which he can expend his love and his hate in terms of physical action. However, this breaks the connection only on the level of act. Hence his repudiation of Addie becomes meaningless, without validity. The horse has been bought to replace the mother, but instead she has become identified with it in Jewel's mind. Because of this identification he insists on bringing the horse with him on the burial journey. His surrendering the horse negates his former deed and the full intensity of act and emotion, no longer separated, reverts to Addie. This explains why during the flood scene Jewel is prevented by the horse from going back to the wagon; whereas during the fire all his energies are directed toward saving her.

The one scene in which Jewel actually reveals his stream of consciousness anticipates and justifies Addie's belief that he will save her from and in the violence of water and fire:

> It would just be me and her on a high hill and me rolling the rocks down the hill at their faces, picking them up and throwing them down the hill, faces and teeth and all by God until she was quiet... [pp. 347–48].

The violence is carried into his contact with the other characters. It is his fury which precipitates the accident at the ford and his wild energy which rescues the coffin from the fire. He has no connection with Dewey Dell, Vardaman, or Anse because there is no common ground for meeting. Each time he meets Cash it is to override his valid action with the impetuosity of his own violence. And it is, of course, between Jewel and Darl, the first fatherless, the second by his own admission motherless, that the greatest tension is generated. It is significant that Jewel is the only character in the novel whose language is filled with the sound of cursing. It is as if the violence of his emotion could be expressed only through the explosion of the curse. After the burial, however, the fury seems to recede both from his actions and his language.

Dewey Dell seems least concerned with the problem of Addie. She exists on the level of conscious thought divorced from action. All her thoughts find their source in her act with Lafe. Yet she disclaims the act itself by disclaiming responsibility for it: "And so it was full when we came to the end of the row and I could not help it. And so it was because I could not help it" [p. 356]. As long as she can maintain herself on the level of unenacted thought she feels herself to be safe: "The reason you will not say it is, when you say it, even to yourself, you will know it is true: is that it? But you know it is true now. I can almost tell you the day when you knew it is true. Why won't you say it, even to yourself?" [p. 365]. However, to admit it is to act, which Dewey Dell is not ready to do.

She and Darl never communicate verbally. There is no need for such intercourse. He has entered her level of consciousness, penetrated her egotism, and so knows without words. But through knowing he also assumes the responsibility for acting. Again, as with Jewel, this establishes not only communication but latent violence between them: "And that's why I can talk to him with knowing with hating because he knows" [p. 356]. The violence finds its expression in her sudden unexpected betrayal of Darl to

Gillespie and in her physical attack on him at the end of the novel.

The style used by Faulkner in the Dewey Dell scenes reflects thought revolving around itself. "It is like a dog outside the house, going back and forth around the house to whatever door you come to, waiting to come in" [p. 380]. There is always the circular, repetitive movement, and always behind it is Darl, provoking the thought to become an act, looking "like one of these bulldogs, one of these dogs that don't bark none, squatting against the rope, watching the thing he was waiting to jump at" [p. 512].

Finally Vardaman, the youngest, the last child of Addie. His thought process is entirely on the level of the unconscious in which relations are formed by association and emotion. Because he is incapable of either conscious ordering or of effective action, things for him become yoked by violence; they are forced together in a sphere beyond his control. Thus the killing of the fish and the death of the mother produce a unity in his mind: "My mother is a fish." The spatial juxtaposition of Dr. Peabody and the sickbed suggests to him that the doctor is the murderer of Addie. Hence he works his vengeance on Peabody's horses. His lack of air in the corn crib and Addie's position in the coffin evolve into the fish "who is my mother," suffocating in the coffin. The distance between the thought and its source and the act produces the madness of the act: his drilling the holes through the coffin to let in air. It is to be remembered that the same distance exists between Darl's compulsion and his act.

Through interaction of the characters and the resultant manifestation of violence the complexity of the central problem has been evoked. And through an understanding of the complexities of the central problem, the motivation and hence the reality of the characters is established. At the end we see them in terms of the problem, "sitting bolt upright in our nakedness, staring at one another and saying 'Now is the truth' " [p. 433]. Because the nakedness is unendurable, Anse begins covering his share in it by new words and a new wife, thus planting the germ of a new problem for his family and incidentally for the reader.

Although the action has been understood in terms of the central problem and the interactions of the family, it is necessary to provide it with a wider frame of reference. The reverberations of the actions penetrate into the non-Bundren world. It is in this capacity that Faulkner introduces his eight vibrators. Moseley and MacGowan respond to the act of Dewey Dell which, in keeping with her character, she makes them state overtly. The first reacts in terms of outraged morality and self-righteousness; the second takes advantage of it. She returns to the wagon, empty of her sullen faith in them, of Lafe's money, even of Darl's enmity. Characteristically she brushes everything concrete from her consciousness and sits nibbling a banana.

Samson, Armstid and Tull are the complementary acts to Anse's words. Because of his ineffectuality they are forced to act. "Trouble is, his quitting was just about to start our doing" [p. 477]. This despite Anse's word protestation that "We wouldn't be beholden . . ." [p. 419]. Again characteristically, Anse believes that his not wanting to be "beholden" disposes of any possibility of his being indebted. Each of these three men recount a stage in the journey to Jefferson in terms of what action it has forced him to take. However, when the family is caught up in the violence of the fire, the action is not related by Gillespie, whose barn is being burnt. It is as if the fire is significant only in terms of the family. Gillespie, at that point, is incapable of comprehending the relation between their act and himself.

Cora Tull and Whitfield react to the family in ethical terms, in words and phrases. Anything done during the death and burial is bound to be another step in Cora's self-justification and the Bundrens' eternal damnation. Addie's soliloquy, which is concerned with emphasizing the separation of words and acts, is flanked by the empty rhetoric of Cora and Whitfield.

Peabody alone seems to make certain statements which act as a general guide for the interpretation of the actions of the family. He makes a separate evaluation of life, love, and death in the sickroom. He speaks on the basis of long experience with people and with the Bundrens; hence his generalizations may be said to rise naturally out of the material. However, they do not seem to have passed through the catalyst of his own character. They are not in keeping with the texture of his actions. It is as if in this instance alone the reverberator was not operating in terms of itself.

While acting as reverberators for the actions of the Bundrens, the eight outside characters offer release from the tension, humorous interludes. Because the actions are seen only through the physical eye, they become humorously distorted. What is horror and violence for the family becomes farce for the non-implicated. The internal action seethes with unresolved tension at Mottson, but to the townspeople it is only a ridiculous effrontery. As the wagon pulls up before the hardware store the ladies scatter up and down the streets, their handkerchiefs held to their noses. Their only comprehension of the situation is through the sense of smell. MacGowan treats Dewey Dell's position on the level of comedy, and again we have the intermingling of horror and humor which insists on seeing all of the action as a country farce.

And of course Cora with her eggs and her God is so completely unconscious of the seriousness of the problem that her intrusion into the family affairs becomes a source of comedy. Her intimate association with the deity makes her quite unable to understand the Bundrens or even to help them effectively. But the picture of her "bounding toward my God and my reward" [p. 404] is irresistibly funny. Into the wake of her unintentional humor she drags Tull, who consequently acts on two levels. He helps Anse and he echoes Cora, thus contributing both to the serious progression of the novel and to the comedy in it:

> I reckon she's right. I reckon if there's ere a man or woman anywhere that He could turn it all over to and go away with His mind at rest, it would be Cora. And I reckon she would make a few changes, no matter how He was running it. And I reckon they would be for man's good. Leastways, we would have to like them. Leastways, we might as well go on and make like we did [p. 391].

The interplay of seriousness which reaches the level of tragedy and humor which is practically farce is part of the complete success of *As I Lay Dying*. It is only when one sees the relationship of these elements as well as of the problem and characters, of action and observers, that the full power of the novel is felt and the mastery of Faulkner realized.

THE STONE AND THE CRUCIFIXION: FAULKNER'S *LIGHT IN AUGUST*

RICHARD CHASE

WITHOUT ado I wish to direct attention to the symbolic texture of *Light in August*. This texture is very much a matter of mechanics and dynamics—a poetry of physics. Repeatedly Faulkner presents appearance, event, and even character in the images of stasis, motion, velocity, weight, lightness, mass, line, relative position, circle, sphere, emptiness, fullness, light, and dark. The phrase "light in August" has at least two meanings. As Mr. Malcolm Cowley informs us in his *Portable Faulkner,* the phrase means "light" as opposed to "heavy" and refers to a pregnant woman who will give birth in August. And it also means "light" as opposed to "dark"—an affirmation of life and human spirit. *Light in August* may be described, in Faulkner's own words (though he is describing something else), as "the mechanics, the theatring of evil." This is not a complete or fully fair description of Faulkner's novel, but it is complete and fair enough to demand that we look at the novel from this point of view—and that we finally ask, How successful is the author in extending his account of the mechanics and theatring of evil into an account of the human situation?

The reader of *Light in August* will be puzzled in the first

Reprinted with permission from *The Kenyon Review,* Autumn, 1948, pp. 539–551.

few pages by what may be called "the string of beads image."
We read that the wagon in which Lena Grove rides through the
August afternoon is like "a shabby bead upon the mild red string
of road" and that the village beside the railroad, from which she
begins her long journey, is like "a forgotten bead from a broken
string." Later our attention is called to the row of iron bars in
the fence which surrounds the orphanage of Joe Christmas' childhood, to the identical windows of a street car, to a picket fence,
and to the rows of identical white houses in which the lower-
middle-class whites live. To these images of linear discreteness
Faulkner opposes images of the curve. Lena Grove—searching
for Lucas Burch, the father of her unborn child—passes through
"a long monotonous succession of peaceful and undeviating
changes from day to dark and dark to day"; but her mode of
action and of consciousness is not of the order of the "string of
beads." She is "like something moving forever and without progress across an urn." For her the road is not linear but like a string
"being rewound onto a spool." These images of linear discreteness
and curve are extended into one of the central images of the
book: flight and pursuit.

We have already encountered the symbolic representation of
two realms of being which are counterposed throughout the
novel. The linear discrete image stands for "modernism": abstraction, rationalism, applied science, capitalism, progressiv-
ism, emasculation, the atomized consciousness and its pathological extensions. The curve image stands for holistic consciousness,
a containing culture and tradition, the cyclical life and death of
all the creatures of earth. Throughout the novel, Lena retains
her holistic consciousness and she is strong, enduring, hopeful.
All the other characters in one way or another are victims of
the linear delusion. For Joe Christmas, in whom the linear consciousness becomes pathological, the curve image is a "cage" or
a "prison" to be broken out of. Or it is something to be gashed
from the outside so that whatever it contains will be spilled mean-
inglessly out. Joe gashes the whiskey tins he and Burch have
buried in the woods as he has a vision of trees in the moonlight,

standing like "a diminishing row of suavely shaped urns," each one cracked and extruding "something liquid, deathcolored, and foul." At the end, when Joe can no longer perform this symbolic act of urn smashing, the curve image becomes the fateful circle of repetition which he has never really either escaped or broken and which is the only path to the only kind of holism he will ever find: death. "I have never got outside that circle. I have never broken out of the ring of what I have already done and cannot ever undo." The tragic irony of the linear consciousness, Faulkner seems to say, is that it is an illusion; all consciousness is holistic, but it may be the holism of life (Lena) or of death (Joe). The remarkable symbol of the wheel in the passage describing the final madness of the Reverend Mr. Hightower presumably coincides with Joe's circle of doom, though here it may symbolize the completion in death of a cycle of legendary family history.

Faulkner's counterposing of motionlessness and motion seems to imply a fairly consistent deploying of polarity of character. Lena, Joe, and Hightower all have a certain kind of motionlessness. Lena, "her voice quite grave now, quite quiet," sitting "quite still, her hands motionless upon her lap," has the inner quiet of the wheel's axle, a stillness within movement. The stillness behind Joe's cold, contemptuous mask is the abstract stillness of separation, a schizoid disengagement from outer action. The motionlessness of Hightower, sitting "rigidly" behind his desk, his "forearms parallel upon the armrests of the chair," is the negation of the will and action by fear, "denial," and impotence.

The quality of Joe's action is simply a willed translation of his separateness. Whenever he is in motion, in fantasy or actuality, he is in flight; and this is true even of his many connections with women–these also he must turn into the pattern of flight whenever they threaten to bring him too close to the kind of central and holistic peace represented by Lena. Although Burch is throughout the book in a sense in flight from Lena, Byron Bunch, or the sheriff, his movements entirely lack Joe's willed abstract control. He is pure aimless motion, a rural poor white uprooted and cast adrift in an industrial-urban society. "He puts me in mind," says

Byron Bunch, "of one of these cars running along the street with a radio in it. You can't make out what it is saying and the car ain't going anywhere in particular and when you look at it close you see that there ain't even anybody in it." A friend of Bunch's replies, "Yes, he puts me in mind of a horse. Not a mean horse. Just a worthless horse." This rude progression of metaphors will serve to indicate that Faulkner's imagination very frequently approaches the level of human character and consciousness beginning with the mechanical, and proceeding to the animal level through an intermediate level of dynamics.

The denouement of the novel can be conceived as the final resolution of several kinds of motion. Byron Bunch separates himself from his spiritual kinship with Hightower and his hitherto meaningless life finds its repose in Lena. Burch moves away from Lena, dooming himself, as it were, to aimless perpetual motion. The final flight of Joe to Hightower's house may seem too little explained as part of the plot. But it has a symbolic significance, since Joe, turning away for the last time from the realm of being which is represented by Lena and which he has tried to find in his various women, finds his ultimate refuge in the castration and death vouchsafed to him by Percy Grimm (only the last of all the symbolic castrations and deaths he has first sought and then endured). Hightower himself had turned away from the Lena-holism when years earlier he had in effect pursued his wife out of existence by believing in his fantasy that his "seed" had died with his grandfather in the Civil War.

2.

Mr. Robert Penn Warren suggests that Faulkner's objection to the modern world is that it lacks the ability to set up "codes, concepts of virtue, obligations" by which man can "define himself as human" and "accept the risks of his humanity." In *Light in August*, Faulkner seems to be concerned with showing that the codes modern man *does* set up do *not* allow him to define himself as human—that codes have become compulsive patterns which man clings to in fear and trembling while the pattern emasculates him. Byron Bunch, wondering why he lives to the split second by his big silver watch and works alone in the planing mill every Saturday afternoon and why the Reverend Mr. Hightower has refused to leave Jefferson, the scene of his ruin and disgrace, reflects, "It is because a fellow is more afraid of the trouble he might have than he ever is of the trouble he's already got. He'll cling to trouble he's used to before he'll risk a change." Byron and Hightower have for years been sustaining one another in their "patterns." Their relationship ends over the question of Bunch's aiding and courting Lena, pregnant with another man's child. The dilemma for each is whether to stick to a pattern of behavior which prohibits accepting "the risks of his humanity" or to become involved responsibly in a human situation. Byron chooses to break the pattern and accept the consequences of intervention. Hightower remains in the pattern (though he makes certain senile excursions from it), choosing to conspire in closing the circle of his destiny, choosing separation and madness. It is not true, as has been said, that all of Faulkner's characters are rigidly controlled by fate: Byron, for one, is left free to choose his own fate.

Joe Christmas is in many ways a masterful portrait of a man whose earliest years have been spent in an institution—an experience, as the psychiatrists show, which definitively affects not only the emotional centers of the victim but also the character of his conceptual thinking. In the forbidding orphanage (a true symbol of the conditions of modern life) Joe finds a surrogate mother— a cynical, suspicious and indeed almost paranoiac dietitian, a mockery of the Nursing Mother of the myths. His surrogate father is an obscenely fanatical inquisitor and peeping tom who functions as the janitor of the orphanage and who later turns out to be Joe's grandfather. The pattern of Joe's life is inexorably formed when the dietitian finds that he has been hiding in her closet eating tooth paste while she has been entertaining an interne on her bed (the tube of tooth paste is another urn symbol). The definitive event is not that Joe has seen the dietitian in the act but that she fails to punish him and instead offers him money not to tell. Having felt terribly guilty, having expected and even wanted to be punished, and having had no idea of giving away the secret, he is irretrievably shocked when she offers him the money. He had wanted the woman to engross him in her life, if only by beating him. Instead she denies him this engrossment and gives him a silver dollar, whose shining circumference forms a circle Joe will never break through. Joe's homosexualism is another theme symbolized by the "string of beads" image. The relationship between Joe and his guardian, McEachern, a fanatical apostle of a parochial and degenerate Presbyterianism who beats Joe with the impersonal violence of a machine, has for both McEachern and Joe the uneasy satisfaction of an abnormal but vehemently pure sexual alliance. McEachern has succeeded with Joe where the dietitian failed. Joe finds the relationship "perfectly logical and reasonable and inescapable," and he quickly learns to hate Mrs. McEachern because her proffered feminine kindnesses always threaten to taint an abstract and predictable relationship—just as the food she offers him makes him sick (all the women in Joe's life try to feed him; one of them is a waitress in a restaurant).

Joe's many adventures with women are attempts to escape the abstract quality of a latently homosexual life. As Joe pauses outside Miss Burden's house before keeping a tryst with her, Faulkner says, "The dark was filled with the voices, myriad, out of all time that he had known, as though all the past was a flat pattern. And going on: tomorrow night, all the tomorrows, to be part of the flat pattern, going on." "Then," says Faulkner, "it was time"—which seems to be a pun (the same one occurs in *The Sound and the Fury*) meaning that now Joe's existence can be measured by time (the urn consciousness) rather than by the abstraction of eternity. But the connection with Miss Burden, like all of Joe's connections with women, turns into a ritual reaffirmation that no such connection is possible, a circular path back to the compulsive pattern—as we see when after various ingenious phases of sexual flight and pursuit, Miss Burden, before Joe kills her, is transmuted in appearance and behavior into a mocking likeness of McEachern. The sexual dilemma of Joe's life is nicely symbolized in the episode where he lolls in the woods (and gashes the whiskey tins) reading a magazine "of that type whose covers bear either pictures of young women in underclothes or pictures of men shooting one another with pistols." He reads as a man "walking along the street might count the cracks in the pavement, to the last final page, the last and final word." He goes through life with this same attachment to his pattern, hating the women in underclothes, longing for a purely masculine annihilation.

In symbolic polarity to the compulsive pattern we have Lena, who does not need to flee from involvement in human life, and Lucas Burch. Distantly adumbrating all the polarities of *Light in August*, the gay irresponsible, aimless Burch symbolizes pure Chaos. Perhaps through the child in Lena's womb, Burch symbolizes the undetermined possibility of a future the direction of which will be decided by the final resolution of forces among the other characters. If so, we may say that *Light in August* is a "hopeful" book. For the future is in the hands of Lena and Byron Bunch— a woman who endures and loves and a man who has decided to "accept the risks of his humanity."

3.

Mr. Warren suggests that we ought not to think of Faulkner as an exclusively Southern writer but as a writer concerned with modern times in general. To this, one might add that Faulkner has many affinities with both Hawthorne and Melville. As Malcolm Cowley has said, the myth of a Southern society which emerges from Faulkner's work as a whole can be compared with Hawthorne's myth of New England. One might add that the dilemma with which Faulkner confronts Bunch and Hightower —whether to take the responsibility of moral intervention in human affairs—is the same dilemma which confronts many of Hawthorne's characters (for example, the painter in "Prophetic Pictures"). Joe Christmas would be recognized by Hawthorne; for he is frightened and obsessed by the inescapable stain on every human life. There is never any real proof that Joe is part Negro, but Joe's gratuitous assumption that he is tainted is at the root of all his actions. He becomes as obsessed with his stain as does Aylmer with the blemish on his wife's face in Hawthorne's "The Birthmark" and with a purpose as relentless and immoral as Aylmer's he goes about removing the stain—an impulse which arises in the central figures of both "The Birthmark" and *Light in August* from what is, in the final moral terms, simply their inability to bear the burden of being human. (The word "burden," by the way, seems to have the same significance for the Southern writers as the pack of the peddler had for Hawthorne and Melville: the "burden" of one's history or of one's continually self-annihilating humanity. Miss Burden, in *Light in August*, is not the only character in Southern fiction so named.)

Faulkner and Melville share a liking for physical, dynamic, and animal images. Both abound in images of light and dark. In Faulkner's novel there is a persistent reference to white "blood" and black "blood," and Joe's ambiguous character is symbolized by the dark serge trousers and white shirt he invariably wears. Both Ahab and Joe Christmas are seeking an elusive *purity*, symbolized by whiteness. Both shape their doom by their sharp rejections of their own humanity. Both are "unmanned," to use Melville's word, by fate or by their own moral acts. Faulkner's manner of handling symbols and themes is like Melville's. His downright spiritual vehemence often produces a wonderful lyric or epic sense of life; but sometimes the symbols are crudely imagined or imperfectly assimilated in context. For example, the uneasy connection of Joe Christmas with Christ: several of Joe's acts take place on Friday, or "on the third day"; Mrs. McEachern washes his feet; Burch betrays him for a thousand pieces of silver; Hines, his grandfather and the only father Joe knows, imagines that he is God. Faulkner seems not to sense exactly how the Christ theme should be handled, sometimes making it too overt and sometimes not overt enough. His attempts to enlarge Joe's character by adducing a willed mythology remind one of Melville's similar attempts in *Pierre*. It may finally seem to us that Faulkner and Melville are most in control of their work when they approach the epic form, as in *As I Lay Dying* and *Moby Dick*; but that when they try novels of complex symbolic human relationships, their effort suffers from their uncertain power of grouping symbols into a close coherent statement.

4.

It has been said of Faulkner that his rhetoric and the actions it expresses are so terrific that they annihilate his characters, that his characters become mere targets for violent emotive bombardments. The measure of truth in this criticism does not destroy Faulkner as an artist. It simply indicates that he is one kind of artist—surely he is not a novelist of manners in quite the way that such a phrase as "the Balzac of the South" would imply. As if in self-criticism, Faulkner writes of Hines and his fanatical sermons: "So they believed that he was a little crazy.... It was not that he seemed to be trying to conceal one thing by telling another. It was that his words, his telling, just did not synchronize with what his hearers believed would (and must) be the scope of a single individual." Yet in one of the utterances of the Reverend Mr. Hightower we find this idea translated into a true definition of tragedy: "Too much happens. That's it. Man performs, engenders, more than he can or should have to bear. That's how he finds that he can bear anything. That's it. That's what is so terrible." In such a statement as this Faulkner begins to justify the overplus of superhuman and subhuman violence in his novels. Nevertheless there remains a discrepancy between the theoretical justification and the artistic practice. We cannot avoid phrasing the aesthetic implication of Hightower's words in some such way as this: "Faulkner attributes more action and emotion to his characters than can meaningfully be attributed to them."

The alienation of man *via* language is a common theme in *Light in August*. The people who have beaten and robbed Joe and left him on the floor of a cheap boarding house, speak "in a language which he did not understand." The sermons of Hightower seem to have been expressly contrived to separate him from his congregation. As for Lena, her separation-by-language is always maintained only to the degree necessary to her total purpose. When she asks along the road for Burch, people direct her to "Bunch," but to her they always seem to say "Burch." She is purposefully separated from irrelevance and relaxed in her vision of reality. Separation by language is surely a fact of human life. But is Faulkner entirely in control of this theme? In the orphanage the dietitian and Hines meet "calm and quiet and terse as two conspirators" and then proceed to discourse in some pseudo-Old Testament language which is anything but calm, quiet, or terse. But perhaps it is another form of dissociation which makes this putatively powerful situation seem defective. Perhaps—in order that the dissociation might be in *his* mind, for it needs to be in *someone's* mind—the five-year-old Joe should have been present, watching and listening in awe to the terrible creatures, his mythical father and mother. It is simply a novelist's mistake to present us with a sharp dislocation between his characters and what they say, without accounting in context for the dislocation. One feels that Faulkner has missed a chance in this scene to form a profound associative human situation.

This leads us to a general question: What is the quality of consciousness displayed in *Light in August?* Surely, it is not a consciousness which broods over the whole range of action, associating people with each other or with a culture, establishing their manners and morals in a whole containment. It is a consciousness in flight and pursuit, wonderfully aware of fact, the physical and animal fact, wonderfully in possession of extreme emotions and the ecstasy of violence, cognizant too of the tender humorousness of love, and in general wonderfully fantastic and magical. *Par excellence*, it is the American folk-literary consciousness. When it seeks to interpret or enlighten the human situation, when Faulkner breaks off the humorous-tragical flow of rhetorical poetry and ventures an observation on human manners, he is likely to sound naïve. He will speak in the manner of the folk proverb: "Yes, sir. You just let one of them get married or get into trouble without being married, and right then and there is where she secedes from the woman race and spends the balance of her life trying to get joined up with the man race. That's why they dip snuff and smoke and want to vote." Or he will attempt a more intellectually formulated observation, with the following unhappy result: "the faces of the old men lined by that sheer accumulation of frustration and doubt which is so often the other side of the picture of hale and respected full years"—What a piece of philosophy! One can hardly help sensing an uncomfortable hiatus between Faulkner's poetic portrayal of manners and his explicit consciousness of them.[1]

Probably the episodes of family and cultural history which accompany Faulkner's account of Miss Burden and Hightower would mean more to a Southerner than they do to me. But especially in the case of Hightower there seems to be a failure of consciousness precisely at the point where we should understand the quality of the association between Hightower and his own history. Hightower has projected his sexual and spiritual impotence back upon a myth of his grandfather. Faulkner goes along with Hightower on this point, assuming too much that a fantasy projected from some center of real causation is the cause itself. He nearly allows Hightower to determine the quality of his (Faulkner's) consciousness. On the other hand, he is capable of involving Burch in a situation which calls for a degree of consciousness far above what seems possible, and then arbitrarily giving him the necessary consciousness; so that we have a dull country lout whose "rage and impotence is now almost ecstatic. He seems to muse now upon a sort of timeless and beautiful infallibility in his unpredictable frustrations" (the qualifiers "almost," "seems to," "a sort of" are significant). And a moment later we find Burch (so it seems) reflecting that a Negro he is talking with "does not appear to have enough ratiocinative power to find the town." In *Anna Karenina* a dog conducts a humorous and anxious conversation with himself. But unlike the Burch episode, this does not seem in the least out of place, because Tolstoy with his great associative consciousness always gives one the feeling that he

1. But the observations I have made in this paragraph would be substantially less true if applied to *The Sound and the Fury*.

knows exactly when and how much to withdraw or extend his mind in the universe of his novel. I do not mean to imply that Faulkner's novel *lacks* consciousness, but only that the consciousness it displays is sometimes unhappily biased, bardic, parochial, and, in the societal or cultural sense, unmannered. Davy Crockett still screams in the Southern wilderness.

But of course any discussion which compares Faulkner unfavorably with a writer like Tolstoy must not be guilty of the assumption that Faulkner's Southern culture is as cohesive and knowable as Tolstoy's Russian culture was; obviously it is not. And Faulkner's claim to be the novelist of a culture (if that is his claim) must be judged on the basis of his whole work. Nevertheless the evidence of *Light in August*, though it shows that Faulkner is capable of very fine and very extensive and complex fictional constructions, also seems to indicate that he can fail us exactly at that level of existence where the subtle complications of human behavior have to be established. Faulkner works inward from the extremities, from the mechanics and the ecstasy of life. And this relentless, bardic-American bias often makes us wish he would reverse the procedure, that his consciousness would work through human manners into the human character and then outward toward the extremities it can contain or fail to contain. Human life submits itself to die at the hands of the artist so that it may be reborn in art, somewhat as Joe Christmas submits himself to the beatings of McEachern: "The boy's body might have been wood or stone; a post or a tower upon which the sentient part of him mused like a hermit, contemplative and remote with ecstasy and selfcrucifixion." One wants to know finally, what manner of man is this *between* the stone and the crucifixion?

5.

But it is only one's high estimation of Faulkner which raises these questions at all. Like the author of *Moby Dick*, Faulkner might say of himself, "I try everything; I achieve what I can." In these bad times, a serious venturesomeness must count heavily with us. But it is also a sense of Faulkner's achievement which makes me think him the equal of any American novelist of his generation.

Perhaps *The Great Gatsby* is the only novel of the time which can be defended as superior to Faulkner's best work.

In the nineteen-thirties the liberal-progressive culture turned away from Faulkner for many of the same bad reasons which caused it, eighty years before, to turn away from Melville. If our liberal thought now begins to return from its disastrous wanderings of the last decades—that era of the great rejections— and to recover its vitality, it is because it grows capable of coming to terms with Faulkner, as it already learns again to come to terms with Hawthorne and Melville.

"STRANGE GODS" IN JEFFERSON, MISSISSIPPI: ANALYSIS OF *ABSALOM, ABSALOM!*

WILLIAM R. POIRIER

ALMOST WITHOUT EXCEPTION, existing criticism of Faulkner has ignored *Absalom, Absalom!* or has examined it either as a naturalistic novel full of Gothic horror and romantic attitudinizing or as little more than a curious source book, significant only for what it can tell us about the problems of Quentin Compson in *The Sound and the Fury*. The only notable exception of which I am aware is Malcolm Cowley's essay "William Faulkner's Legend of the South."[1] But the commentary on *Absalom, Absalom!* which is included in that essay is not meant by Mr. Cowley to be extensive, and it only partially succeeds, it seems to me, in suggesting the true character of the novel.

An understanding of the environment which we see conditioning Quentin in *The Sound and the Fury* is of course helpful. We can perhaps better appreciate his response to experience in

1. *Sewanee Review,* LIII (Summer, 1945), 343–361.

Absalom, Absalom! if we have learned from the earlier book
that Quentin's disillusionment, the vacuity of purpose which
plagues him, cannot be divorced from the spiritual dead end
which his mother represents and which his father pathetically
articulates. The latter, summing up his view of life, tells Quentin
that "Time is your misfortune."[2] The remark is characteristic of
Mr. Compson's teaching throughout *The Sound and the Fury*. In
terms of it, his son has been deprived of the possibility of abstracting human values from a historical context. The father has slowly
undermined for Quentin the myth of any spiritual transcendence
of what seems to be the mechanism of historical fact. This is in
great part the problem faced by Quentin in *Absalom, Absalom!*
as well. It is a problem which makes Quentin, as an organizer of
Thomas Sutpen's story, the dramatic center of this novel. Indeed,
in *Absalom, Absalom!* Quentin is nearly allowed to appropriate
the position of the author.

But this is not to say, as many have, that Quentin or some
other character is Faulkner's spokesman. Faulkner is extremely
careful to prevent his novels from ever being controlled by the
"efficient confessionals" which Kenneth Burke claims to find in
them.[3] The form in both *The Sound and the Fury* and *Absalom,
Absalom!* prevents any one of the narrators from seducing the
reader to a restricted, wholly individual point of view. It is quite
clear that the author sympathizes in the earlier book with Benjy
and Quentin. But if we are looking for Faulkner to express himself, we shall find that he does so impersonally in the structure of
the work itself. Benjy, Quentin, and Jason tend, in different
degrees, to neutralize one another. It is the structure of *The Sound
and the Fury* which emphasizes the wholeness of Dilsey's point
of view and which affirms the presence, if only as a choral effect,
of a traditional and moral context in which we can place the
whole novel.

The adaptation of this method to a new set of circumstances

2. *The Sound and the Fury* (New York: Random House, 1946), p. 123.
3. Kenneth Burke, *The Philosophy of Literary Form* (Baton Rouge, 1941),
p. 117.

constitutes the most significant connection between *The Sound and the Fury* and *Absalom, Absalom!* In the formal arrangement of this later novel, for example, we see Faulkner's sense of history played off against the social irresponsibility of Rosa Coldfield, the most consciously incantatory of all his narrators. We see Thomas Sutpen try to make history begin in his own image and, when the damage is done, Quentin Compson attempt to discover the meaning of his historical background with Sutpen as the central figure. The attempt to create history is both the story of Sutpen and, with a difference, the conscious effort of Quentin as a narrator of that story. Faulkner has joined the two themes so that the persisting disruptions caused by Sutpen almost fatally affect Quentin's attempt to discover the meaning of his heritage.

Because Quentin, if he is to define himself, must confront these persisting disruptions, it is little wonder that Faulkner is so obviously fond of him. The preoccupations and the difficulties of the two are not dissimilar. Within the chaotic nature of Sutpen's history and Rosa's "demonizing," Quentin tries to find some human value adhering to what is apparently a representative anecdote of his homeland. In doing so, he must somehow overcome a problem such as confronts the contemporary writer. As T. S. Eliot defines it, it is the problem of overcoming "the damage of a lifetime and of having been born into an unsettled society."[4] And Quentin is "older at twenty," he tells Shreve, "than a lot of people who have died" [p. 377].[5]

In Quentin's mind, the career of Thomas Sutpen is the most persistently disturbing element in the history of his native region, and one in which all of his family have been involved. Indeed, his preoccupation with the meaning of the story is so distressing that he can see no respite from it even in the future: "Nevermore of peace. Nevermore of peace. Nevermore Nevermore Nevermore" [p. 373]. The reader who is acquainted with *The Sound and the Fury* may understandably wish to view Quentin's problem here

4. *After Strange Gods* (London, 1934), p. 54.
5. Page references to *Absalom, Absalom!* are to the Random House edition, 1936.

in terms of his experience in the earlier novel. Quentin cannot, for example, hear Rosa continue the story past her recounting of the murder of Charles Bon. He may see in this incident a distorted image of his own failure in *The Sound and the Fury* to defend the honor of his sister, Caddy, and of the incest which he claims to have committed. At different times Quentin associates himself both with Bon, who feels compelled to threaten incest, and with Henry, Judith's brother, who must kill his friend to prevent it and the accompanying evil of miscegenation. Quentin, who could neither dignify Caddy's immorality by the damning sin of incest nor properly defend his sister's honor, discovers something of himself in history by recreating the circumstances which led to Bon's murder. But it is well to remember that Quentin's interest in Sutpen's story transcends any reference he finds in it for such personal problems, which, after all, we are acquainted with only from observing his activity outside the context of *Absalom, Absalom!* Had Quentin assumed the luxury of treating the Sutpen story merely as an objectification of some personal obsession, the total effect of the novel would have partaken of the overindulgent and romantic self-dramatization of Rosa's soliloquy.

Quentin tries to place Sutpen in a social and historical context. By doing so he can perhaps discover his own tradition and the reasons for its collapse. His father tells him that in Sutpen's day, in Quentin's past, the circumstances in which people operated at least simplified what Mr. Robert Penn Warren refers to as the risks of being human:[6]

of that day and time, of a dead time; people too as we are, and victims too as we are, but victims of a different circumstance, simpler and therefore, integer for integer, larger, more heroic . . . not dwarfed and involved but distinct, uncomplex who had the gift of living once or dying once instead of being diffused and scattered creatures . . . [p. 89].

Quentin will discover that the times were not so "simple" as his father imagines. But he is still painfully aware of the deprivation

6. "Cowley's Faulkner," *The New Republic,* CXV (August 12, 1946), 177.

his father defines, a deprivation which Shreve, who lays no claim either on the past or to a tradition, cannot fully understand. Perhaps Malcolm Cowley is right and the Sutpen story represents for Quentin the essence of the Deep South.[7] But *Absalom, Absalom!* is not primarily about the South or about a doomed family as a symbol of the South. It is a novel about the meaning of history for Quentin Compson. The story of Sutpen simply represents that part of the past which Quentin must understand if he is to understand himself. In this respect, Quentin's dilemma is very similar to that of Stephen Dedalus in *Ulysses*. Whether the scene is Ireland or the South, the problem of extracting value from a cultural heritage remains about the same. Indeed, Quentin has his own Buck Mulligan in his roommate, Shreve McCannon. When Shreve and other students at Harvard ask Quentin about the South, they really demand that he justify his own existence: *Tell about the South. What's it like there. What do they do there. Why do they live there. Why do they live at all...* [p. 174]. The painful consequence of Quentin's reply—which is the story of Sutpen—is that all of the questions remain for Shreve unanswered. Part of the history which Quentin reconstructs is a record of violence and evil. But Quentin hopes, when he begins, that in the world in which Sutpen lived, unlike his own world in *The Sound and the Fury*, violence was of some moral consequence and evil was at least a violation of a corruptible but not wholly devitalized moral code.

Regardless of what Sutpen might represent in Quentin's mind, it is soon made obvious to the reader, though the point is often missed, that he is above all a special case. In the context of the novel he is not even a typical Southern planter. It is emphasized that at least three of the other characters, Wash Jones, Charles Bon, and Mr. Coldfield, were at one time confronted respectively with the very things which injured Sutpen: the same social antagonism, nearly the same act of repudiation, and an almost identical opportunity to exploit the evils of the economic system. Sutpen alone seems able to pursue his ambition, what he calls his "design," not only in defiance of an outraged community but

7. Cowley, *Sewanee Review,* LIII (Summer, 1945), 344.

in ignorance of its codes and customs and with a complete insensitivity to human character.

Like the violence of Joe Christmas in *Light in August*, Sutpen's "design" is directed as much against a terrifying sense of his own insufficiency as against a society which apparently standardizes that insufficiency by caste or class systems. When his family moves from the primitively communal society of their mountain home to settle in the Tidewater, young Sutpen finds everything in the new environment phenomenal: the Negroes, the social customs, the differences in living standards among the white men employed, like his father, on the plantation. The boy cannot understand how or why this place should differ from the mountain settlement where "the land belonged to anybody and everybody" [p. 221]. He is naturally humiliated and confused when, carrying a message to the plantation owner, he is ordered away from the front door by a Negro in livery. Because he has been brought up in a society outside the one in which he now lives, he cannot fit the action of the "monkey nigger" into any acknowledged social pattern. It can be seen by young Sutpen only as a wholly personal affront. At the door, he finds himself "looking out from within the balloon face" of the Negro [p. 234], and at himself. Having no past, no background of his own by which he could appreciate the social complexity of the incident, he prejudicially assumes the position of his insulter, or the agent of his insulter, and both pities and degrades himself. At first he considers immediate revenge: he will shoot the Negro and the owner of the house. But he finally decides that the best thing he can do is to become as rich and powerful as the man from whose door he has been turned. This ambition develops into what he later calls his "design."

When Sutpen tells Quentin's grandfather about this incident, he claims that he felt then that "he would have to do something about it in order to live with himself for the rest of his life" [p. 234]. Years later he explains to General Compson that the "design" was "not what he wanted to do but what he just had to do, had to do it whether he wanted to or not" [p. 220]. He justifies himself by an appeal not to any moral code which might have been violated at the plantation door, but to some inexplicable compulsion over which he apparently can exert no discipline. It might be argued that Sutpen makes the worst of what someone like Wash Jones would have assimilated into the accepted order of things. In any case, the rest of his life is dedicated to a vindication of that little boy at the door, what he himself calls "the boy symbol" [p. 261].

The "boy symbol" motif persists throughout the novel and becomes connected with Sutpen's desire for a son. Indeed, the whole "design" is a calculated bid for a kind of immortality. His son and the rest of his descendants shall have all Sutpen lacked: wealth, power, untainted respectability. To that end, he first goes to Haiti to make a fortune only to abandon it and to repudiate his first wife and son, Charles Bon, when he discovers that she has a trace of Negro blood. The hundred-square-mile plantation called Sutpen's Hundred which he later builds in Mississippi is really a second and, it seems, unassailable foundation of the power and wealth that his heir, Henry Sutpen, shall perpetuate. And for respectability he chooses, much to the town's indignation, Ellen Coldfield, daughter not of the richest but of the most primly respectable and most religious family in Jefferson. It is characteristic of Sutpen that in selecting his wife he chooses, in place of the aristocratic connection he wishes to make, a marriage into a family which is merely priggishly proud. Without any sense or knowledge of the past, Sutpen, through his son, would belong only to the future. Quentin imagines that Bon recognized Henry as his brother by seeing in his face the image of *"the man who shaped us both out of that blind chancy darkness which we call the future"* [p. 317]. As a reflection of the vindicated boy symbol, Henry becomes for his father a means of disowning the past.

When Sutpen arrived in Jefferson to upset the town first by his unorthodox and dishonest methods and then by apparently corrupting the Coldfields, he was, Rosa says, "a man who so far as anyone . . . knew, either had no past or did not dare reveal it— a man who rode into town out of nowhere" [p. 16]. It is significant that Sutpen gives a very poor account of his own experiences and that he treats his activity prior to Jefferson with boredom, almost with disinterest. Quentin's grandfather, who is really the one person in town who befriends Sutpen, manages to induce him to recount some of his past life. When Sutpen does so, it is as if he were just

...telling a story about something a man named Thomas Sutpen had experienced, which would still have been the same story if the man had had no name at all, if it had been told about any man or no man over whiskey at night [p. 247].

He shows no regard whatever for cause and effect and, General Compson complains, little for logical sequence. Such an inability to tell his own story is indicative of Sutpen's refusal to believe that anyone could have any interest in his past activity. He can ignore the details of his past because, as far as he is concerned, they hold no portent of his future. In terms of his "design," he has achieved a self-identification beyond anything that has been done or can be done to him.

But ironically enough, that part of his past which he outlines for General Compson will later indicate to Quentin the source and the reasons for the retribution which overtakes him. The general himself is aware of the perilous quality of this man's calculated activity when he hears Sutpen bombastically explain the disposition of his first wife. He has dared treat her as an abstract, expendable counter to be used by him with "fairness" but with complete impersonality:

I found that she was not and could never be, through no fault of her own, adjunctive or incremental to the design which I had in mind, so I provided for her and put her aside [p. 240].

According to Quentin, "Sutpen's trouble was 'innocence' ":

...that innocence which believed that the ingredients of morality were like the ingredients of pie or cake and once you had measured them and balanced them and mixed them and put them into the oven it was all finished and nothing but pie or cake could come out [p. 263].

Part of that "innocence" is, of course, the belief that any woman will accept money as a final recompense for desertion. Bon's sudden and ironically unintentional appearance with Henry at Sutpen's Hundred makes that expression of Sutpen's "innocence" seem purblind indeed. Sutpen, who at least gave Bon the name he bears, is the only one in the family who is aware of the guest's real identity. But all he can do for the present is to remain silent. To acknowledge that Charles Bon is his son would be to infuse humanity into the "ingredients" of his "design." He is simply incapable of doing it. He fails to realize that Bon is demanding only the same sort of recognition denied him as a boy at the plantation door. And he can forget human need so completely that he cannot understand how or why his plans could be so affected by what he calls "a maelstrom of unpredicable and unreasoning human beings" [p. 275].

Sutpen's story might well be about his opportunities for becoming human. There are countless opportunities, like the appearance of Bon, which he has ignored. Potentially there were others during his childhood experience on the plantation which, for someone with his particular background, the social order simply did not make available. But Sutpen, as we have seen, comes totally to express the very inhumanity and injustice which he would have us believe compelled the "design" in the first place. When Judith's life is ruined as a consequence of the complications which lead to the murder of Bon, she complains to Quentin's grandmother that the fulfillment of her life was frustrated by forces over which she had no control.

Because you make so little impression, you see. You get born and you try this and dont know why only you keep on trying it and you are born at the same time with a lot of other people, all mixed up with them, like trying to, having to, move your arms and legs with strings only the same strings are hitched to all the other arms and legs and the others all trying and they dont know why either except that the strings are all in one another's way like five or six people all trying to make a rug on the same loom only each one wants to weave his own pattern into the rug...[p. 127].

Actually, it is her father's "innocence" of anything but his own compulsion which disorders her life and the lives of "a lot of other people." Quentin, only with much pain, finally discovers in the career of Thomas Sutpen not the essence of his past so much as a force which disrupts all that was possibly coherent, orderly, and humane in the past.

Both in *Go Down, Moses* and in this novel, Faulkner clearly recognizes the evil tendencies of the plantation system. But Sutpen acts as a wholly "modern" element in that system. He unknowingly abstracts those evil tendencies from the controlling fiber of the community and its traditions, simply exploiting them without discipline for the purposes of his own ambition. It is no wonder that Mr. Compson feels able to observe that perhaps the Civil War was "instigated by that family fatality" [p. 118] for which Sutpen is largely responsible. We are told that Rosa's father, who actually equates the force of the Civil War with the exploitations of his son-in-law, firmly believed that in both of these the South "was now paying the price for having erected its economic edifice not on the rock of stern morality but on the shifting sands of opportunism and moral brigandage" [p. 260]. Faulkner, in these and other remarks made in *Absalom, Absalom!*, gives full notice to the opinion that the true nature of the plantation system and of Sutpen's "design" was revealed negatively at the moment and in the act of breakdown.

But the novel itself does not allow us to be so categorical. We have already seen how factitious is so close an identification between the character of Sutpen and that of the social system he exploits. As Faulkner sees it, the system was corrupt enough not to be able to control its Thomas Sutpens. And we may even view the Civil War as a consequence of such a further corruption of existing order as that which was carried on by Sutpen. It is well to remember, however, that a civil war was lost by Jefferson, Mississippi, when Sutpen finished his home and married Ellen Coldfield in 1838. The terrible result of both his "design" and the war between the states was fratricide. Faulkner's metaphorical use of the Sutpen story does not go much further than that; it is never extended into allegory. Sutpen is not what is called the Old South, but rather a force in it which was so corrupting that possibly, as Quentin thinks Rosa believes, *"only through the blood of our men and the tears of our women could He stay this demon and efface his name and lineage from the earth"* [p. 11]. But such a statement, in itself, is merely a rephrasing of Quentin's problem and of the theme of the novel. Quentin is trying to find in the issues of the conflicts within the Sutpen family and within the community of Jefferson some expression of a sense of human and moral value.

The structure of *Absalom, Absalom!* is a reflection of both the nature and the method of Quentin's search, in a confusion of historical fact, for value. Consideration of that structure might begin simply by dividing the novel into two parts of four chapters each, leaving Rosa's monologue, which separates them by exclusively occupying all of Chapter V, for special consideration. The first four chapters, in which the whole of Sutpen's story is continually repeated with changing emphases, are really a dramatization of Quentin's activity at the sources of his information. In the last four chapters, during which he is at Harvard College, Quentin, with the help of his roommate, Shreve, pieces together all of the facts and opinions about the story held by Rosa, his father, and his grandfather along with a good deal of information which is apparently a part of his heritage. All of the data, as it comes to him in the early chapters, is confused, contradictory, and phenomenal in character. It is like the letter which Judith had given to his grandmother and which is now a document in his attempt to order the story coherently:

the writing faded, almost indecipherable, yet meaningful, familiar in shape and sense, the name and presence of volatile and sentient forces; you bring them together in the proportions called for, but nothing happens; you re-read, tedious and intent, poring, making sure that you have forgotten nothing, made no miscalculation; you bring them together again and again nothing happens: just the words, the symbols, the shapes themselves, shadowy, inscrutable and serene, against that turgid background of a horrible and bloody mischancing of human affairs [p. 101].

The events of the Sutpen narrative are neither so contemporary nor, except for Rosa, so personally consequential to the speakers here as are those in *The Sound and the Fury*. Yet neither Rosa nor Mr. Compson, both of whom first tell the story to Quentin in the early chapters, are wholly trustworthy narrators. In the first chapter, Quentin becomes directly involved in the story, parts of which he has heard throughout his childhood, when he visits Rosa Coldfield in compliance with a note she has sent him. Before revealing the task she has planned, Rosa, by way of justifying herself, begins to tell her version of Sutpen's character and activity. As he listens, Quentin does not yet realize that, like her handwriting, Rosa's "demonizing" of Sutpen is indicative of a character which is "cold, implacable, and even ruthless" [p. 10].

Her description of Sutpen's first years in Jefferson is wild and incredible. Sutpen becomes *"an ogre, some beast out of tales to frighten children with"* [p. 158]. But the distortions resulting from her nightmarish sensibility are continually being revealed to the reader by the contradictory nature of Rosa's own testimony. At other times, her version of an incident may remain consistent throughout her conversation, only to be invalidated by some other narrator who is either more informed or at least less prejudiced. Her "outraged recapitulation" evokes for Quentin a vision of Sutpen's arrival in Jefferson—"Out of quiet thundercap he would abrupt (man-horse-demon)...with grouped behind him his band of wild niggers like beasts" [p. 8]. We are given quite a different picture, however, in the next chapter. Mr. Compson describes Sutpen's first appearance in Jefferson as it was viewed by Quentin's grandfather. We see in place of Rosa's "demon," a man "gaunt now almost to emaciation" [p. 32] trying to reach his property before dark so that he can find food for his Negroes, who, though wild, sit quietly in the wagon. The point is not that Rosa is unfair to Sutpen. He is a "demon" to be sure. But, as I hope to show presently, her reasons for calling him one are as ambiguous and questionable as her version of the event just discussed.

The detailing of incidents by Quentin's father, in Chapters II, III, and IV, if not as distorted as Rosa's, is no less riddled with faulty information. On the basis of what he knows, Mr. Compson believes, for example, that Sutpen forbade Judith's marriage merely because her fiancé, Charles Bon, kept an octoroon mistress in New Orleans. Considering the final consequences of the father's refusal, Mr. Compson understandably remarks: "It's just incredible. It just does not explain" [p. 100]. But Quentin, after his trip to Sutpen's Hundred with Rosa, comes into possession of more information. In the process of retelling the story in Chapter VII, he corrects his father's error in Chapter II. We learn what only Sutpen knew at the time: the real identity of Charles Bon. Judith's betrothal to him was forbidden by Sutpen because it would have resulted not only in incest, but in miscegenation. This new information not only partially invalidates Mr. Compson's analysis, but also reflects adversely on the already questionable account of the story given by Rosa. In the first chapter she tells Quentin that she "saw Judith's marriage forbidden without rhyme or reason or shadow of excuse" [p. 18]. It is this belief, based on ignorance of the facts, which partly explains the peculiar quality of her hatred of Sutpen. Rosa's bitterness and frustration at being the last child of cold and unloving parents finds total expression in the collapse of the romantic life she had lived vicariously in that of her niece, Judith.

In the light of the new facts uncovered by Quentin, the reader must now re-evaluate Rosa's emotional state which has its reference in the incredibility for her of Sutpen's prohibition of the marriage. By doing so the reader sees that the attitude of Rosa, or it might be of any other narrator, is understandable not in terms of what actually has happened but because of either her lack of information or her inability to change her mind when new information is made available. To Quentin's already prodigious task of finally ordering the story is added the responsibility of reinterpreting all that Rosa has told him and, at the same time, of giving an understandable context to her "incredulous and unbearable amazement" [p. 14]. Quentin's version of the Judith-Bon affair causes a reorientation of the whole Sutpen story. Sutpen's attitude toward the marriage becomes a coherent element in his "design" and Bon's insistence on returning to marry his half-sister becomes a dramatically powerful gesture activated by his need for paternal recognition.

This correction of Mr. Compson's statement in Chapter IV [p. 100] by Quentin in Chapter VII [p. 266] is superficially indicative of the form of the novel. But as I have pointed out, the dramatization in the early chapters of Quentin's attempt to assemble all the facts is separated from his painful effort in the later chapters meaningfully to order this material by the long soliloquy of Rosa Coldfield. The novel seems to turn upon her chapter. Indeed, before Quentin begins to piece the whole story together in his room at Harvard, the opposition to Sutpen seems most strenuously represented by her.

Before dealing with Rosa Coldfield in greater detail, I want to suggest once again that the emphasis here is primarily upon Quentin, that neither Rosa nor Sutpen can serve as the dramatic center of this novel. Quentin's acts of remembrance actually determine the form of the novel. Rosa's soliloquy is apparently a product of her mind. But it is presented as if it were being recalled in Quentin's even as he sits listening to her. Before he and Shreve begin the job of historical recreation, Quentin can see in Rosa's approach to the Sutpen story the great difficulty which will beset him in his effort to discover the human content of his heritage. From her involvement in the "design," Rosa seems to conclude that history fulfills itself not through the efforts or aspirations of human beings, but wholly in an impersonal, antagonistic universe, through abstract "designs" or by the action of Fate. If that is the case, Quentin's tradition is devoid of human value. Eventually, his attempt to discover a meaningful tradition depends for its success upon his discovery of a participant in the conflict with Sutpen with whom he can share an active sense of association. Whoever that individual is, he must be able, as Rosa is not, to acknowledge the world outside himself; he must surrender some of his individuality in order actively to participate in society. Rosa simply compounds for Quentin the already frightening phenomena of Sutpen. She is no more aware than her "demon" of any necessary relationship between her aspirations and the moral codes and social disciplines of the community.

Considering the possibility that Sutpen's "design" has denied to Rosa any hope for the future, it is a not-unimportant irony, for its effect on the total meaning of the novel, that Rosa's association with Sutpen is actually only intermittent and largely vicarious. Even before seeing him for the first time, Rosa is conditioned by her guardian, a spinster aunt, to think of Sutpen as an "ogre," a "demon." Her only direct involvement with him, other than the yearly visits discontinued at her father's death, occurs when Miss Rosa is Judith's companion and Sutpen suddenly proposes to her. But the most injurious contact exists without Sutpen's knowledge and operates in Miss Rosa's dream state as part of her romantic illusions about Charles Bon.

Although she has never seen him, Rosa has fallen deeply in love with her vision of the man who she never learns is Sutpen's unrecognized son. She has heard him discussed by Ellen, whose plans for an engagement between him and Judith, also made in ignorance of Bon's identity, come to objectify Rosa's own romantic longings. Her dream of Bon is a dream of a future, a "living fairy tale" [p. 76]. Like Sutpen's dream of the future, it is a "fairy tale" which is foolishly isolated from the world of other human beings in which it must, if at all, exist. Rosa's dream was concocted in the hallways of her darkened house. Only there could she remain *"shod with the very damp and velvet silence of the womb"* [p. 145], unapprehended by what she calls *"some cold head-nuzzling forceps of the savage time"* [p. 144].

When Wash Jones shouts beneath her window that Henry has "kilt" Charles Bon "dead as a beef" [p. 133], she leaves this "hallway" and rushes out to Sutpen's Hundred. She does not go, as she claims, to rescue Judith from the curse which seems to be on the house. Rather, she is trying desperately to save some of the enchantment of Judith's proposed wedding, her own "vicarious bridal" [p. 77]. But when she rushes into the hall calling for Judith, her *"shadow-realm of make-believe"* [p. 147] comes into direct conflict with Sutpen's *"factual scheme"* [p. 143]. This is embodied for Rosa in Clytie, Sutpen's daughter by a Negro slave and, Rosa claims, *"his own image the cold Cerberus of his private hell"* [p. 136]. Clytie has blocked Rosa's path which leads to Judith's room, to Bon's body, which has been placed there. The moment of conflict has finally been achieved. But even Rosa knows that her involvement in the Sutpen tragedy is indirect: *"we seemed to glare at one another not as two faces but as two abstract contradictions which we actually were"* [p. 138].

At this point the narrative stops. Attention is focused by Rosa upon the significance of Clytie's grip on her arm. She cries out, not at Clytie but at what she calls the *"cumulative over-reach of despair itself"* [p. 140]. In attempting to define its elements, Rosa expands this single moment, which is in a sense out of time, into her whole experience of life. Her immediate response becomes enlarged into the total response of an individual who has encountered the disabling grip of a damaging past as she tries to realize her dream of the future. But even as she stands there, Rosa persists in believing that there *"is a might-have-been which is more true than truth"* [p. 143]. Only when she is released by Clytie are her illusions completely shattered. She finds that though Bon is dead, she still is denied by Judith the chance to look at him, that Judith, left nearly a widow, refuses to grieve for him. Rosa at last faces what Sutpen optimistically refused to face: *"that sickness somewhere at the prime foundation of this factual scheme"* [p. 143]. That "sickness," one might say, is primarily an ignorance of context. The pattern of events which Rosa had chosen to recognize was only a dream. One action, which to a narrator like Quentin might fit naturally into the sequence of events, can suddenly thrust a *"maelstrom of unbearable reality"* [p. 150] into her dream life.

The collapse of Rosa's illusions is roughly equivalent to Sutpen's sudden discovery, also due to Bon's activity, that in pursuit of his "design" he seems to have arrived "at a result absolutely and forever incredible" [p. 263]. Sutpen still believes that it is merely a matter of miscalculation and that "whether it was a good or a bad design is beside the point" [p. 263]. But he feels compelled to go to General Compson in order to "review the facts for an impartial...mind to examine and find and point out to him" his mistake [p. 267]. Similarly, Rosa must reassess her whole experience in relation to her fatal excursion into the "factual scheme" of things. And she tells the story of her life to Quentin after she has experienced the effects of having been awakened out of the dream state. The shock and revulsion resulting from the stair episode is imposed back upon situations from which the necessity of Rosa's emotions would not seem naturally to have arisen. Rosa can acknowledge the past only through the retroactive distortions of her own rage and frustration. Her version of the story is infinitely more complex than Sutpen's. But it cannot assist Quentin in his task even as much as that superficial outline of his experience which is all Sutpen could give to General Compson.

The poverty of Sutpen's imagination and the neurotic richness of Rosa's place the two figures at poles. Yet in their different ways, both express a wholly nonsocial, dangerously individualistic point of view. This polar equality between Sutpen and Rosa is similar in kind to the thematic relationship existing in *Light in August* between Hightower and Joe Christmas, neither of whom even meet until the climax of that novel. Hightower's hysterical suggestion that he and Joe Christmas had spent the evening of the murder in an illicit relationship is only factually implausible. Rosa and Sutpen were, as pathetically, made for each other. That is the ironic appropriateness of Sutpen's proposal. What Rosa confesses to Quentin, and to us, is the story of a woman who, confronting a world as furiously antagonistic as Sutpen's, feels that she can come to life only as a man:

But it was no summer of a virgin's itching discontent; no summer's caesarean lack which should have torn me, dead flesh or even embryo, from the living: or else, by friction's ravishing of the male-furrowed meat, also weaponed and panoplied as a man instead of hollow woman [p. 145].

It is sufficient to say that Sutpen represents all that she would but cannot be. In her soliloquy he is given alternately the face of an ogre and the *"shape of a hero"* [p. 167]. She recalls that her life *"was at last worth something"* [p. 162] when she helped care for him after the war. His proposal is accepted simply because he is a man and, she thinks then, a heroic one: she *"lost all the shibboleth erupting of cannot, will not, never will in one red instant's fierce obliteration"* [p. 163]. The breaking of the engagement occurs only when he intimates that she is merely the means to provide him with another son to carry on the "design." In a rage, she returns to her "womb-like corridor" [p. 112] to live on the charity of the town and to continue her "demonizing" of Sutpen, a role which her aunt "seems to have invested her with at birth along with the swaddling clothes" [p. 61].

But the very attitudes implicated in her final revulsion and hatred of Sutpen further the ironic similarities already suggested as existing between Sutpen and Rosa Coldfield. Both of them try desperately to disown the past. Rosa has had her own design, one by which she was obsessed with a future even more impossible of achievement than Sutpen's. Sutpen's scapegoat is the "monkey nigger"; Rosa's is Sutpen. She uses him, as Sutpen used his experience at the plantation door, to objectify an exclusively egocentric and romantic view of life which has been wrenched apart by forces and events for which she holds this remarkably childish man too exclusively responsible. She never sees in the very nature of her illusions—nor does he in his—the source of their destruction.

Faulkner's own literary position is powerfully suggested by the dramatic function in the novel of Rosa's self-negating soliloquy. Chapter V is comparable, in this respect, to Yeats' poem *Meditations in Time of Civil War*. If I read that poem correctly, it dramatizes the dilemma of a literary artist attempting to find his metaphors in an unsettled society, a society bent on disvaluation. Recognizing this feature in *Absalom, Absalom!*, one is almost obliged to associate the problems of the author with the problems of Quentin Compson. In Rosa Coldfield's soliloquy, Faulkner has dramatically fused literary with social disorders. These very disorders are in large part what T. S. Eliot is concerned with in *After Strange Gods*. Both Rosa's point of view and the career of Thomas Sutpen, which concerns her, are illustrative of the heretical sensibility on the loose, of the danger, which Eliot defines for us, of overindulgent individualism: "when morals cease to be a matter of tradition and orthodoxy . . . and when each man is to elaborate his own, then *personality* becomes a thing of alarming importance."[8]

This sort of "elaboration" is clearly dramatized by Rosa's obliviousness to anything but her own needs and compulsions. But its literary applications are made most evident by the stylistic quality of her version of the Sutpen story. Through the style of Rosa's soliloquy, we are made aware that Sutpen is not alone in his pursuit of "strange Gods." A rather peculiar Eros intrudes upon Agape despite Rosa's incantations to an avenging God. Perhaps because of this, her soliloquy is reminiscent of the Gerty McDowell sequence in Joyce's *Ulysses*. Such a parallel is particularly noticeable in those passages in which Rosa's poetic sensibility seems to function in the soul of a pathetic, antebellum "bobby-soxer." She remarks of Bon's picture:

And I know this: if I were God I would invent out of this seething turmoil we call progress something (a machine perhaps) which would adorn the barren mirror altars of every plain girl who breathes with such as this—which is so little since we want so little—this pictured face. It would not even need a skull behind it; almost anonymous, it

8. P. 54.

*would only need vague inference of some walking flesh and blood
desired by someone else even if only in some shadow-realm of make-
believe* [p. 147].

Such tortuous, verbalized relieving of emotion, and there are
more obvious examples throughout this soliloquy, is a consequence of Rosa's neurotic self-absorption. She is bringing herself to life through emotional paroxysms. Eliot observes much
the same thing happening, but not with Faulkner's ironic purpose, in the novels of Hardy. Indeed, Eliot's definition of the
kind of "heresy" Hardy is supposed to have committed in his
novels applies exactly to those qualities of Rosa's soliloquy which
I am anxious to point out. Eliot observes

. . . an interesting example of a powerful personality uncurbed . . . by
submission to any objective beliefs; unhampered by any ideas, or even
by what sometimes acts as a partial restraint . . . the desire to please a
large public. [Hardy] . . . seems to me to have written as nearly for
the sake of self-expression as a man well can. . . .[9]

The point I should like to make is that Eliot's remarks can
apply to Rosa but cannot in any sense be applied to Faulkner.
This is precisely the mistake made by those critics who have
accused Faulkner of being irresponsibly romantic. Mr. Alfred
Kazin, for example, asserts that Faulkner represents "a tormented
individualism in the contemporary novel, a self-centered romanticism."[10] If this were true, we might use Rosa Coldfield's soliloquy to direct irony against the author himself. Obviously, the
novel does not allow us to do this. The context in which Faulkner places her soliloquy prevents it from having any persuasively
incantatory effect upon the reader. Rosa's romantic verbaliza-

9. *Ibid.*
10. Alfred Kazin, *On Native Grounds* (New York, 1942), p. 466.
See also J. Donald Adams, *The Shape of Books to Come* (New York,
1944), p. 131; Elizabeth Hardwick, "Faulkner and the South Today,"
Partisan Review, October, 1948, pp. 1130–35; Granville Hicks, *The Great
Tradition* (New York, 1935), p. 291; Wyndham Lewis, *Men Without Art*
(London, 1934), pp. 44–48; Edmund Wilson, "William Faulkner's Reply
to the Civil Rights Program," *The New Yorker,* October 23, 1948, p. 106.

tion is consistent with her avocation as a poet but reflects only in a most negative way Faulkner's sense of his own vocation. When Quentin first visits Rosa, he remarks that even in his father's youth she had composed over one thousand poems to the soldiers of the Confederacy,

> . . . had already established herself as the town's and county's poetess laureate by issuing to the stern and meager subscription list of the county newspaper poems, ode, eulogy and epitaph, out of some bitter and implacable reserve of undefeat [p. 11].

The "undefeat" of what? Certainly not the war, since Rosa pretends on several occasions to subscribe to the moral necessity of the South's defeat. Rosa's indiscriminate outrage has a primarily personal and an ambiguously sexual content. Quentin, even before he begins his re-creation of the story, listens to Rosa as the last and most vociferous opponent of Sutpen. But the reader will be disappointed who tries to discover in Rosa's soliloquy the moral basis for her hatred of Sutpen. All that she can reveal to Quentin is the "undefeat" not of moral rigor but of an essentially unregenerate personality.

When Rosa is finished, Sutpen remains where Quentin found him, bewilderingly inexplicable. The explanation for this is part of the logic of Faulkner's method which is really the method of historical research and re-creation. But the historical method has to this point proved, so far as Quentin is concerned, tragically unsuccessful. Rosa's inability to place events in their human and historical context, an inability which she shares with Sutpen, results quite naturally in the treatment of both individuals and complex social action as phenomena. The "phenomenon" for Sutpen was the "monkey nigger." It compelled the "design." Rosa's inability to give human proportions to Sutpen, "the demon," results eventually in her romantic and pessimistic view of history. The implications are obvious. Both Rosa and Sutpen are really ignorant of what is going on about them. Knowledge is the basis of historical perspective and knowledge is essentially an act of remembrance, an awareness of tradition.[11]

The form of *The Sound and the Fury*, of *Absalom, Absalom!*, and of most of Faulkner's major works is determined by this conception. The reader is witness to a conscious stockpiling of information by the characters as the story is repeated over and over again with a different focus upon the material, a persistent encirclement of alien facts and enigmatic personalities by all the accumulated knowledge of an individual, a family, or an entire community. In *Knight's Gambit*, this form is used to allow a gathering of anecdotes by the attorney Gavin Stevens from the whole countryside. Eventually, the form of each of Gavin's stories is the same as the process of community justice in the solution of the crime and in the judging of the criminal.

Quentin's persistent acts of remembrance in the last four chapters finally are successful in placing Sutpen in a comprehensible human context. Quentin and his roommate, Shreve McCannon, bring both a fairly complete knowledge of the facts and an inventive curiosity to the job of historical re-creation. Sutpen himself ceases to be a phenomenon in Quentin's past.

In their final ordering of the story, Quentin and Shreve are primarily concerned with the activity of Charles Bon and Henry Sutpen. Quentin's perceptive awareness of the meaning of that activity infuses a wholly human content into what has been the mechanical abstract nature of those past experiences which seem to constitute his heritage. It is specifically this human content, we have seen, which Sutpen tacitly ejected from his "design" by his refusal ever to recognize Bon as his son. And it is ironic, in view of Quentin's presentation of Bon, that in Rosa's soliloquy, as well as in Mr. Compson's version of the story, Sutpen is never more inhuman. Rosa herself never seems more fantastic than in their relationships to Charles Bon.

The account of the Bon story which finally emerges from

11. I am remembering some observations by Nicholas Berdyaev on the general problem of value in history. Nicholas Berdyaev, *The Meaning of History* (London, 1936).

the conversations of Quentin and Shreve may be viewed as an attempted rejection by Quentin of both his father's and Rosa's points of view. The effect, in terms of the novel, is a rejection of naturalism. The activity of Bon and Henry, as it is seen by Quentin, simply does not sustain a conception of history either as an impersonal mechanism or in which "blind Fate" slowly and solemnly triumphs. Faulkner quite admirably makes his own job extremely difficult. He endows Bon's career with all the material which should by its very nature keep Rosa's "current of retribution and fatality" [p. 269] moving on unaffected by Bon's own feelings and desires. Bon's childhood, according to Shreve, was almost a ritual in which his mother prepared him as an agent of her revenge on her husband. And, as we have already seen, Bon's experience at Sutpen's Hundred is made equivalent to that of Sutpen as a child standing before the plantation door.

Actually, however, Bon gives Sutpen numerous opportunities to correct his "mistake." Rather than revenge for his mother, all he is seeking is his father *out of the shadow of whose absence my spirit's posthumeity has never escaped* [p. 317]. If Sutpen had for one moment equally transcended the effects of his childhood and of his repudiation, if he had once perceived Bon's human motive, then the latter would, he claims, have sacrificed the love of Henry and whatever claim he might have to the love of Judith:

Yes. Yes. I will renounce her; I will renounce love and all; that will be cheap, cheap, even though he say to me "never look upon my face again; take my love and my acknowledgment in secret, and go" I will do that; I will not even demand to know of him what it was my mother did that justified his action toward her and me [p. 327].

But he at last falls victim, as Sutpen himself is a victim, to the ravages of this abstract "design." Incest with Judith or death at the hands of his brother become the only ways in which Bon can identify himself as Sutpen's son. Henry, after four years of painful indecision, kills his friend and brother at the gates of Sutpen's Hundred. For Bon, this was the ultimate recognition of his sonship. For Henry, it was a terribly difficult moral act. It had to be carried out in a world which his father, like Quentin's mother in *The Sound and the Fury*, has almost wholly corrupted. Henry acts not in obedience to his father, but to an inherent sense of a moral code which is stronger than his love for Bon. The act, though Sutpen insisted upon it, is really a transcendence by Henry of the dehumanized quality of his father's "design." This part of the story is proof for Quentin, if he needed proof, that life in the past was not as easily heroic as his father once imagined, the circumstances neither so "simple" nor the people so "distinct, uncomplex." What is important is that Quentin can see in the activity of Charles and Henry an active expression, however confused and frustrated, of human value responding to the inhumanity of Sutpen.

Shreve is genuinely moved by the account he and Quentin are able to make of Bon's and Henry's dilemmas. By the time that element of the story is finished, he has ceased both his self-conscious demonizing of Rosa and the picayune, witty interjections at which Quentin is silently but visibly annoyed. At one point, both he and Quentin become so engrossed in their own efforts fully to re-create the story that "it did not matter to either of them which one did the talking" [p. 316]. As the story develops, it becomes profoundly human, profoundly noumenal in content. So much so that for the first time the two boys at Harvard find themselves understandably situated within the destinies of the "shades" they create:

They were both in Carolina and the time was forty-six years ago, and it was not even four now but compounded still further since now both of them were Henry Sutpen and both of them were Bon [p. 351].

But the conversations of Quentin and Shreve do not end with the killing of Bon, with a personal action carried out in painful recognition of a moral code. As they continue with the Sutpen story, its natural sequence is significantly disrupted. Chronologically, though all of the details are made available to us in earlier chapters, the death of Bon should be followed by Wash

Jones' murder of Thomas Sutpen and by the violent escapades of Bon's son, Velery Bon, who has been brought by Clytie and Judith to Sutpen's Hundred. Structurally, however, the next incident with which Quentin and Shreve concern themselves is the final catastrophe of the Sutpen family, a catastrophe which seems to affirm the workings of a grotesquely deterministic universe. Such a focus on the material as a chronological ordering of the Wash Jones and Velery Bon stories would have allowed might have permitted Quentin a more substantial mitigation of the meaning which Shreve desperately assigns in the end to the idiot who alone survives at Sutpen's Hundred.

The actions of Wash Jones and of Velery Bon suggest as clearly as the final actions of Bon and Henry a distorted but eloquent sense of moral revulsion at the corruption and inhumanity of Sutpen's "design." When there seems no hope of reinstituting that "design," Sutpen perhaps consciously provokes Wash into killing him. In Wash's hearing, he crudely repudiates Milly, Wash's granddaughter, when she fails to bear him a son. But we can as easily view the murder less as a credit to Sutpen's scheming than as an assertion by Wash of human pride. In order to reaffirm his manhood and his dignity, he must destroy the man who has been his hero. His conduct partakes of the same traditional morality which justifies, in the short story "Tomorrow," the murder of Buck Thorpe by an outraged father. The murder in both instances can be viewed as punishment for a gross violation of primitive social mores.

Like Milly and Wash, Velery Bon discovers that he, too, is a part of the rejected residue of his grandfather's career. His subsequent conduct is a comment upon the consequences of Sutpen's invalidation of the habits and customs of the community which, taken together, constitute a kind of moral or social discipline. Having no family of his own, his real identity hidden from the town, Velery Bon seeks literally to make a name for himself by violent and extraordinary action. Though he could pass for a white man, he marries a woman who is an extremely dark Negress, and insists on being recognized as a Negro himself. Considering the

social consequences, this is really a conscious form of self-degra-
dation similar in its motivation to that of Joe Christmas in
Light in August. Velery Bon's violence, like Joe's unkindness
to Mrs. McEachern, is directed against the feminizing pity of
those about him. They are aware of their own incompleteness;
and symbolically this may be viewed as a dimly Christian awareness of the possible glory of being human. Joe and Velery Bon
can define themselves only horribly. In Sutpen's world, all Velery
Bon can do is to assert negatively his potential dignity as a man.

But the structure of the final episodes dramatically excludes
from the immediate attention of Quentin and Shreve the moral
affirmations, however deformed, of Wash and Velery Bon. Instead, we have in the sharpest possible juxtaposition, the circumstances of Bon's death and the almost theatrical horror of the
burning of Sutpen's Hundred. Velery Bon's son, the heir to the
estate and a Negro idiot, is left to "lurk around those ashes and
howl" [p. 376]. The howling of Jim Bon is totally devoid of
the kind of value which was tragically dramatized by Henry's
murder of his friend. Quentin actually trembles in his bed as
he remembers it.

The structure insists on the persistent quality of Quentin's
problem. The Negro idiot seems powerfully to reintroduce the
apparently inhuman and mechanistic nature of Sutpen's history
and of Quentin's heritage. Shreve is moved almost as much as
Quentin by the ambiguous quality of the story they have finally
pieced together, by the insoluble tension between the human
needs and passions inherent in the tale and the impersonally
deterministic form it seems to take. But he rather pathetically
disguises his feelings and doubts. He grasps what is for him the
easiest solution, what is for Quentin an emotionally impossible
solution—the cliché of the idiot as symbol of predestined doom.
This final catastrophe, he tells Quentin, "clears the whole ledger,
you can tear all the pages out and burn them, except for one
thing" [p. 378]. That one thing, Shreve facetiously concludes, is
the mechanism itself by which "the Jim Bonds are going to
conquer the western hemisphere":

So it took Charles Bon and his mother to get rid of old Tom, and Charles Bon and the octoroon to get rid of Judith, and Charles Bon and Clytie to get rid of Henry; and Charles Bon's mother and Charles Bon's grandfather got rid of Charles Bon. So it takes two niggers to get rid of one Sutpen, dont it? [pp. 377–378].

Shreve ends his remarks, to which Quentin has listened silently and unwillingly, with a final question: "Why do you hate the South?" What he assumes is that Quentin can afford to hate not simply the South, but his past, his paternity, and himself as a product of all three.

Quentin gives the only possible answer with a terrifying urgency:

"I dont hate it," Quentin said quickly, at once, immediately; "I dont hate it," he said. *I dont* hate it, he thought, panting in the cold air, the iron New England dark; *I dont. I dont. I dont! I dont hate it! I dont hate it!*

His only other possible answer would be a telling of the whole story of Sutpen over again. But Quentin speaks to himself as much as to his friend. Annoying to Quentin as Shreve's easy and terrible solution might seem, the possibility exists for him even at the end of the novel that man and his history are mutually hostile and alien; that he is merely the reflex of some impersonal and abstract historical process. But it is a possibility to which he refuses wholly to succumb. Inherent in the tragically suggestive ambiguity of the conclusion is the justification for the structure of *Absalom, Absalom!* The form of the novel itself insists that the act of placing Sutpen in the understandable context of human society and history is a continually necessary act, a never-ending responsibility and an act of humanistic faith.

Two Contrasting Views of
Intruder in the Dust

FAULKNER AND THE SOUTH TODAY

ELIZABETH HARDWICK

THERE ARE probably very few novelists in America who have not in some depressed, sterile hour wished for Faulkner's madness. He is authentically, romantically possessed by his genius; he can lose himself not only in the act of writing in the world his imagination has created and populated. He believes all of it, concretely, amazingly: the map of Yoknapatawpha County is not a joke. Here is a man who can take a walk in the morning and point to the spot where Wash Jones killed Sutpen or visit Compson's Mile for which Jason I swapped Ikkemotubbe a race horse. And he is so beautifully our young writer's image of the artist: he has done it by himself, in solitude, far from New York, in spite of critics, little magazines, fads, and professors—our natural genius, isolated, sure of himself, magnificently hallucinated as we feel the artist ought to be. And what a happy man he must have been, for what is there except the furious ecstasy of art's triumph over the artist's life in his extraordinary recent comments on the characters in *The Sound and the Fury*? He tells us that Candace, the heroine of a novel published in 1929, has vanished in Paris with the German occupation in 1940, that she is still beautiful and does not show her age. He's mad, of course;

A review of *Intruder in the Dust*, reprinted with permission from *Partisan Review,* October, 1948, pp. 1130-1135. This and the following review by Andrew Lytle have been included as representatives of two quite opposing views of *Intruder in the Dust*; the advantage gained from including them comes chiefly from their very different readings of a controversial work. [editors]

we remind ourselves that there is no Candace, nor a Jason, after the pages of the book are closed, to live on into a sour middle age and to sneak up the steps with his "big, plain, brazenhaired" mistress from Memphis. Still we cannot help but envy a writer so splendidly deluded; we feel an irrevocable calling to art ought to give us indifference to reality, that creative work should heal the misery of an unhappy love affair, pull us through nervous breakdowns, discount personal deficiencies, and in that sense most artists strive desperately for the same fantastic identification with their work and characters, the wondrous involvement with the imagination which Faulkner's little map symbolizes with an accuracy and simplicity almost beyond credulity. For it is either this or the slow, painful workings of the mind; either Faulkner's madness, large and self-sufficient, his stunning belief in his imaginary world, or something we secretly believe to be smaller: autobiographies, social observation, the neat situation, "the interesting but not creative."

His limitations, his overwriting and obfuscation are apparent; it is easy enough, if reckless, for Clifton Fadiman to satirize one of his most dazzling works ("One may sum up both substance and style by saying that every person in *Absalom, Absalom!* comes to no good end, and they all take a hell of a time coming even that far."), or to be really dreary about him, as Maxwell Geismar is, and hint at Fascism, the great "hatred," and the threat to the body politic in Faulkner's love of the past. But his six or seven superb novels insinuate themselves, no matter, and someone is always discovering that Faulkner is our greatest living novelist and saying it with a chip on his shoulder, belligerently, as though he expected to be booted out of the room. Indeed, Faulkner's reputation is curiously incomplete, somehow not authorized and catalogued. Like a patch of thrilling and famous scenery, almost everyone admires him but no one has anything very thrilling or famous to say about him.

One does not know whether to be glad or sorry that even Faulkner, the possessed, legendary writer, could not escape forever from the real Mississippi. His new novel, *Intruder in the Dust*, is astonishing: it is a tract, a polemic, even in its odd way a "novel of ideas." It is not what we expected and in it Faulkner appears as a hermit, perfect and necessary to our urban sentiments, who by chance picked up yesterday's newspaper, became annoyed with the state of the world and ran down from the hills to make a speech in the public square. It is less than his previous work, but fascinating because of that work and because it reveals the desperation of his present condition, the possibility that his inspired madness has disintegrated, leaving him, like everyone else, hollow and uncertain with the sickness and perplexity not of the past but of the present. The sickness of *Intruder in the Dust*, the fear and despair, are intimately connected with the future of Faulkner's career, a career which demands that there be a South, not just a geographical section and an accent, but a reasonably autonomous unit, a kind of family ready, and even with a measure of geniality, to admit the existence of the people next door and to cooperate in the necessary civic responsibilities, such as the removal of garbage and the maintenance of highways, but beyond that unique and separate, not to be reproached, advised, or mourned for the goings on behind the door.

The bare situation of the novel is brilliant: an old Negro, Lucas Beauchamp, a man apart, "not arrogant, not scornful, just intractable and composed," *pretends* to be a murderer, wants to be innocently lynched, to add his own blood to the South's dishonor, as his last act of contempt for his oppressors. He is not successful because of the intense need of several white people to prevent his martyrdom, and not only in Lucas' private interest, but in their own interest as white men who already have more shame than they can bear. Lucas, or the mass Negro, has at last conquered the South by giving the white man an unendurable burden of guilt. "Lucas Beauchamp, once the slave of any white man within range of whose notice he happened to come, now tyrant over the whole country's white conscience."

The brilliance of this situation is that it is not so much about the Negro as about the South's appalled recognition of its sins, its confusion before the unforgiving, alienated faces of the Negroes whose suffering has given them immense pride and dignity, the moral superiority of the victim. The Negro must be saved, Faulkner seems to be saying, so that the white man can become his moral equal, be relieved of the bondage to his terrible mistake.

Lucas' innocence is proved by a sixteen-year-old boy, Charles Mallison. The boy had been haunted for years by his feeling that he was in debt to Lucas for having, as a child, eaten part of the old man's dinner. Lucas refused money for the dinner and when the boy sent a Christmas present he was immediately repaid by a gallon jar of molasses from Lucas. By proving the Negro's innocence, the boy hopes to reassert his position again, and again he is defeated, because Lucas puts his escape from death on a business basis, insists upon paying the boy's uncle, a lawyer, two dollars for services, and thereby repudiating the equalizing gesture. The Negro is triumphant: he will not allow the white man to reduce even a penny of the incalculable debt.

Seen through the boy's eyes this situation has great subtlety, in spite of the ludicrous improbability of some of Faulkner's inventions, which include vanishing corpses and grave-robbing scenes more suitable to Tom Sawyer and Injun Joe than to the tragic momentum suggested here. And then suddenly the novel ceases to belong to the Negro and the boy and is given over to the boy's uncle, the lawyer who also wished to save Lucas. The uncle delivers absurd, strident lectures, written with frantic bad taste (the conglomerate Negro is called Sambo) and a flippant effort in the direction of political satire. The South must "defend not Lucas nor even the union of the United States but the United States from the outlanders North East and West who with the highest motives and intentions (let us say) are essaying to divide it at a time when no people dare risk division by using federal laws and federal police to abolish Lucas' shameful condition . . . . " and again, "I'm defending Sambo from . . . the outlanders who will fling him decades back not merely into injustice but into grief and

agony and violence too by forcing on us laws based on the idea
that man's injustice to man can be abolished overnight by
police . . . ." and, "I only say the injustice is ours, the South's. We
must expiate and abolish it ourselves, alone and without help nor
even (with thanks) advice."

Faulkner acknowledges the Negro's moral victory over the
South, yields and desires his total civic equality ("Someday
Lucas Beauchamp . . . will vote anywhen and anywhere a white
man can and send his children to the same school anywhere the
white man's children go and travel anywhere the white man
travels as the white man does it"), scorns as he always has the
depraved Southern murderer, the Percy Grimm who killed and
emasculated Joe Christmas, and whose portrait Faulkner has
drawn with a passionate condemnation not achieved to my
knowledge by any other writer.

This perception of the final emancipation of the Negro is
real and historical, a fact and a victory only Stalinists and certain
liberals feel compelled to underestimate. The sadistic passion
these people take in disowning every triumph of the Negro in
America, in predicting greater and greater injustice to him, is
one of the most detestable aberrations of their minds. One can
only believe they want violence in order to prove themselves
right, as the deluded maniac, faced with the infuriating reason
of the doctor, wishes to have a great bloody wound the next
day to testify to the actual existence of his imaginary attackers.
And when the Negroes are won over to the Communist Party have
they not fallen in love with their own misfortune, since at no
time is there so much discussion of lynchings, humiliating segre-
gation, such delicious examination of white deceitfulness as between Stalinists and Negroes? The one never tires of "exposing"
to the other an endless chronicle of dangers past and to come,
as if the Negro did not know them well enough but had to taste,
touch, and fondle them over and over until both are in a frenzy
of indescribable perversity.

Faulkner's best intuitions have something to do with this
phenomenon and there is at least a measure of psychological

truth in his understanding that a cruel, lost South is necessary to the idea of America held by certain radicals. This intuition partly informs his plea that the South be allowed to redeem itself. Unfortunately he was not content with psychological perceptions, but had to compose a states' rights, leave-us-alone, don't-be-coming-down-here-and-telling-us-what-to-do pamphlet which falsifies and degrades his fine comprehension of the moral dilemma of the decent guilt-ridden Southerner.

I think he was compelled to this not alone by a compulsive love of the South but also by the fact that he has lost his belief in the South as a unique region; he can reaffirm that belief only by imagining a mystic separation from the North, since his will to justice does not want a South unique because of its brutality to Negroes. He must believe that the contemporary Southerner is still close to his history, still romantically doomed, unable to forget the old disgrace, a proud, driven, image of the past. "For every Southern boy fourteen years old, not once but whenever he wants it, there is the instant when it's still not yet two o'clock on that July afternoon in 1863, the brigades are in position behind the rail fence, the guns are laid and ready in the woods and the furled flags are already loosened to break out and Pickett himself with his long oiled ringlets and his hat in one hand probably and his sword in the other looking up the hill waiting for Longstreet to give the word...."

But this is unimaginable; it is literary, flamboyant, historically ridiculous in terms of America today. And it is also inconceivable, that the citizens of a few states are actually prepared, as Faulkner suggests, to risk their lives, their children, their futures, their wealth, or even their time in any sustained, hopeless revolt against the will of the country to which they are tied and which they need as much as anyone else. This is romantic, cowboy play acting, the election of Talmadge, the hootings and posturings of the Dixiecrats notwithstanding. The rebel yell on the radio—an unmistakable scream of buffoonery and self-mockery. It is the end, not the beginning, the end of Faulkner's imaginary kingdom and he is terrified by it.

The Negroes have migrated in vast numbers to the North and those who are left no longer feel tragically or gloriously fused with the destiny of the South. There are no Dilseys today, neither in the South nor in the North, neither black nor white, and Faulkner's immense, loving memorial to the Negro servant is not only a remarkable creative achievement but a contribution to social history, a painstaking study of a lost relationship which will appear, a few generations from now, as queer and archaic to the American as the role of the duenna. The white Southerner himself is ruled by the ambitions of the rest of the country, which are all he can call upon if he is to survive and manage the American present.

Faulkner has caught up with the confusion of the country today, and with bitterness he finds that it cannot be controlled and ordered or even thought about in the intimate, vitalizing way in which he knew and used the past. The language of *Intruder in the Dust* is fatefully indicative of what has happened to him and his vision. Upon a realistic, contemporary situation he has tried hopelessly, impossibly, to impose the grandiloquent cadences of *Absalom, Absalom!* and nothing could be more out of key, more jarring and defeating. The rhetoric of that gloomy marvel cannot give epic grandeur, vast passionate design to his parable of the present. Here everything is real, small, and practical. What we hear, in spite of every effort to disguise it, is not the old Faulknerian music, but the sour stutters and complaints of a writer fretting over his new, urgent, difficult material.

REGENERATION FOR THE MAN

ANDREW LYTLE

IN THIS NOVEL[1] Faulkner has taken a subject, and almost it seems deliberately taken it, which the propagandists of the party line have pre-empted as theirs to have and to hold and fulminate about; or for that matter, any of the intruders upon the art of fiction who violate the Muse for pragmatic purposes, whether at the state's command or out of private need, or through sociology's quasi revelations. These last pretend to illuminate situation and performance, but, in effect, by meddling with the craft, obfuscate even their debased cult of good works. It is irrelevant, actually, whether Faulkner either out of irony or from some more private impulse chose what seems a current issue as subject for this novel. Such choice is beyond the artist's capacity. He does not choose his subject; his subject chooses him. And because this imagination functions in a certain way, craft against reverie, even if he deliberately set out to make a plea to action, or to treat the accidental accidentally, he wouldn't be able to do it. The artist is simply one who cannot debase his work even when, pressed, he thinks he gives in to circumstance; certainly not after his apprenticeship is behind him. There always seem to be a few exceptions to prove the rule; but on close scrutiny I doubt that these could show more than a technical virtuosity such as magic shows.

Dickens' passionate interest in the social evils of his day and *Bleak House*, that one of his books which stirred England to reform the Courts in Chancery, together give the best example I know of the artist's inviolability. The excitement of the day and the social action *Bleak House* set afoot were residual to the

Reprinted with permission from *The Sewanee Review,* Winter, 1949, pp. 120–127.
1. *Intruder in the Dust.*

central experience, the literary truth, of the novel. It happened that the injustices of the Courts in Chancery served Dickens as the complication which discovered his subject. The effect of the inertia, the circumlocutions, the mazelike ritual of the Court upon the characters, gave to its injustice the absolute quality of Fate with which man struggles but about which he can do little but realize the combinations of his character against circumstance; so that the proportion of good and evil in the nature of man is implied in all its variety through the central drive of the action. If Dickens' concern had been with the evils of banking, say, instead of the cases in Chancery, the literary truth would have been the same. The book would merely have lacked the residual effect of reforming the banking system, which at that time the public interest had not identified with its sorrows. The artist may use anything, since whatever he uses will be absorbed by his imagination and rendered by his technical skill, and this is the artist's integrity. He will use only what his vision sees, and that according to the degree of its intensity. The surface and density of the object, illuminated in its totality, is form. Whatever failure there is is a failure of human fallibility, not of intention.

Intruder in the Dust bears comparison with *Bleak House*, with the difference that Dickens' concern is with a single institution while Faulkner deals with the complex and fundamental involvement of a whole society. The supposed murder of a white man by a Negro, a threat of lynching, and even the bill of rights, which certainly brings the material up to the moment, has all the appearance of being the author's subject; but actually this is only one aspect of it. In the first paragraph Faulkner reports sparely, tersely even, an act of violence. At noon the high sheriff has reached the jail with Lucas Beauchamp, although the entire county has known since the night before that Lucas killed a white man. The act of violence has already happened. But the pastness of it is not static. There is a continuum in the information about the spread of the news; and given the particular kind of news it is and the lapse of time between the murder and the jailing of Lucas we are made to feel a mounting suspense which gives to the delay, as the story unfolds, a quality of mystery. This suspense and a feeling of the dark unknown is further tightened by the emphasis on time, not any hour but the hour of noon, a crucial division of time which we sense will be of importance, if for no more than the narrow limits it suggests will contain the action. That it also will imply a symbolical reference we cannot know but later find ourselves prepared for. This introduces us to the structure. Instead of leading up to the murder as the final release to the tensions of involvement, by putting it into the past Faulkner uses the act as the compulsive force to catalyze the disparate fragments of appearance into reality, for the story is not about violence at all. It is about a sixteen-year-old boy's education in good and evil and his effort to preserve his spiritual integrity.

Charles Mallison, Jr. (he is called by name once) is not merely a sensitive boy in whom resides the consciousness of his race, although he is this, too. More particularly he has a grief. The cause for this grief comes out of the dichotomy between the races, brought about by the long assault from the outside which has isolated Southern people and made him, along with them, overly sensitive to his racial distinction, to the extent that the integrity of his manhood has become identified with his distinction. This identification between race and manhood represents for the boy-man both Nemesis and Fate, since he is neither responsible for the imperfection of his view nor for the pattern of the action which the dead white man releases. He resists flight (washing his hands of it). His effort to escape his predicament lies in his decision to discover the truth by digging up the grave of the dead man to see what bullet killed him. He will face dangers both physical and metaphysical comprised in an undertaking beyond his capacity to perform, but in his decision he assumes the moral responsibility for his humanity. The impulse behind this decision, however, is mixed. On the one hand he hopes to wipe out the shame his manhood has suffered at the attitude of Lucas four years before the story opens (Lucas's denial of his racial pre-eminence; or so it seemed); on the other, it is to avoid the shame of lynching that attaches to any mob action, since this is another kind of emasculation both for the individual and society, as in either case the will is deprived of its function. Or, to put it another way, the individual's violation of his code of conduct and society's subversion of its laws become a kind of suicide; especially in the instance of traditional man and a homogeneous society. It is his innocence as a boy but his pride and conscience as man which in the end clarify the confused impulses and bring him into a fuller knowledge of the truth. In one sense the historic isolation of the Southern culture by a victorious and hostile force serves for the fateful drive of the story: is at once the cause for action and the clue to its meaning. By focusing it in the moral destiny of a boy, the story becomes dramatic instead of didactic: that is, a novel and not propaganda.

There is for any Southern writer of imagination an inescapable preoccupation with his native scene and especially with its historic predicament. He can no more escape it than a Renaissance painter could escape painting Her Ladyship the Virgin and the Court of Angels. He has been made to feel too sharply his uniqueness and the uniqueness of his society in the modern world. His self-consciousness does for him what blindness did for Homer. He has been forced to achieve aesthetic distance. It is this which gives to the boy protagonist in this book the authority for his undertaking (a cult hero almost) and allows him to absorb into the working out of his fate the entire complex set of relationships which represent the contradictions, the mixed virtues and vices, the agonies even of the Southern sensibility, containing a vision at once objective and involved: the poet-prophet who defines a civilization bereft of historic destiny but which refuses the role.

It seems to me that criticism all too often attempts to isolate an author's truth by abstracting it from the context of his performance. It is the writer's nature to discover for himself his meaning by matching his knowledge of experience against his imagination. This never comes in a burst of light, but out of a gradual exploration into the dark places of the mind and heart of man. The process of writing forces the discovery; or rather it is the discovery. What saves the writer from losing himself (the points of darkness are infinite) is his point of view. To this he may return and by this he may relate, reduce, and absorb the seemingly unrelated matters of experience until they become what to him is truth. Given the creative function, what follows is style; and style is that breath of life which makes of texture and structure, or body and bone, an organic whole. In this novel Faulkner has achieved a oneness of style and point of view which is of the first order of literary distinction. It is all effortless and so fused (which has not always been the case in his other books —he has not always removed his scaffolding) that to probe for purposes of analysis becomes a kind of bloody operation.

I shall let the point of view more or less envelop what I have to say. It lies in the close sympathy which exists between the boy and his uncle, a sympathy so intimate that at times the transference of thought does not need speech. There are many advantages to this. The novel is freed, but not entirely so, from the indistinct image the narrator-actor must present to the reader. By having two sensibilities instead of one—he would have done better had he made them more personally distinct—each is able to give to the other the grace of humanity. The boy's innocence and the uncle's maturity set up an interplay both at the center and on the periphery of the structure. Their relationship becomes strophe and antistrophe, enforcing the formal pause, defining the action as it is taking place. The center of the structure depends upon the treatment of time. For the physical action a very narrow limit is set; but the physical action, while performing at its own level, releases the flow of reverie and comment which becomes the embodiment of the intrinsic meaning. Since within this area lies the realm of truth, where all is timeless, the dual consciousness moves through past, present, and even into the future, according to the needs of the particular stage of the story's development. But for this flexibility the continuous beat of the prose would grow monotonous—with its inversions and parentheses, and the dreamlike quality of its tone (again the sense of timelessness) often threatening to make the skill of its complex delivery too apparent, which would be fatal. But always at the right moment there comes the pause, the break of dialogue—and Faulkner's dialogue surpasses itself—the added information when it is needed, or the image in a new light subtly changing the texture, or the posturing of a character as sudden as the shock of the tragic mask.

Gradually as we come to understand the achievement of the boy's education, and the achievement is manhood, we discover that the point of view has not shifted but was more inclusive than it first appeared. It is still posted firmly with the boy-uncle relationship but it has expanded beyond the boy's discoveries, though still contingent upon them. It rests at last not upon the boy's coming into manhood, but upon manhood, or its essence: The Man. The boy set out to restore a spurious manhood (appearance), but thanks to his innocence and the guidance of his uncle reaches instead true manhood (reality). The Man is the representative of the homogeneous society. His symbol is the fire and the hearth. He maintains the right relationships between the sexes, preserving to each his natural function; guards the blood's purity; is ultimately responsible for order in his household and therefore in the state; attends to his business, does not intrude or allow intrusion. He punishes and rewards toward this end and is the trustee for the earth out of which life comes and by which it is maintained. He, not Freedom, which history has shown no man can stand, is the realizable image for society.

But in the South as it is now there are half-men or men hamstrung out of their instinct to preserve this manhood. The uncle who understands so much is blinded by "the facts and circumstances." The sheriff, the hunter who guards the jail for five dollars as he reads the funnies, the jailkeeper who is outraged that he may lose his life for seventy-five dollars a month but will still risk it, and the old Gowrie, the father of the murdered man, are all men in Faulkner's sense, but each is circumscribed by some phase of the South's darkened image. In Miss Habersham's action the functions of the sexes are transposed. She, an old woman, does what a man should have done, if it had to be done, dig up a grave at midnight for justice's sake. And yet she was the only one who could assist the boys. Her caste and feminine intuition both informed her beforehand of what she would find, intuition acting truly, her caste function misplaced; she, a lady peddling eggs and vegetables at the town's back doors, wearing Sears-Roebuck dresses, but thirty-dollar handmade shoes and fourteen-dollar gloves—symbols of gentility, whereas the dress was not and therefore could represent her economic status. But slavery or any like subordination is the specific image of emasculation. The South's hope for regeneration lies in its struggle itself to restore, not from outside pressure, to that part of its population the rights of manhood of which it is deprived. Understanding of this is proof of the boy's initiation and his right to the toga virilis. But his possession is still precarious. He has not yet, as individual or symbol, established himself, because one man cannot maintain this state alone, against an environment where the spurious image is predominant and where the unrecognizable sin, the impossible sin, has been committed: fratricide. A Gowrie cannot kill a Gowrie, but one has. The fraternity of the state cannot be destroyed by internecine conflict, but it has been. Out of the South's resistance to this impossibility, which exists, has come an integrity mixed with turpitude, the misplaced functions of the sexes, a misdirected and fragmentary homogeneity.

When this is understood, Lucas's relationship to the novel grows clear. He is the basic symbol of the Southern predicament. He never actually performs as a character; that is not to say he is not characterized. He is the hone upon which all is sharpened. He is the society, both black and white, his white grandfather the founder of the plantation. He has inherited the man-ness (the signs of this the handmade beaver hat, which was the grandfather's, the gold toothpick, the pistol, the old frock coat) while his white cousin, the present owner, has inherited through the distaff side. Each is misplaced; each is confined by the isolation of this displacement, and will remain so, so long as Lucas says, "I ain't got no friends. I pays my way."

But there is hope. The boy's uncle tells him, "Don't stop." Don't stop trying to rectify injustice or to restore the true order. It is still possible to regenerate Southern homogeneity, because of and not in spite of the sheriff, the old one-armed Gowrie, the hunter, the jailkeeper, Miss Habersham, and himself. The uncle says, "[The white and the black in the South] . . . should confederate: swap him the rest of the economic and political and cultural privileges which are his right, for the reversion of his capacity to wait and endure and survive. Then we would prevail. . . ." For at this time the man will dominate again, justice be restored, and all ordered according to place and function, even to the exact degree of place and function. Then will the blood be purified of its foreign bodies.

There is one other point to make: the boy's active identity with the basic symbol. At the opening of the book on a hunting trip to the plantation he falls into a creek of icy water, in November, goes under three times and comes up to confront Lucas: the first encounter. The shock of the experience and the sight of Lucas immediately afterwards (he appears almost miraculously), who does not help him, who even orders the boy's colored playmate to remove the pole, the only assistance offered (the crutch of matter), so that the boy can get out by his own effort, is a kind of baptism from which he will be forevermore changed. Even the time of year marks it, the dead season which always precedes regeneration. The boy's recognition of his involvement, in spite of his efforts to free himself, even to the temptation of flight, sends him to Lucas's cell and commits him to the central adventure of the book. Lucas's attitude toward him at the creek and in the cell emphasizes the underlying symbolism of his presence. He asks nothing of anybody, not even the boy. He is intractable, even indifferent to the inherent threat in his situation. He merely directs the boy to go dig up the grave. Even in this he is impersonal and without specific information of what he will find; so that the burden of the action is shifted to the boy as his, not Lucas's, responsibility, as baptism in the Church puts the burden of salvation upon the communicant.

This extends the point of view still further, saying in effect that in the action of the boy, or such as he and Miss Habersham, will the South's crucifixion be prevented; since it is such as they who can or will restore the true image by removing from within the initial injustice which has obscured it, at which time the threat of crucifixion, which comes out of the North, will have lost its excuse for being. This is the final enlargement of the point of view. The use of time in the action, from high noon until midnight (actually it becomes longer) is suggestive, even the three before the grave is suggestive; but quite rightly Faulkner does not belabor this. Within the needs of the action of a story the symbol to work must perform at every level as it does in this book. To do more than suggest the specific Crucifixion would weaken his narrative by introducing comparisons extraneous to his own truth and so compromise him.

ATMOSPHERE AND THEME IN
FAULKNER'S "A ROSE FOR EMILY"

RAY B. WEST, JR.

THE FIRST CLUES to meaning in a short story usually arise from a detection of the principal contrasts which an author sets up. The most common, perhaps, are contrasts of character, but when characters are contrasted there is usually also a resultant contrast in terms of action. Since action reflects a moral or ethical

Reprinted with permission from *Perspective,* Summer, 1949, pp. 239–245.

state, contrasting action points to a contrast in ideological perspectives and hence toward the theme.

The principal contrast in William Faulkner's short story
"A Rose for Emily" is between past time and present time: the
past as represented in Emily herself, in Colonel Sartoris, in the
old Negro servant, and in the Board of Aldermen who accepted
the Colonel's attitude toward Emily and rescinded her taxes;
the present is depicted through the unnamed narrator and is
represented in the *new* Board of Aldermen, in Homer Barron
(the representative of Yankee attitudes toward the Griersons
and through them toward the entire South), and in what is called
"the next generation with its more modern ideas."

Atmosphere is defined in the *Dictionary of World Literature* as "The particular world in which the events of a story or
a play occur: time, place, conditions, and the attendant mood."
When, as in "A Rose for Emily," the world depicted is a confusion between the past and the present, the atmosphere is one
of distortion—of unreality. This unreal world results from the
suspension of a natural time order. Normality consists in a
decorous progression of the human being from birth, through
youth, to age and finally death. Preciosity in children is as monstrous as idiocy in the adult, because both are *unnatural*. Mon-
strosity, however, is a sentimental subject for fiction unless it is
the result of human action—the result of a willful attempt to
circumvent time. When such circumvention produces acts of
violence, as in "A Rose for Emily," the atmosphere becomes one
of horror.

Horror, however, represents only the extreme form of
maladjusted nature. It is not produced in "A Rose for Emily"
until the final act of violence has been disclosed. All that has
gone before has prepared us by producing a general tone of
mystery, foreboding, decay, etc., so that we may say the entire
series of events that have gone before are "in key"—that is, they
are depicted in a mood in which the final violence does not
appear too shocking or horrible. We are inclined to say, "In such
an atmosphere, anything may happen." Foreshadowing is often

accomplished through atmosphere, and in this case the atmosphere prepares us for Emily's unnatural act at the end of the story. Actually, such preparation begins in the very first sentence:

When Miss Emily Grierson died, our whole town went to her funeral: the men through a sort of respectful affection for a fallen monument, the women mostly out of curiosity to see the inside of her house, which no one save an old manservant—a combined gardener and cook—had seen in at least ten years.

Emily is portrayed as "a fallen monument," a *monument* for reasons which we shall examine later, *fallen* because she has shown herself susceptible to death (and decay) after all. In the mention of death, we are conditioned (as the psychologist says) for the more specific concern with it later on. The second paragraph depicts the essential ugliness of the contrast: the description of Miss Emily's house "lifting its stubborn and coquettish decay above the cotton wagons and the gasoline pumps—an eyesore among eyesores." (A juxtaposition of past and present.) We recognize this scene as an emblematic presentation of Miss Emily herself, suggested as it is through the words "stubborn and coquettish." The tone—and the contrast—is preserved in a description of the note which Miss Emily sent to the mayor, "a note on paper of an archaic shape, in a thin, flowing calligraphy in faded ink," and in the description of the interior of the house when the deputation from the Board of Aldermen visit her: "They were admitted by the old Negro into a dim hall from which a stairway mounted into still more shadow. It smelled of dust and disuse—a close, dank smell." In the next paragraph a description of Emily discloses her similarity to the house: "She looked bloated, like a body long submerged in motionless water, and of that pallid hue."

Emily had not always looked like this. When she was young and part of the world with which she was contemporary, she was, we are told, "a slender figure in white," as contrasted with her father, who is described as "a spraddled silhouette." In the picture of Emily and her father together, framed by the door, she frail and apparently hungering to participate in the life of her time, we have a reversal of the contrast which has already been presented and which is to be developed later. Even after her father's death, Emily is not monstrous, but rather looked like a girl "with a vague resemblance to those angels in colored church windows—sort of tragic and serene." The suggestion is that she had already begun her entrance into that nether-world (a world which is depicted later as "rose-tinted"), but that she might even yet have been saved, had Homer Barron been another kind of man.

By the time the deputation from the new, progressive Board of Aldermen wait upon her concerning her delinquent taxes, however, she has completely retreated into her world of the past. There is no communication possible between her and them:

> Her voice was dry and cold. "I have no taxes in Jefferson. Colonel Sartoris explained it to me. Perhaps one of you can gain access to the city records and satisfy yourselves."
>
> "But we have. We are the city authorities, Miss Emily. Didn't you get a notice from the sheriff, signed by him?"
>
> "I received a paper, yes," Miss Emily said. "Perhaps he considers himself the sheriff. . . . I have no taxes in Jefferson."
>
> "But there is nothing on the books to show that, you see. We must go by the—"
>
> "See Colonel Sartoris. I have no taxes in Jefferson."
>
> "But Miss Emily —"
>
> "See Colonel Sartoris." [Colonel Sartoris had been dead almost ten years.] "I have no taxes in Jefferson. Tobe!" The Negro appeared. "Show these gentlemen out."

Just as Emily refused to acknowledge the death of her father, she now refuses to recognize the death of Colonel Sartoris. He had given his word, and according to the traditional view, "his word" knew no death. It is the Past pitted against the Present —the Past with its social decorum, the Present with everything set down in "the books." Emily dwells in the Past, always a world of unreality to us of the Present. Here are the facts which set the tone of the story and which create the atmosphere of un-reality which surrounds it.

Such contrasts are used over and over again: the difference between the attitude of Judge Stevens (who is over eighty years old) and the attitude of the young man who comes to him about the "smell" at Emily's place. For the young man (who is a member of the "rising generation") it is easy. For him, Miss Emily's world has ceased to exist. The city's health regulations are on the books. "Dammit, sir," Judge Stevens replied, "will you accuse a lady to her face of smelling bad?" Emily had given in to social pressure when she allowed them to bury her father, but she triumphed over society in the matter of the smell. She had won already when she bought the poison, refusing to comply with the requirements of the law, because for her they did not exist.

Such incidents seem, however, mere preparation for the final, more important contrast between Emily and Homer Barron. Emily is the town's aristocrat; Homer is a day laborer. Homer is an active man dealing with machinery and workmen—a man's man. He is a Yankee—a Northerner. Emily is a "monument" of Southern gentility. As such she is common property of the town, but in a special way—as an ideal of *past* values. Here the author seems to be commenting upon the complex relationship between the Southerner and his past and between the Southerner of the present and the Yankee from the North. She is unreal to her compatriots, yet she impresses them with her station, even at a time when they considered her *fallen*: "as if [her dignity] had wanted that touch of earthiness to reaffirm her imperviousness." It appeared for a time that Homer had won her over, as though the demands of reality as depicted in him (earthiness) had triumphed over her withdrawal and seclusion. This is the conflict that is not resolved until the final scene. We can imagine, how-ever, what the outcome might have been had Homer Barron, who was not a marrying man, succeeded, in the town's eyes, in seducing her (violating her world) and then deserted her. The view of Emily as a monument would have been destroyed. Emily might have become the object of continued gossip, but she would have become susceptible to the town's pity—therefore, human. Emily's world, however, continues to be the Past (in its extreme form it is death), and when she is threatened with desertion and disgrace, she not only takes refuge in that world, but she also takes Homer with her, in the only manner possible.

It is important, too, to realize that during the period of Emily's courtship, the town became Emily's allies in a contest between Emily and her Grierson cousins, "because the two female cousins were even more Grierson than Miss Emily had ever been." The cousins were protecting the general proprieties against which the town (and the times) was in gradual rebellion. Just as each succeeding generation rebels against its elders, so the town took sides with Emily against her relations. Had Homer Barron been the proper kind of man, it is implied, Miss Emily might have escaped both horns of the dilemma (her cousins' traditionalism and Homer's immorality) and become an accepted and respected member of the community. The town's attitude toward the Grierson cousins represents the usual ambiguous attitude of man toward the past: a mixture of veneration and rebelliousness. The unfaithfulness of Homer represents the final act in the drama of Emily's struggle to escape from the past. From the moment that she realizes that he will desert her, tradition becomes magnified out of all proportion to life and death, and she conducts herself as though Homer really had been faithful—as though this view represented reality.

Miss Emily's position in regard to the specific problem of time is suggested in the scene where the old soldiers appear at her funeral. There are, we are told, two views of time: (1) the world of the present, viewing time as a mechanical progression in which the past is a diminishing road, never to be encountered again; (2) the world of tradition, viewing the past as a huge meadow which no winter ever quite touches, divided from (us) now by the narrow bottleneck of the most recent decade of years. The first is the view of Homer Barron and the modern generation in Jefferson. The second is the view of the older members of the Board of Aldermen and of the confederate soldiers. Emily holds the second view, except that for her there is no bottleneck dividing her from the meadow of the past.

Emily's small room above stairs has become that timeless meadow. In it, the living Emily and the dead Homer have remained together as though not even death could separate them. It is the monstrousness of this view which creates the final atmosphere of horror, and the scene is intensified by the portrayal of the unchanged objects which have surrounded Homer in life. Here he lay in the roseate atmosphere of Emily's death-in-life: "What was left of him, rotted beneath what was left of the nightshirt, had become inextricable from the bed in which he lay; and upon him and upon the pillow beside him lay that even coating of the patient and biding dust." The symbols of Homer's life of action have become mute and silent. Contrariwise, Emily's world, though it had been inviolate while she was alive, has been invaded after her death—the whole gruesome and unlovely tale unfolded.

In its simplest sense, the story says that death conquers all. But what is death? Upon one level, death is the past, tradition, whatever is opposite to the present. In the specific setting of this story, it is the past of the South in which the retrospective survivors of the War deny changing customs and the passage of time. Homer Barron, the Yankee, lived in the present, ready to take his pleasure and depart, apparently unwilling to consider the possibility of defeat, either by tradition (the Griersons) or by time (death) itself. In a sense, Emily conquered time, but only briefly and by retreating into her rose-tinted world of the past, a world in which death was denied at the same time that it is shown to have existed. Such retreat, the story implies, is hopeless, since everyone (even Emily) is finally subjected to death and the invasion of his world by the clamorous and curious inhabitants of the world of the present.

In these terms, it might seem that the story is a comment upon tradition and upon those people who live in a dream world of the past. But is it not also a comment upon the present? There is some justification for Emily's actions. She is a tragic—and heroic—figure. In the first place, she has been frustrated by her father, prevented from participating in the life of her contemporaries. When she attempts to achieve freedom, she is betrayed by a man who represents the new morality, threatened by disclosure and humiliation. The grounds of the tragedy is depicted in the scene already referred to between Emily and the deputation from the Board of Aldermen: for the new generation, the word of Colonel Sartoris meant nothing. This was a new age, a different time; the present was not bound by the promises of the past. For Emily, however, the word of the Colonel was everything. The tax notice was but a scrap of paper.

Atmosphere, we might say, is nothing but the fictional reflection of man's attitude toward the state of the universe. The atmosphere of classic tragedy inveighed against the ethical dislocation of the Grecian world merely by portraying such dislocation and depicting man's tragic efforts to conform both to the will of the gods and to the demands of his own contemporary society. Such dislocation in the modern world is likely to be seen mirrored in the natural universe, with problems of death and time representing that flaw in the golden bowl of eighteenth- and nineteenth-century natural philosophy which is the inheritance of our times. Perhaps our specific dilemma is the conflict of the pragmatic present against the set mores of the past. Homer Barron was an unheroic figure who put too much dependence upon his self-centered and rootless philosophy, a belief which suggested that he could take whatever he wanted without considering any obligation to the past (tradition) or to the future (death). Emily's resistance is heroic. Her tragic flaw is the conventional pride: she undertook to regulate the natural time-universe. She acted as though death did not exist, as though she could retain her unfaithful lover by poisoning him and holding his physical self prisoner in a world which had all of the appearances of reality except that most necessary of all things—life.

The extraction of a statement of theme from so complex a subject matter is dangerous and never wholly satisfactory. The subject, as we have seen, is concerned not alone with man's relationship to death, but with this relationship as it refers to all the facets of social intercourse. The theme is not one directed at presenting an attitude of Southerner to Yankee, or Yankee to Southerner, as has been hinted at in so many discussions of William Faulkner. The Southern Problem is one of the objective facts with which the theme is concerned, but the theme itself transcends it. Wallace Stevens is certainly right when he says that a theme may be emotive as well as intellectual and logical, and it is this recognition which explains why the extraction of a logical statement of theme is so delicate and dangerous an operation: the story *is* its theme as the life of the body *is* the body.

Nevertheless, in so far as a theme represents the *meaning* of a story, it can be observed in logical terms; indeed, these are the only terms in which it can be observed for those who, at a first or even a repeated reading, fail to recognize the implications of the total story. The logical statement, in other words, may be a clue to the total, emotive content. In these terms, "A Rose for Emily" would seem to be saying that man must come to terms both with the past and the present; for to ignore the first is to be guilty of a foolish innocence, to ignore the second is to become monstrous and inhuman, above all to betray an excessive pride (such as Emily Grierson's) before the humbling fact of death. The total story says what has been said in so much successful literature, that man's plight is tragic, but that there is heroism in an attempt to rise above it.

Bibliography

When an item is a review or a study of a work by Faulkner and the work is not specified by the title of the item, then the work is named in parentheses after the item. Every review cited is indicated by the abbreviation "rev."

Adams, J. Donald. "Mr. Faulkner's Astonishing Novel," *New York Times Book Review* (October 9, 1932), 6, 24 (rev. *Light in August*).

Aiken, Conrad. "William Faulkner: The Novel as Form," *The Atlantic Monthly*, CLXIV (November, 1939), 650–654.

Algren, Nelson. "Faulkner's Thrillers," *New York Times Book Review* (November 6, 1949), 4 (rev. *Knight's Gambit*).

Allen, Walter. "Mr. Faulkner's Humanity," *The New Statesman and Nation*, XXXVIII (October 15, 1949), 428–429 (rev. *Intruder in the Dust*).

Anonymous. "War's Aftermath," *New York Times Book Review* (April 11, 1926), 8 (rev. *Soldiers' Pay*).

————. "A Southern Family," *New York Times Book Review* (March 3, 1929), 8 (rev. *Sartoris*).

Ansermoz-Dubois, Félix. *L'Interprétation française de la littérature américaine d'entre-deux-guerres*. Lausanne: Imprimerie la Concorde, 1944. Pages 133–134, 181–184, *passim*.

Arland, Marcel. "*Lumière d'août*," *La Nouvelle Revue française*, XLV (October, 1935), 584–586 (rev.).

Arthos, John. "Ritual and Humor in the Writing of William Faulkner," *Accent*, IX (Autumn, 1948), 17–30.

Beach, Joseph Warren. *American Fiction, 1920–1940*. New York: Macmillan, 1941. Pages 123–172.

Beck, Warren. "Faulkner and the South," *Antioch Review*, I (Spring, 1941), 82–94.

————. "Faulkner's Point of View," *College English*, II (May, 1941), 736–749.

————. "William Faulkner's Style," *American Prefaces*, VI (Spring, 1941), 195–211.

————. "A Note on Faulkner's Style," *Rocky Mountain Review*, VI (Spring-Summer, 1942), 6–7, 14.

Benét, Stephen Vincent. "Flem Snopes and His Kin," *Saturday Review of Literature*, XXI (April 6, 1940), 7 (rev. *The Hamlet*).

Benét, William Rose. "Faulkner as Poet," *Saturday Review of Literature*, IX (April 29, 1933), 565 (rev. *A Green Bough*).

———. "Fourteen Faulkner Stories," *Saturday Review of Literature*, X (April 21, 1934), 645 (rev. *Doctor Martino*).

Bergel, Lienhard. "Faulkner's *Sanctuary*," *Explicator*, VI (December, 1947), item 20.

Birney, Earle. "The Two William Faulkners," *The Canadian Forum*, XVIII (June, 1938), 84–85 (rev. *The Unvanquished*).

Bowling, Lawrence. "Faulkner: Technique of *The Sound and the Fury*," *Kenyon Review*, X (Autumn, 1948), 552–566.

Boyle, Kay. "Tattered Banners," *The New Republic*, XCIV (March 9, 1938), 136–137 (rev. *The Unvanquished*).

Boynton, Percy H. *America in Contemporary Fiction*. Chicago: University of Chicago Press, 1940. Pages 103–112.

Bradford, Roark. "The Private World of William Faulkner," *'48, the Magazine of the Year*, II (May, 1948), 83–90. Photographs by Bradley Smith.

Breit, Harvey. "Faulkner after Eight Years: A Novel of Murder and Morality," *New York Times Book Review* (September 26, 1948), 4 (rev. *Intruder in the Dust*).

Breuil, Roger. "William Faulkner: *Lumière d'août*," *Esprit*, I (January, 1936), 612–614 (rev.).

Brodin, Pierre. *Les Écrivains américains de l'entre-deux-guerres*. Montreal: Éditions Bernard Valiquette, 1945. Pages 147–170.

Brooks, Cleanth, and Robert Penn Warren. *Understanding Fiction*. New York: F. S. Crofts, 1943. Pages 409–414 ("A Rose for Emily").

Brumm, Ursula. "William Faulkner im alten Süden," *Weltstimmen*, XIX (May, 1950), 374–380.

Bunker, Robert. "Faulkner: A Case for Regionalism," *New Mexico Quarterly*, XIX (Spring, 1949), 108–115 (rev. *Intruder in the Dust*).

Burgum, Edwin Berry. *The Novel and the World's Dilemma*. New York: Oxford University Press, 1947. Pages 205–222.

Buttitta, Anthony. "William Faulkner: That Writin' Man of Oxford," *Saturday Review of Literature*, XVIII (May 21, 1938), 6–8.

Cahen, Jacques-Fernand. "Du Roman américain," *Le Divan*, No. 267 (July-September, 1948), 393–406; continued, No. 268 (October-December, 1948), 455–469.

Calvo, Lino Novas. "El Demonio de Faulkner," *Revista de Occidente,* XXXIX (January, 1933), 98–103.

Campbell, Harry M. "Experiment and Achievement: *As I Lay Dying* and *The Sound and the Fury,*" *The Sewanee Review,* LI (Spring, 1943), 305–320.

―――. "Faulkner's *Sanctuary,*" *Explicator,* IV (June, 1946), item 61.

―――. "Faulkner's *Absalom, Absalom!,*" *Explicator,* VII (December, 1948), item 24.

―――. "Structural Devices in the Works of Faulkner," *Perspective,* III (Autumn, 1950), 209–226.

Canby, Henry Seidel. "The School of Cruelty," *Saturday Review of Literature,* VII (March 21, 1931), 673–674 (rev. *Sanctuary*). Reprinted in *Seven Years' Harvest.* New York: Farrar and Rinehart, 1936. Pages 77–83.

―――. "The Grain of Life," *Saturday Review of Literature,* IX (October 8, 1932), 153, 156 (rev. *Light in August*).

Cargill, Oscar. *Intellectual America: Ideas on the March.* New York: Macmillan, 1941. Pages 370–386.

Cecchi, Emilio. "William Faulkner," *Pan,* II (May, 1934), 64–70.

Cestre, C. "William Faulkner: *Light in August,*" *Revue anglo-américaine,* X (June, 1933), 466–467 (rev.).

Chamberlain, John. "Dostoyefsky's Shadow in the Deep South," *New York Times Book Review* (February 15, 1931), 9 (rev. *Sanctuary*).

Chase, Richard. "The Stone and the Crucifixion: Faulkner's *Light in August,*" *Kenyon Review,* X (Autumn, 1948), 539–551.

Coindreau, Maurice E. "William Faulkner," *La Nouvelle Revue française,* XXXVI (June 1, 1931), 926–930.

―――. "Le Puritanisme de William Faulkner," *Cahiers du sud,* XII (April, 1935), 259–267.

―――. "*Absalom, Absalom!*" *La Nouvelle Revue française,* XLVIII (January, 1937), 123–126 (rev.).

―――. "Panorama de la actual literatura joven norteamericana," *Sur,* VII (March, 1937), 49–65.

Coindreau, Maurice E. "Quadrille américain," *Les Œuvres nouvelles.* New York: Editions de la Maison Française, 1946. I, 137–181.

Colum, Mary M. "Faulkner's Struggle with Technique," *The Forum and Century,* XCVII (January, 1937), 35–36 (rev. *Absalom, Absalom!*).

Connolly, Cyril. *"Pylon,"* *The New Statesman and Nation,* IX (April 13, 1935), 525 (rev.).

Cowley, Malcolm. "Voodoo Dance," *The New Republic,* LXXXII (April 10, 1935), 284–285 (rev. *Pylon*).

———. "Poe in Mississippi," *The New Republic,* LXXXIX (November 4, 1936), 22 (rev. *Absalom, Absalom!*).

———. "Sanctuary," *The New Republic,* XCVII (January 25, 1939), 349 (rev. *The Wild Palms*).

———. "Faulkner by Daylight," *The New Republic,* CII (April 15, 1940), 510 (rev. *The Hamlet*).

———. "Go Down to Faulkner's Land," *The New Republic,* CVI (June 29, 1942), 900 (rev. *Go Down, Moses*).

———. "William Faulkner's Human Comedy," *New York Times Book Review* (October 29, 1944), 4.

———. "William Faulkner Revisited," *Saturday Review of Literature,* XXVIII (April 14, 1945), 13–16.

———. "William Faulkner's Legend of the South," *The Sewanee Review,* LIII (Summer, 1945), 343–361. Reprinted in *A Southern Vanguard,* ed. Allen Tate. New York: Prentice-Hall, 1947. Pages 13–27.

———. "Introduction," *The Portable Faulkner.* New York: Viking Press, 1946. Pages 1–24.

———. "William Faulkner's Nation," *The New Republic,* CXIX (October 18, 1948), 21–22 (rev. *Intruder in the Dust*).

Cushing, Edward. "A Collection of Studies," *Saturday Review of Literature,* VIII (October 17, 1931), 201 (rev. *These Thirteen*).

Daniel, Robert W. *A Catalogue of the Writings of William Faulkner.* New Haven: Yale University Library, 1942.

Davenport, Basil. "Tragic Frustration," *Saturday Review of Literature,* VI (December 28, 1929), 601–602 (rev. *The Sound and the Fury*).

———. "In the Mire," *Saturday Review of Literature,* VII (November 22, 1930), 362 (rev. *As I Lay Dying*).

De Voto, Bernard. "Witchcraft in Mississippi," *Saturday Review of Literature,* XV (October 31, 1936), 3–4, 14 (rev. *Absalom, Absalom!*). Reprinted in *Minority Report.* Boston: Little, Brown, 1940. Pages 209–218.

De Voto, Bernard. "Faulkner's South," *Saturday Review of Literature,* XVII (February 19, 1938), 5 (rev. *The Unvanquished*).

Dickmann, Max. "William Faulkner, escritor diabólico," *Revista de las Indias,* XIII (March, 1942), 107–116.

Evans, Medford. "Oxford, Mississippi," *Southwest Review,* XV (Winter, 1929), 46–63.

Fadiman, Clifton. "The World of William Faulkner," *The Nation,* CXXXII (April 15, 1931), 422–423 (rev. *Sanctuary*).

———. "Mississippi Frankenstein," *The New Yorker,* XIV (January 21, 1939), 60–62 (rev. *The Wild Palms*).

Fäy, Bernard. L'École de l'infortune," *Revue de Paris,* XLIV (August, 1937), 644–665.

Fiedler, Leslie A., "William Faulkner: An American Dickens," *Commentary,* X (October, 1950), 384–387.

Fischer, W. "William Faulkner: *The Unvanquished,*" *Beiblatt zur Anglia,* LI (December, 1940), 283–284 (rev.).

Foster, Ruel E. "Dream as Symbolic Act in Faulkner," *Perspective,* II (Summer, 1949), 179–194.

Frohock, W. M. "William Faulkner: The Private versus the Public Vision," *Southwest Review,* XXXIV (Summer, 1949), 281–294. Reprinted in *The Novel of Violence in America.* Dallas: Southern Methodist University Press, 1950. Pages 101–124.

Garnett, David. "Books in General," *The New Statesman and Nation,* VI (September 30, 1933), 387 (rev. *These Thirteen*).

Geismar, Maxwell. *Writers in Crisis.* Boston: Houghton Mifflin, 1942. Pages 141–183.

———. "Ex-Aristocrat's Emotional Education," *Saturday Review of Literature,* XXXI (September 25, 1948), 8 (rev. *Intruder in the Dust*).

Giles, Barbara. "The South of William Faulkner," *Masses and Mainstream,* III (February, 1950), 26–40.

Glicksberg, Charles I. "William Faulkner and the Negro Problem," *Phylon,* X (Second Quarter, 1949), 153–160.

Gloster, Hugh M. "Southern Justice," *Phylon,* X (First Quarter, 1949), 93–95 (rev. *Intruder in the Dust*).

Gordon, Caroline. "Mr. Faulkner's Southern Saga," *New York Times Book Review* (April 5, 1946), 1, 45 (rev. *The Portable Faulkner*).

Gordon, Caroline. "Notes on Faulkner and Flaubert," *The Hudson Review,* I (Summer, 1948), 222–231.

———, and Allen Tate. *The House of Fiction.* New York: Scribner's, 1950. Pages 531–534 ("The Spotted Horses").

Green, A. Wigfall. "William Faulkner at Home," *The Sewanee Review,* XL (Summer, 1932), 294–306.

Greene, Graham. "The Furies in Mississippi," *The London Mercury*, XXXV (March, 1937), 517–518 (rev. *Absalom, Absalom!*).

Gregory, Horace. "New Tales by William Faulkner," *New York Times Book Review* (May 10, 1942), 4 (rev. *Go Down, Moses*).

———. "In the Haunted, Heroic Land of Faulkner's Imagination," *New York Herald Tribune* (Books) (August 20, 1950), 1, 12 (rev. *Collected Stories*).

Hardwick, Elizabeth. "Faulkner and the South Today," *Partisan Review*, XV (October, 1948), 1130–1135 (rev. *Intruder in the Dust*).

Harnack-Fish, Mildred. "William Faulkner, ein amerikanischer Dichter aus grosser Tradition," *Die Literatur*, XXXVIII (October, 1935), 64–67.

Hartwick, Harry. *The Foreground of American Fiction*. New York: American Book Co., 1934. Pages 160–166.

Hatcher, Harlan. *Creating the Modern American Novel*. New York: Farrar and Rinehart, 1935. Pages 234–243.

Hawkins, Desmond. *"The Hamlet," The New Statesman and Nation*, XX (September 28, 1940), 312–314 (rev.).

Hicks, Granville. "The Past and Future of William Faulkner," *The Bookman*, LXXIV (September, 1931), 17–24.

———. *The Great Tradition*. New York: Macmillan, 1933. Pages 262–268.

Hirshleifer, Phyllis. "As Whirlwinds in the South: *Light in August*," *Perspective*, II (Summer, 1949), 225–238.

Hopper, Vincent F. "Faulkner's Paradise Lost," *Virginia Quarterly Review*, XXIII (Summer, 1947), 405–420.

Howe, Irving. "The South and Current Literature," *The American Mercury*, LXVII (October, 1948), 494–503.

Howe, Irving. "Minor Faulkner," *The Nation*, CLXIX (November 12, 1949), 473–474 (rev. *Knight's Gambit*).

———. "William Faulkner and the Quest for Freedom," *Tomorrow*, IX (December, 1949), 54–56 (rev. *The Wild Palms*).

Hudson, Tommy. "William Faulkner: Mystic and Traditionalist," *Perspective*, III (Autumn, 1950), 227–235.

Jack, Peter M. "Mr. Faulkner's Clearest Novel," *New York Times Book Review* (January 22, 1939), 2 (rev. *The Wild Palms*).

Jackson, James Turner. "Delta Cycle: A Study of William Faulkner," *Chimera*, V (Autumn, 1946), 3–14.

Jarlot, Gérard. *"Pylône," Fontaine,* X (November, 1946), 653–657 (rev.).

Johnson, C. W. M. "Faulkner's 'A Rose for Emily,'" *Explicator,* VI (May, 1948), item 45.

Jones, Howard Mumford. "Loyalty and Tiresias of Yoknapatawpha," *Saturday Review of Literature,* XXXII (November 5, 1949), 17 (rev. *Knight's Gambit*).

Kazin, Alfred. "In the Shadow of the South's Last Stand," *New York Herald Tribune* (Books) (February 20, 1938), 5 (rev. *The Unvanquished*).

————. "A Study in Conscience," *New York Herald Tribune* (Books) (January 22, 1939), 2 (rev. *The Wild Palms*).

————. "Faulkner: The Rhetoric and the Agony," *Virginia Quarterly Review,* XVIII (Summer, 1942), 389–402. Reprinted in *On Native Grounds.* New York: Reynal & Hitchcock, 1942. Pages 453–470.

Kildal, Arne. *Amerikas stemme fra amerikansk litteratur og kulturliv.* Oslo: Steenske forlag, 1935. Pages 103–108.

Kohler, Dayton. "William Faulkner and the Social Conscience," *College English,* XI (December, 1949), 119–127.

Korn, Karl. "Moira und Schuld," *Die Neue Rundschau,* IL (December, 1938), 603–607 (rev. *Absalom, Absalom!*).

Kronenberger, Louis. "Faulkner's Dismal Swamp," *The Nation,* CXLVI (February 19, 1938), 212, 214 (rev. *The Unvanquished*).

————. "The World of William Faulkner," *The Nation,* CL (April 13, 1940), 481–482 (rev. *The Hamlet*).

Kubie, Lawrence S. "William Faulkner's *Sanctuary*: An Analysis," *Saturday Review of Literature,* XI (October 20, 1934), 218, 224–226.

LaBudde, Kenneth. "Cultural Primitivism in William Faulkner's 'The Bear,'" *American Quarterly,* II (Winter, 1950), 322–328.

Larbaud, Valery. *Ce Vice impuni, la lecture...domaine anglais.* Paris: Gallimard (*La Nouvelle Revue française*), 1936.

Leavis, F. R. "Dostoevsky or Dickens?" *Scrutiny,* II (June, 1933), 91–93 (rev. *Light in August*).

Le Breton, Maurice. "William Faulkner: *Pylon,*" *Revue anglo-américaine,* XII (October, 1935), 81–82 (rev.).

————. "Technique et psychologie chez William Faulkner," *Études anglaises,* I (September, 1937), 418–438.

Leibowitz, René. "L'Art tragique de William Faulkner," *Cahiers du sud*, XVII (November, 1940), 502–508.

Levin, Harry. "Some European Views of Contemporary American Literature," in *The American Writer and the European Tradition*, eds. Margaret Denny and William H. Gilman. Minneapolis: University of Minnesota Press, 1950. Pages 168–184.

Lewis, Wyndham. "The Moralist with the Corn-cob: A Study of William Faulkner," *Life and Letters*, X (June, 1934), 312–328. Reprinted in *Men without Art*. London: Cassell, 1934. Pages 42–64.

Linn, James W., and Houghton W. Taylor. *A Foreword to Fiction*. New York: Appleton-Century, 1935. Pages 144–157.

Linn, Robert. "Robinson Jeffers and William Faulkner," *The American Spectator*, II (1933), 1. Reprinted in *The American Spectator Year Book*, eds. George Jean Nathan, Ernest Boyd, et al. New York: Frederick A. Stokes, 1934. Pages 304–307.

Longley, John L., Jr., and Robert Daniel. "Faulkner's Critics: A Selective Bibliography," *Perspective*, III (Autumn, 1950), 202–208.

Lovati, Georgio. "Faulkner, Soldati and America," *The Living Age*, CCCLI (September, 1936), 71–72.

Lundkvist, Artur. "Amerikansk prosa," *Bonniers litterara magasin*, VI (March, 1937), 197–204.

Lytle, Andrew. "Regeneration for the Man," *The Sewanee Review*, LVII (Winter, 1949), 120–127 (rev. *Intruder in the Dust*).

Maclachlan, John M. "William Faulkner and the Southern Folk," *Southern Folklore Quarterly*, IX (June, 1945), 153–167.

Madge, Charles. "Time and Space in America," *The London Mercury*, XXXII (May, 1935), 83 (rev. *Pylon*).

Magny, Claude-Edmonde. *L'Age du roman américain*. Paris: Éditions du Sueil, 1948. Pages 196–243.

Malraux, André. "Préface à *Sanctuaire* de William Faulkner," *La Nouvelle Revue française*, XLI (November, 1933), 744–747.

Marichalar, Antonio. "William Faulkner," *Revista de Occidente*, XLII (October, 1933), 78–86 (rev. *Sanctuary*).

Maxwell, Allen. "*The Wild Palms*," *Southwest Review*, XXIV (April, 1939), 357–360 (rev.).

McCole, Camille J. "The Nightmare Literature of William Faulkner," *The Catholic World*, CXLI (August, 1935), 576–583.

———. *Lucifer at Large*. New York: Longmans, 1937. Pages 203–222.

Milano, Paolo. "Faulkner in Crisis," *The Nation,* CLXVII (October 30, 1948), 496–497 (rev. *Intruder in the Dust*).

Morra, Umberto. "William Faulkner: *Luce d'Agosto,*" *Letteratura,* III (July, 1939), 173–174 (rev.).

Neville, Helen. "The Sound and the Fury," *Partisan Review,* V (June, 1938), 53–55 (rev. *The Unvanquished*).

O'Donnell, George M. "Faulkner's Mythology," *Kenyon Review,* I (Summer, 1939), 285–299.

Oliver, María Rosa. "La Novela norteamericana moderna," *Sur,* IX (August, 1939), 33–47.

Paterson, Isabel. "An Unquiet Ghost Out of the Old South," *New York Herald Tribune* (Books) (October 25, 1936), 3 (rev. *Absalom, Absalom!*).

Patten, Mercury. *"Light in August,"* *The New Statesman and Nation,* V (February 11, 1933), 163 (rev.).

Perdeck, A. "William Faulkner," *Critisch Bulletin,* 1934, 209–213.

Peyre, Henri. "American Literature through French Eyes," *Virginia Quarterly Review,* XXIII (Summer, 1947), 421–437.

Pick, Robert. "Old-World Views on New-World Writing," *Saturday Review of Literature,* XXXII (August 20, 1949), 7–9, 35–38.

Pilkington, James Penn. "Faulkner's *Sanctuary,*" *Explicator,* IV (June, 1946), item 61.

Pouillon, Jean. "William Faulkner, un Témoin," *Les Temps modernes,* II (October, 1946), 172–178 (rev. *Pylon*).

Powell, Sumner C. "William Faulkner Celebrates Easter, 1928," *Perspective,* II (Summer, 1949), 195–218 (*The Sound and the Fury*).

Prins, A. P. "Faulkner en het negervraagstuk," *Critisch Bulletin,* 1950, 126–127 (rev. *Intruder in the Dust*).

Proteus. *"Soldiers' Pay,"* *The New Statesman,* XXXV (June 28, 1930), 369 (rev.).

Rabi. "Faulkner et la génération de l'exil," *Esprit,* XIX (January, 1951), 47–65.

Rascoe, Burton. "Faulkner's New York Critics," *The American Mercury,* L (June, 1940), 243–247.

Redman, Ben Ray. "Flights of Fancy," *Saturday Review of Literature,* XI (March 30, 1935), 577, 581 (rev. *Pylon*).

———. "Faulkner's Double Novel," *Saturday Review of Literature,* XIX (January 21, 1939), 5 (rev. *The Wild Palms*).

Rice, Philip Blair. "The Art of William Faulkner," *The Nation,* CXXXVIII (April 25, 1934), 478 (rev. *Doctor Martino*).

Riva, Arturo Sanchez. "William Faulkner: *Luz de Agosto*," *Sur*, XII (November, 1942), 75–77 (rev.).

Rosati, Salvatore. "William Faulkner," *Nuova Antologia*, CCCXCV (January 16, 1938), 225–230.

Roth, Russell. "The Brennan Papers: Faulkner in Manuscript," *Perspective*, II (Summer, 1949), 219–224.

———. "William Faulkner: The Pattern of Pilgrimage," *Perspective*, II (Summer, 1949), 246–254.

Rugoff, Milton. "Out of Faulkner's Bog," *New York Herald Tribune* (Books) (March 31, 1940), 4 (rev. *The Hamlet*).

———. "The Magic of William Faulkner," *New York Herald Tribune* (Books) (May 17, 1942), 2 (rev. *Go Down, Moses*).

Saint Jean, Robert de. *"Sanctuaire,"* *La Revue hebdomadaire*, XLIII (April 21, 1934), 487–491 (rev.).

Sartre, Jean-Paul. *"Sartoris,* par William Faulkner," *La Nouvelle Revue française*, L (February, 1938), 323–328.

———. "A Propos de *Le Bruit et la Fureur*: La Temporalité chez Faulkner," *La Nouvelle Revue française*, LII (June, 1939), 1057–1061; continued, LIII (July, 1939), 147–151. Reprinted in *Situations* I (Paris, Gallimard, 1947). Pages 70–81.

———. "American Novelists in French Eyes," *The Atlantic Monthly*, CLXXVIII (August, 1946), 114–118.

Schappes, Morris U. "Faulkner as Poet," *Poetry: A Magazine of Verse*, XLIII (October, 1933), 48–52 (rev. *A Green Bough*).

Schneider-Schelde, Rudolf. *"Absalom, Absalom!"* *Die Literatur*, XL (July, 1938), 693–694 (rev.).

Schwartz, Delmore. "The Fiction of William Faulkner," *The Southern Review*, VII (Summer, 1941), 145–160.

Scott, Evelyn. *On William Faulkner's "The Sound and the Fury."* New York: Jonathan Cape and Harrison Smith, 1929.

Smith, Marshall J. "Faulkner of Mississippi," *The Bookman*, LXXIV (December, 1931), 411–417.

Snell, George. "The Fury of William Faulkner," *Western Review*, XI (Autumn, 1946), 29–40. Reprinted in *The Shapers of American Fiction*. New York: E. P. Dutton, 1947. Pages 87–104.

Stallings, Lawrence. "Gentleman from Mississippi," *The American Mercury*, XXXIV (April, 1935), 499–501 (rev. *Pylon*).

Starke, Aubrey. "An American Comedy: An Introduction to a Bibliography of William Faulkner," *Colophon*, V, 1934, part 19.

Stone, Geoffrey. *"Light in August,"* *The Bookman*, LXXV (November, 1932), 736–738 (rev.).

Stone, Phil. "William Faulkner, the Man and His Work," *Oxford Magazine* (Oxford, Miss.), Copy 1 (1934), 13–14; continued in Copies 2 and 3; unfinished.

———. "William Faulkner and His Neighbors," *Saturday Review of Literature*, XXV (September 19, 1942), 12.

Strauss, Harold. "Mr. Faulkner's New Novel Strikes a Fresh Vein," *New York Times Book Review* (March 24, 1935), 2 (rev. *Pylon*).

Strong, L. A. G. "Mr. Faulkner Again," *The Spectator* (London), CXLVI (April 25, 1931), 674 (rev. *The Sound and the Fury*).

Thiébaut, Marcel. "*Tandis que j'agonise*," *Revue de Paris*, XLI (July 15, 1934), 474–476 (rev.).

Thompson, Alan R. "*Sanctuary*," *The Bookman*, LXXIII (April, 1931), 188–189 (rev.).

———. "The Cult of Cruelty," *The Bookman*, LXXIV (January-February, 1932), 477–487.

Thorp, Willard. "Four Times and Out?" *Scrutiny*, I (September, 1932), 172–173 (rev. *Sartoris*).

Trilling, Lionel. "Mr. Faulkner's World," *The Nation*, CXXXIII (November 4, 1931), 491–492 (rev. *These Thirteen*).

Trilling, Lionel. "The McCaslins of Mississippi," *The Nation*, CLIV (May 30, 1942), 632–633 (rev. *Go Down, Moses*).

———. "Contemporary Literature in Its Relation to Ideas," *American Quarterly*, I (Fall, 1949), 195–208. Reprinted in *The American Writer and the European Tradition*, eds. Margaret Denny and William H. Gilman. Minneapolis: University of Minnesota Press, 1950. Pages 132–153.

Troy, William. "And Tomorrow," *The Nation*, CXL (April 3, 1935), 393 (rev. *Pylon*).

———. "The Poetry of Doom," *The Nation*, CXLIII (October 31, 1936), 524–525 (rev. *Absalom, Absalom!*).

Van Doren, Dorothy. "More Light Needed," *The Nation*, CXXXV (October 26, 1932), 405 (rev. *Light in August*).

Van Doren, Mark. "*Pylon*," *New York Herald Tribune* (Books) (March 24, 1935), 3 (rev.).

Vaucher-Zananiri, Nelly. *Voix d'Amerique*. Cairo: R. Schindler, 1945. Pages 29–31.

Vernon, Grenville. "Fallen Angel?" *The Commonweal*, XV (January 20, 1932), 332–333 (rev. *These Thirteen*).

Veruly, A. "Vliegerromans," *Critisch Bulletin*, 1935, 313–317 (rev. *Pylon*).

Vickery, Olga Westland. "*As I Lay Dying*," *Perspective*, III (Autumn, 1950), 179–191.

Vittorino, Elio. "William Faulkner: *Oggi si Vola*," *Letteratura*, I (July, 1937), 174–175 (rev.).

Waldman, Milton. "Tendencies of the Modern Novel, America," *The Fortnightly Review*, CXL (December, 1933), 709–725.

Warren, Robert Penn. "The Snopes World," *Kenyon Review*, III (Spring, 1941), 253–257 (rev. *The Hamlet*).

———. "Cowley's Faulkner," *The New Republic,* CXV (August 12, 1946), 176–180; continued (August 26, 1946), 234–237. Reprinted in *Forms of Modern Fiction*, ed. William Van O'Connor. Minneapolis: University of Minnesota Press, 1948. Pages 125–143 (rev. *The Portable Faulkner*).

Welty, Eudora. "In Yoknapatawpha," *The Hudson Review,* I (Winter, 1949), 596–598 (rev. *Intruder in the Dust*).

West, Ray B. "Faulkner's 'A Rose for Emily,'" *Explicator,* VII (October, 1948), item 8.

West, Ray B. "Atmosphere and Theme in Faulkner's 'A Rose for Emily,'" *Perspective,* II (Summer, 1949), 239–245.

———, and Robert Wooster Stallman. *The Art of Modern Fiction.* New York: Rinehart, 1949. Pages 270–276 ("A Rose for Emily").

Whan, Edgar W. "*Absalom, Absalom!* as Gothic Myth," *Perspective,* III (Autumn, 1950), 192–201.

Whittemore, Reed. "Notes on Mr. Faulkner," *Furioso,* II (Summer, 1947), 18–25.

Wilson, Edmund. "William Faulkner's Reply to the Civil Rights Program," *The New Yorker*, XXIV (October 23, 1948), 106, 109–112. Reprinted in *Classics and Commercials*. New York: Farrar, Straus, 1950. Pages 460–470 (rev. *Intruder in the Dust*).

Young, Stark. "New Year's Craw," *The New Republic*, XCIII (January 12, 1938), 283–284.